HTML & CSS

FOR COMPLETE BEGINNERS

A Step by Step Guide to Learning HTML5 and CSS3

IKRAM HAWRAMANI

2018

STEWARDS PUBLISHING

Copyright © 2018 Ikram Hawramani

First Edition

First Published in 2018

Hawramani.com

About the Author

Ikram Hawramani is a veteran web designer and developer who has been building websites since 2001. He has worked as a full stack web developer and lead engineer for startups and runs his own web publishing business. His other technical works include *Cloud Computing for Complete Beginners* and *Object-Oriented PHP Best Practices*.

This page intentionally left blank

Contents

1.

An Introduction to HTML and CSS

HTML stands for Hypertext Markup Language, while CSS stands for Cascading Style Sheets. HTML and CSS were designed to solve the problem of telling computers how to display a document. Below is a typical computer file before the invention of HTML and CSS. The file was created almost 50 years ago, on April 7, 1969. It belongs to a series of documents called RFCs which have continued to this day. These documents are used by the maintainers of the Internet to discuss the development of the infrastructure and technologies related to it.

```
Network Working Group                           Steve Crocker
Request for Comments: 1                                 UCLA
                                                 7 April 1969


                    Title:   Host Software
                    Author:   Steve Crocker
                    Installation:   UCLA
                    Date:   7 April 1969
        Network Working Group Request for Comment:   1


CONTENTS

INTRODUCTION

   I. A Summary of the IMP Software

      Messages

      Links

      IMP Transmission and Error Checking

      Open Questions on the IMP Software

  II. Some Requirements Upon the Host-to-Host Software

      Simple Use
```

Notice how bland the document looks. This is because it is a "plaintext" document. It is made up of alphabetical characters, numbers, spaces and a few other things. There is no room for creating borders, colors and beautiful and complex designs with such a limited technology.

To illustrate what HTML is and how it works, we will start by creating a similarly bland plaintext file, then transform it to an HTML file with a few simple steps. On a Windows system, you can create a plaintext file in any folder by right-clicking on an empty area and choosing New -> Text Document (shown below).

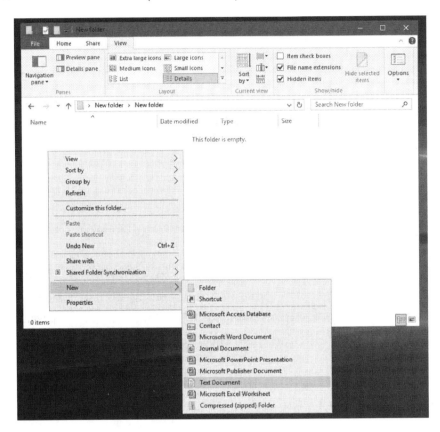

Below is our newly created document:

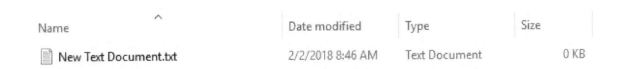

In the above screenshot, if instead of "New Text Document.txt" you see "New Text Document" (without the ".txt" part), this means your computer is set up to hide file extensions. It is important to make file extensions visible for the purposes of the rest of this book. A file extension like ".txt" tells you that this is a text document and affects what program will be used to open the document. In order to make file extensions visible, open any folder, go to the View tab, then click the "Options" button:

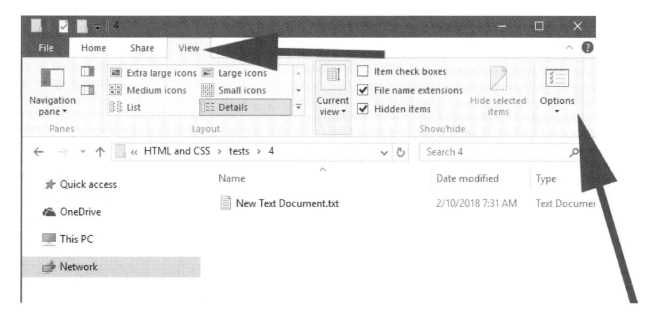

Next, click "Change File and Folder Options" in the little menu that opens up:

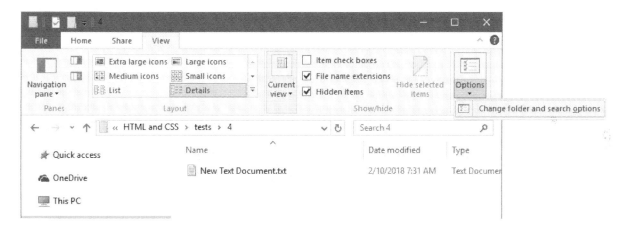

The "Folder Options" window opens up as below, click on the "View" tab at the top of the window:

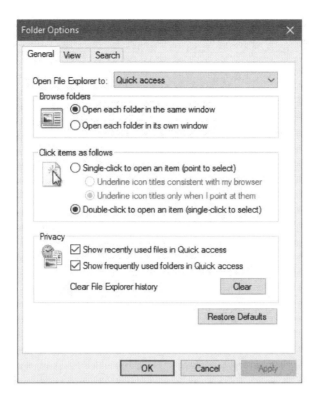

Uncheck "Hide extensions for known file types":

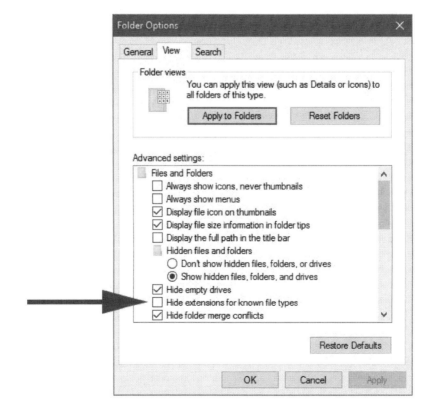

Now, click the OK button at the bottom left and you should be able to start seeing extensions.

Creating an HTML Document

If you open New Text Document.txt, you are presented with a text-editing program called Notepad that lets you type anything you want:

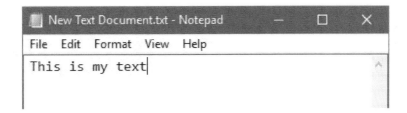

The problem with this program is that it doesn't let you add any formatting. You can't make anything bold, italic, or colorful. You are limited to 'plain' text. If you wanted to draw something, you'd be forced to use dashes and pipes to make crude drawings, as follows:

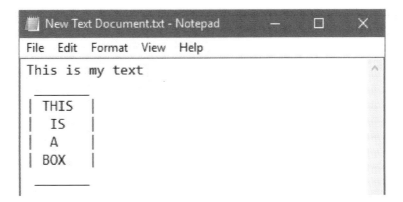

HTML and CSS give us a way of going beyond the limits of plain text. They help us create the sophisticated and occasionally beautiful designs we see on the websites we visit daily.

In the screenshot below, I add HTML 'markup' to the sentence shown earlier:

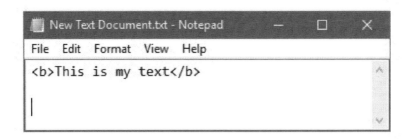

Markup is a way of giving the computer hints for how to understand and show a piece of text or other data. The markup above is HTML that tells the computer this text should be 'understood' as bold text. In HTML, anything enclosed between a <b> and a </b> is bold and will be displayed as bold in a web browser.

If we save the text document, close Notepad and open it again, the text will not become bold, because Notepad continues to assume we are dealing with plain text. In order for the HTML markup to 'come to live', we need to open the file in a program that actually understands HTML. First, we save the file as an HTML file:

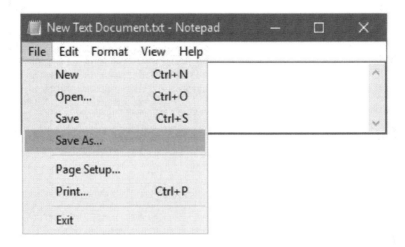

Below, the 'Save As' dialog box opens and here we type 'My New HTML Document.html' in the 'File name' box. Note the ".html" at the end, this lets the computer know that this file is an HTML file.

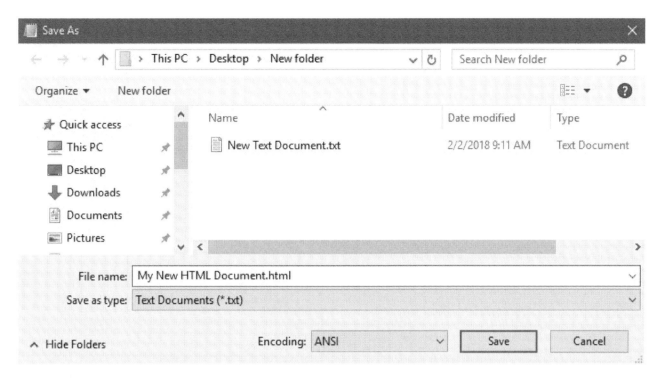

If we look inside the folder, we will now see a new HMTL document:

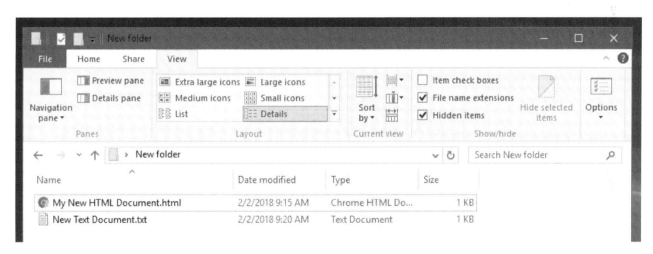

If we open this document by double-clicking on it, this is what shows up:

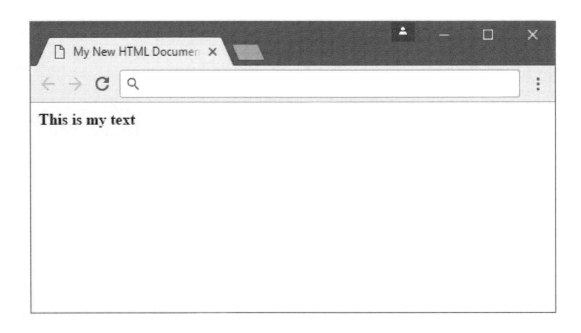

As can be seen, the text now appears bold, and we do not see the markup (the <b> and </b>), because this markup has been 'interpreted' by the program[1]. When the program sees the <b> and </b> markup, it interprets this as an instruction to display everything between them as bold text.

In this way, we are, in effect, programming the computer. We are telling it 'what to think' about the text.

We can still open the HTML file in Notepad in order to edit it, by right-clicking on it, going to 'Open with', then choosing 'Notepad' in the list (if Notepad isn't showing up, click on 'Choose another app' and you will find it there).

---

[1] The program shown in the screenshot is Chromium, which is a web browser used for…browsing websites. Other browsers include Firefox, Safari, Microsoft Edge, Microsoft Internet Explorer and Opera. A website is merely a bunch of HTML documents linked to one another.

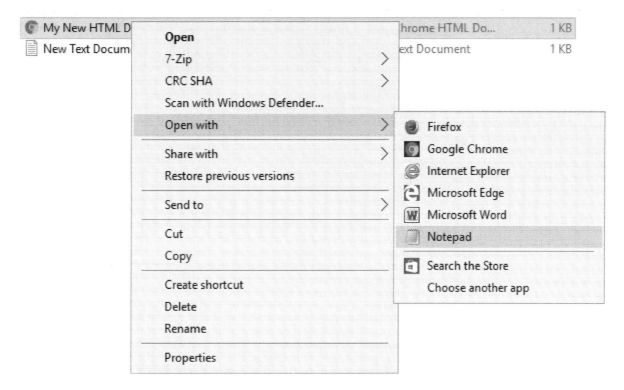

Since Notepad is not designed to understand HTML, the text and its markup both show up, as already mentioned:

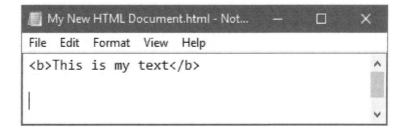

We can now add a new line, this time giving it italic markup using the <i> HTML tag:

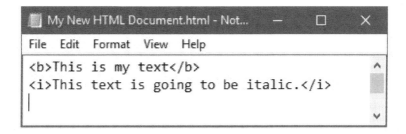

We can now save this document by going to File -> Save.

Now, opening the file again by double-clicking on it, we see the following:

The italic text and the bold text show up on the same line, despite being on different lines when we open the document in Notepad. This is because HTML ignores new lines. The way to create a new line in HTML is to tell HTML to show a new line. There are various ways of achieving this. One way is to use the <br> tag, which tells the program to show a 'break', i.e. a line break or new line. Opening the HTML document in Notepad, we add a '<br>' to the end of the bold line:

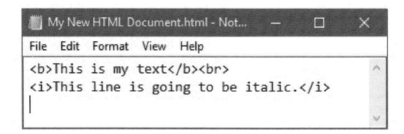

Now, opening the HTML file again in the browser, we see the difference that the <br> tag made:

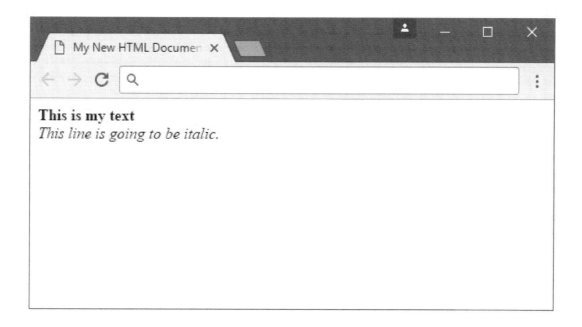

JSTinker

It gets tiresome to have to keep going back and forth between Notepad and the web browser in order to see the results of our changes. Instead, we can use one of many programs that enable us to edit HTML in 'real time' and see its effects immediately. Among such sites are CodePen.io and JSFiddle.net. There is also an open source program called JSTinker that has the same functionality which I will use in this book. You can use this program at my website and other websites.[2] These programs give us a 'playground' or 'sandbox' in which we can play with HTML and CSS, making them very useful for learning. You can follow along by opening the JSTinker link in the footnote below. You can even invite a friend to play along with you by clicking the "collaborate" button shown below.

Opening JSTinker, we see a page with four boxes on it:

---

[2] See http://hawramani.com/wp-content/jstinker/index.html

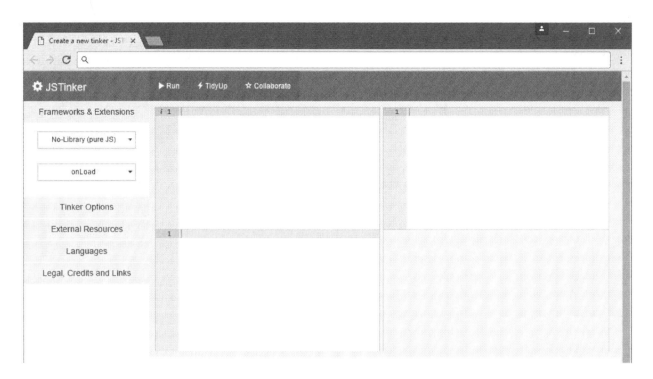

The top left box is where we type our HTML, and the bottom right box is where we see the result.[3] Below is a screenshot of JSTinker with the HTML pasted in the top left box:

Now, if we click the 'Run' button, the program 'interprets' the HTML and displays the result in the bottom right box:

---

[3] The bottom-left box is for JavaScript, which is a language used by coffee-gorging programmers and does not concern us in this book.

The numbers you see on the left of the HTML merely tells us the number of that line, which can be helpful when writing code. Let's now add a heading to our HTML. In HTML we use the 'h' tags for headings. These tags start at <h1>, used for the main heading of the document:

```
1  <h1>Title</h1>
2  <b>This is my text</b><br>
3  <i>This line is going to be italic.</i>
4
5
```

Title

This is my text
This line is going to be italic.

For a subtitle, we can use the <h2> tag, as follow (line 2 of the HTML):

```
i 1  <h1>Title</h1>
  2  <h2>Subtitle</h2>
  3  <b>This is my text</b><br>
  4  <i>This line is going to be italic.</i>
  5
  6
```

Title

Subtitle

This is my text
This line is going to be italic.

Above, you may have noticed that the title and the subtitle are showing up on separate lines in the bottom right box even though we didn't add a line break between them. The reason for this is that some tags are interpreted as 'blocking' (taking up a whole line) and other tags are interpreted as non-blocking or inline, meaning that they do not take up whole lines.

At this point we can introduce CSS. CSS, which stands for Cascading Style Sheets, is a language that helps us add 'styling' to an HTML document. HTML by itself is only for 'markup'. It enables us to add a few instructions to a document that helps the computer know the difference between a title and a paragraph for example. In technical terms, HTML is for 'semantics', it is not for styling. HTML merely defines the structure of the document, so that we can separate the title from the subtitle, and one section of a document from another. Without HTML or another markup language, a computer would have no way of telling the difference between a title and a subtitle. Both of them are merely lines of text. But thanks to the <h1> and <h2> tags, a computer knows that the <h1> is the main title, the <h2> is the subtitle, and the (as of yet unused) <p> tag is a paragraph.

HTML doesn't do much beyond defining the structure of document. If we want to do more, to add complex grids, borders, backgrounds and other nifty things, we need CSS. The simplest way to add CSS to a document is using the 'style' attribute, as follows (line 1 of the HTML below):

```
1    <h1 style="color:gray">Title</h1>
2    <h2>Subtitle</h2>
3    <b>This is my text</b><br>
4    <i>This line is going to be italic.</i>
5
```

Note how the word 'style' is *inside* the <h1> tag. This tells the browser that we are adding CSS styling to this particular tag. The style we have added is "color:gray". In the CSS language, this means that the tag's content (the heading) should be shown in gray. The CSS is enclosed in quotes, without the quotes the program doesn't know where the CSS ends and the HTML resumes again. Below is the result of the code, which we see once we click the "Run" button mentioned earlier:

Title

Subtitle

This is my text
This line is going to be italic.

We can now also add a border (lines 1 and 2 of the HTML below):

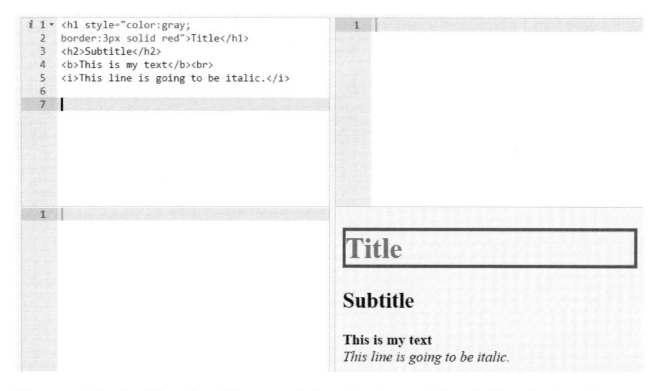

We expand the "style" tag by adding a semicolon after the word "gray". Here, in the HTML code, we add a new line in order to tidy up the appearance of the code. This new line has no effect on the appearance of the document. On the next line we have the text "border:3px solid red". In CSS, this means that the tag should have a border whose thickness is 3 pixels, and whose appearance is solid (rather than dashed, for example).

Looking at the appearance of the border, we can see how the <h1> tag is 'blocking' and takes up the whole line. The border does not merely enclose the word 'Title', it encloses the whole of the line, since it does not care about the text, it only cares about the space that is technically taken up by the <h1> tag. That space, as said, is the whole line.

Another way of adding CSS to a document is to use the <style> tag, as shown (lines 1-4 of the HTML below):

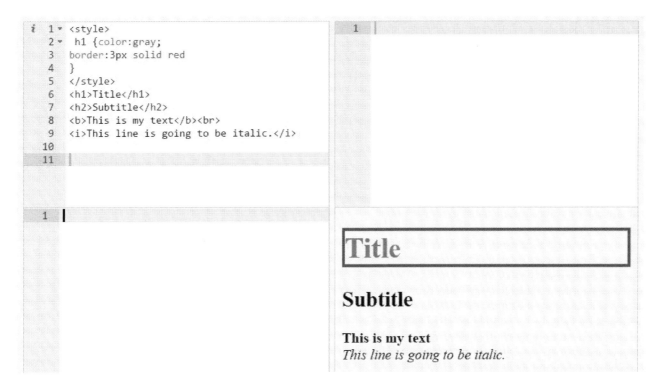

```
i  1 ▾ <style>
   2 ▾  h1 {color:gray;
   3    border:3px solid red
   4    }
   5    </style>
   6    <h1>Title</h1>
   7    <h2>Subtitle</h2>
   8    <b>This is my text</b><br>
   9    <i>This line is going to be italic.</i>
  10
  11
```

The result of the above is exactly the same as before. Inside the <style> tag, we use the CSS language to tell the web browser that the <h1> tag should have the color gray and a red border. Everything enclosed in the curly braces { } applies to the tag mentioned before it.

On a new line, we can add styling to <h2> tag, as follows (line 5):

```
i  1 ▾ <style>
   2 ▾  h1 {color:gray;
   3    border:3px solid red
   4    }
   5    h2 {font-style:italic}
   6    </style>
   7    <h1>Title</h1>
   8    <h2>Subtitle</h2>
   9    <b>This is my text</b><br>
  10    <i>This line is going to be italic.</i>
  11
  12
```

The word 'Subtitle' is now in italics. In CSS, it does not matter how we organize the code, for example the code below has the same meaning as the one above:

```
i   1 ▾ <style>
    2 ▾   h1 {color:gray;border:3px solid red
    3     } h2 {font-style:italic}
    4     </style>
    5     <h1>Title</h1>
    6     <h2>Subtitle</h2>
    7     <b>This is my text</b><br>
    8     <i>This line is going to be italic.</i>
```

We generally add new lines in order to make the code more readable. However, we cannot break words, as this would change the meaning of the CSS. For example if we write "ita lic" (with a space between "ita" and "lic"), this breaks the CSS:

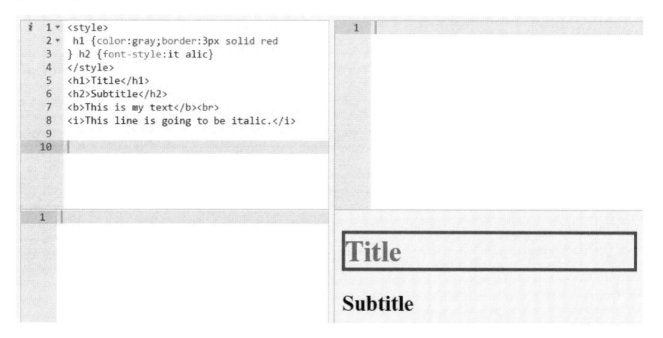

The word 'Subtitle' is now no longer italic. Web browsers are designed to be resilient to broken HTML and CSS, therefore as you can see, the rest of the HTML and CSS continue to function as expected.

JSTinker allows us to separate the HTML from the CSS as follows by putting the CSS inside the box on the right. This helps us keep the code better organized:

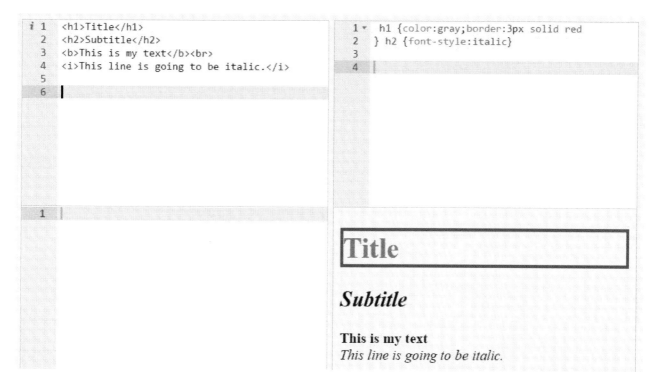

Below, I have reorganized the CSS to make it easier to read. This does not affect the meaning of the code.

```
1 ▾ h1 {
2       color:gray;
3       border:3px solid red;
4   }
5 ▾ h2 {
6       font-style:italic;
7   }
8
```

Below, I change the border of the <h1> from solid to dashed (line 3 below):

```
1 ▾ h1 {
2       color:gray;
3       border:3px dashed red;
4   }
5 ▾ h2 {
6       font-style:italic;
7   }
```

Here is the result:

Below, I add a 'dotted' border to the <h2> (line 7):

```
1 ▾ h1 {
2        color:gray;
3        border:3px dashed red;
4 }
5 ▾ h2 {
6        font-style:italic;
7        border:1px dotted black;
8 }
```

Here is the result:

Paragraphs

Earlier, we used the <br> tag to create a line break between the bold and the italic sentences that we wrote:

```
<b>This is my text</b><br>
<i>This line is going to be italic.</i>
```

Another way of achieving the same effect is to use the <p> tag, which stands for "paragraph":

```
<p><b>This is my text.</b></p>
<p><i>This line is going to be italic.</i></p>
```

Above, I have added two paragraphs. Each line begins with a <p> and ends with a </p>, which in HTML means each line is a paragraph. Note the way that at the end of each line, there is a </p> tag, this is a 'closing tag', it tells the computer that this paragraph ends there. After it, a new <p> starts ands ends at the end of the line. This causes each line to be in its own paragraph:

This is my text.

This line is going to be italic.

A paragraph, however, is more than just a line-break. Note how there is no some space between the two lines, when earlier there wasn't. This is because in CSS, by default, paragraphs have a 'margin' associated with them. A margin is space associated with a tag that is outside the tag's 'box'. We can check this out by giving the <p> tag a border in our CSS:

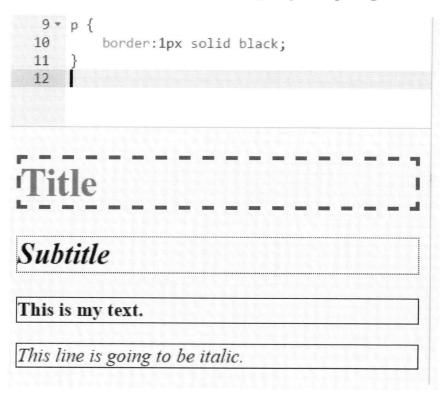

```
 9 ▾ p {
10      border:1px solid black;
11   }
12   |
```

See the way each box has some space under it. We can take away this space by setting the 'margin' CSS property to 0 in the CSS section:

```
 9 ▼ p {
10       border:1px solid black;
11       margin:0;
12 }
13
```

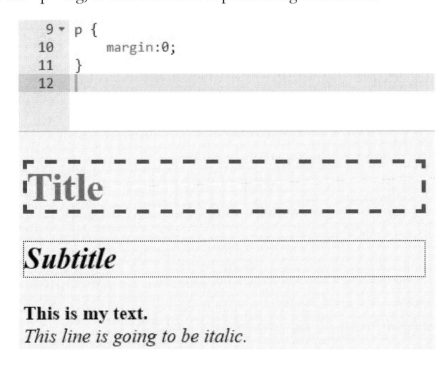

Now, the boxes are collapsed onto each other. The border between the two boxes is thicker than the rest because that is where the two borders meet, each one adds 1 pixel of length, so that the two together make a thickness of two pixels.

We can now hide the borders to see only the texts by removing the border definition from the CSS for the <p> tag, as follows. I have kept the margin definition.

```
 9 ▼ p {
10       margin:0;
11 }
12
```

Now, the two paragraphs have no additional space between them. It is as if the two lines are separated by a <br> only.

Spans and Classes

You may remember the <b> tag which we used to create bold text. HTML also offers the <span> tag, which allows to enclose a piece of text to style it. By default, the <span> has no styling of its own, unless we give it a style.

```
1    <span>Cat</span> <span>Apple</span>
2    <span>Dog</span> <span>Orange</span>
3
```

```
1
```

Cat Apple Dog Orange

In the top left box where the HTML is, we have written the names of four items on two lines. Since this is HTML, the fact that they are on two lines doesn't matter, on the bottom right box they all show up as one line. The way to make them show up on two lines would be to add a <br> tag at the end of the first line, or enclose each line in a <p> and </p>, to turn them into separate paragraphs.

Let's say we want the animal names to have a distinct appearance compared to the fruit names. We can do this through the use of classes:

```
<span class="animal">Cat</span>
<span>Apple</span>
<span class="animal">Dog</span>
<span>Orange</span>
```

In the above, we tell the computer that the stuff inside two of the <span> tags belong to the class 'animal'. Note how the class is enclosed in double quotes. Without that, the computer does not know where the class name begins and where it ends.

By giving the <span> tags class names, we accomplish nothing as of yet. The appearance of the text remains the same. What we need to do is add the CSS that will give the class "animal" a distinct appearance, as follows:

```
1  <span class="animal">Cat</span>
2  <span>Apple</span>
3  <span class="animal">Dog</span>
4  <span>Orange</span>
5
6
7
```

```
1  .animal {
2      font-weight:bold;
3      font-size:150%;
4  }
5
```

Cat Apple **Dog** Orange

In the CSS box, we create a new definition that starts with a dot. In CSS, this denotes that the thing that follows is a class. Without this dot, CSS will think that the thing is a tag name. Inside the curly braces, we give the animal class a bold appearance and we also increase its font size by giving it a font size of 150%, which means one and a half times larger than default.

We can repeat the same process for the fruits:

```
1  <span class="animal">Cat</span>
2  <span class="fruit">Apple</span>
3  <span class="animal">Dog</span>
4  <span class="fruit">Orange</span>
5
6
7
```

```
1  .animal {
2      font-weight:bold;
3      font-size:150%;
4  }
5  .fruit {
6      font-style:italic;
7      text-transform:uppercase;
8  }
9
```

Cat *APPLE* **Dog** *ORANGE*

Using the font-style CSS property, we give the fruits an italic appearance. Using text-transform, we turn the fruit names into all-caps text. Note how in the HTML, the words "Apple" and "Orange" are not in all-caps. But using CSS, we can make them appear as if they are in all-caps. We can also make them all-small:

```
1  <span class="animal">Cat</span>
2  <span class="fruit">Apple</span>
3  <span class="animal">Dog</span>
4  <span class="fruit">Orange</span>
5
6
7
```

```
1  .animal {
2      font-weight:bold;
3      font-size:150%;
4  }
5  .fruit {
6      font-style:italic;
7      text-transform:lowercase;
8  }
9
```

Cat *apple* **Dog** *orange*

Note that above, the text-transform property is given a value of "lowercase", meaning the text should be transformed to all-lowercase when it is displayed.

An HTML tag can have more than one class, as follows:

```
<span class="animal thing">Cat</span>
<span class="fruit thing">Apple</span>
<span class="animal thing">Dog</span>
<span class="fruit thing">Orange</span>
```

A cat is an animal and a thing, while an apple is a fruit and a thing. We can now give a distinct style to the class "thing", as follows:

```
1  .animal {
2      font-weight:bold;
3      font-size:150%;
4  }
5  .fruit {
6      font-style:italic;
7      text-transform:lowercase;
8  }
9  .thing {
10     text-decoration:underline;
11 }
12
```

<u>Cat</u> *<u>apple</u>* <u>**Dog**</u> *<u>orange</u>*

Since all four <span> tags have the class "thing", all four words get an underlined appearance.

A class name cannot begin with a number, although it can contain numbers elsewhere. For example if we add the number zero before the class name "animal", even if we do everything else correctly, the class stops working:

```
1  <span class="0animal thing">Cat</span>          1 ▾ .0animal {
2  <span class="fruit thing">Apple</span>           2      font-weight:bold;
3  <span class="0animal thing">Dog</span>           3      font-size:150%;
4  <span class="fruit thing">Orange</span>          4  }
5                                                   5 ▾ .fruit {
6                                                   6      font-style:italic;
7                                                   7      text-transform:lowercase;
                                                    8  }
                                                    9 ▾ .thing {
                                                   10      text-decoration:underline;
                                                   11  }
                                                   12
```

Cat <u>*apple*</u> <u>Dog</u> <u>*orange*</u>

We can, however, start a class name with a dash or underscore.

Class Conflict

If we give the class "animal" bold styling, while giving the "thing" class normal styling, the two cancel each other out. The computer takes the last definition (the one at the bottom) as the final word.

```
1 ▾ .animal {
2      font-weight:bold;
3  }
4 ▾ .thing {
5      font-weight:normal;
6  }
7
```

Cat Apple Dog Orange

We can define the same class multiple times in the same CSS passage. Below, while the "thing" class's normal styling cancels out the "animal" class's bold styling, the final "animal" class definition has the final word, making the words appear bold.

```
1  .animal {
2      font-weight:bold;
3  }
4  .thing {
5      font-weight:normal;
6  }
7  .animal {
8      font-weight:bold;
9  }
10  |
```

Cat Apple Dog Orange

Using the keyword "!important", we can force one of the definitions to become the final word, as follows:

```
1  .animal {
2      font-weight:bold;
3  }
4  .thing {
5      font-weight:normal !important;
6  }
7  .animal {
8      font-weight:bold;
9  }
10  |
```

Cat Apple Dog Orange

!important tells the computer that this definition should be treated as the final word. The use of !important is useful when solving problems, but it is bad practice to use it when doing professional work, and it can make life very difficult, because you can end up with a situation where everything is "important", so that the word loses its meaning.

Romeo and Juliet

Juliet. O Romeo, Romeo! wherefore art thou Romeo?
Deny thy father and refuse thy name;
Or, if thou wilt not, be but sworn my love,
And I 'll no longer be a Capulet.
    Romeo. [*Aside*] Shall I hear more, or shall I speak at this?
    Juliet. 'T is but thy name that is my enemy;
Thou art thyself, though not a Montague.
What 's Montague? it is nor hand, nor foot,   40
Nor arm, nor face, nor any other part
Belonging to a man. O, be some other name!
What 's in a name? that which we call a rose
By any other name would smell as sweet;

The above design is taken from a 1881 print of Shakespeare's *Romeo and Juliet*. Using HTML and CSS, we can recreate the design so that we can put it on a website. You may notice the number "40" at the center right of the excerpt, we will ignore that. We will begin with the first part.

We use a <p> tag to enclose each character's set of lines. Inside it, we use <span> tags to differentiate between different parts of the text. The character names are given a "character-name" class (line 1 of the HTML below), while the things they speak are given a "text" class (line 2 of the HTML below). Using <br> tags, we can separate lines as needed (line 3 of the HTML):

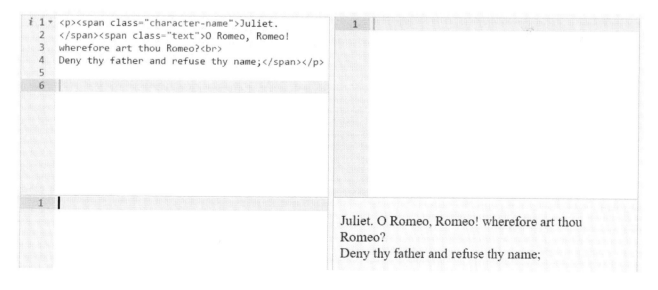

```
1  <p><span class="character-name">Juliet.
2  </span><span class="text">O Romeo, Romeo!
3  wherefore art thou Romeo?<br>
4  Deny thy father and refuse thy name;</span></p>
5
6
```

Juliet. O Romeo, Romeo! wherefore art thou Romeo?
Deny thy father and refuse thy name;

So far, we have not given any styling to the text, therefore, as can be seen above on the bottom right, the text doesn't have anything special going for it. We give the "character-name" class an italic appearance; we also give it a new font:

```
1 ▾  .character-name {
2        font-style:italic;
3        font-family:'Monotype Corsiva';
4    }
5
```

The result is as folows:

Juliet. O Romeo, Romeo! wherefore art thou Romeo?
Deny thy father and refuse thy name;

The font we used is Monotype Corsiva. This is not exactly the font used in the 1881 print, but it is a good enough approximation. When using fonts, we must take into account the fact that some users may not have that particular font on their computers. Monotype Corsiva is a commonly available font on most computers, while if we used a rarer but more ornate font, it may not show up properly on most users' computers since they will not have the font.[4]

You may notice that the word 'Juliet' is smaller than the rest of the text, which causes it to have an unbalanced appearance. This happens because this word is in a different font compared to the rest, and each font has its own peculiar size. When using multiple fonts side-by-side, we must correct for any imbalance using the font-size CSS property, as follows:

```
1 ▾  .character-name {
2        font-style:italic;
3        font-family:'Monotype Corsiva';
4        font-size:118%;
5    }
```

Here is the result:

---

[4] To get beyond this restriction, we can use the technology known as 'web fonts', which enables a website to carry its own font with it so that it shows up correctly regardless of the user's computer.

30

Juliet. O Romeo, Romeo! wherefore art thou
Romeo?
Deny thy father and refuse thy name;

Above, the word "Juliet" is now slightly larger (18% larger, to be exact) then before.

You may recall that the word "Juliet" had some space before it in the 1881 design. We can recreate that using the "padding" CSS property, as follows on line 5:

```
1 ▾ .character-name {
2       font-style:italic;
3       font-family:'Monotype Corsiva';
4       font-size:118%;
5       padding-left:15px;
6   }
```

Above, we added 15 pixels of padding to the left of the <span>. If we had used "padding:15px" rather than "padding-left:15px", the padding would have been added all around the <span>. Using "padding-left" we restrict the padding only to the left of the <span>.

Juliet. O Romeo, Romeo! wherefore art thou
Romeo?
Deny thy father and refuse thy name;

Padding is similar to margins in that it adds space around a tag. It is different from it in that padding adds space *inside* the tag, while margin adds space outside of it. We can see this visually by adding a border around the tag, as follows on line 6:

```
1 ▾  .character-name {
2        font-style:italic;
3        font-family:'Monotype Corsiva';
4        font-size:118%;
5        padding-left:15px;
6        border:1px solid black;
7    }
8
```

The result is as follows:

> *Juliet.* |O Romeo, Romeo! wherefore art thou
> Romeo?
> Deny thy father and refuse thy name;

The space created by the "padding-left" propety is inside the border. If we were using a margin, the space would be outside the border, as follows. Below, I have replaced "padding-left" with "margin-left":

```
1 ▾  .character-name {
2        font-style:italic;
3        font-family:'Monotype Corsiva';
4        font-size:118%;
5        margin-left:15px;
6        border:1px solid black;
7    }
```

> *Juliet.* |O Romeo, Romeo! wherefore art thou
> Romeo?
> Deny thy father and refuse thy name;

Whether one uses margins or padding can make all the difference in the outcomes of certain designs. For now it is sufficient to know that the two things are distinct. Their different effects will be made clearer throughout this book.

Below is the 1881 design for comparison:

> *Juliet.* O Romeo, Romeo! wherefore art thou Romeo?
> Deny thy father and refuse thy name;

Note how there is some space *after* the word "Juliet", not just before it. We can add this using "padding-right" (line 6 below):

```
1 ▾ .character-name {
2        font-style:italic;
3        font-family:'Monotype Corsiva';
4        font-size:118%;
5        padding-left:15px;
6        padding-right:5px;
7 }
```

Juliet. O Romeo, Romeo! wherefore art thou Romeo?
Deny thy father and refuse thy name;

Below, I use CSS to reduce the size of the font of the <p> tag to 80%, this makes all of the text smaller so that the first line has enough space to show up as one line (line 10 below):

```
1 ▾ .character-name {
2        font-style:italic;
3        font-family:'Monotype Corsiva';
4        font-size:118%;
5        padding-left:15px;
6        padding-right:5px;
7 }
8
9 ▾ p {
10        font-size:80%;
11 }
12 |
```

Juliet. O Romeo, Romeo! wherefore art thou Romeo?
Deny thy father and refuse thy name;

The word "Juliet" retains its 118% size. What is happening is that the style on the <p> tag reduces everything so that it is only 80% as large as before, then Juliet's 118% size, starting from this reduced size, increases it by 18%. In this case, the two size definitions do not conflict, they merely change one another. This is because we are using percentages. If we were using pixels, then one font size would overwrite the other (lines 4 and 10):

```
1 ▾  .character-name {
2        font-style:italic;
3        font-family:'Monotype Corsiva';
4        font-size:17px;
5        padding-left:15px;
6        padding-right:5px;
7    }
8
9 ▾  p {
10       font-size:14px;
11   }
12   |
```

Juliet. O Romeo, Romeo! wherefore art thou Romeo?
Deny thy father and refuse thy name;

Even though the 14 pixel font size on the <p> tag is last, it does not have the final word. The size of "Juliet" remains at 17 pixels. This is because in CSS, a style added to a *class name* takes precedence over a style added to a *tag name*. Whatever we add to "character-name" is considered more important by CSS than whatever we added to the <p> tag, and for this reason it overrules it.

We gave the "character-name" class italic styling. We could have instead used an <i> tag, as follows (line 1 of the HTML):

```
i 1 ▾ <p><i class="character-name">Juliet.
  2   </i><span class="text">O Romeo, Romeo!
  3   wherefore art thou Romeo?<br>
  4   Deny thy father and refuse thy name;</span></p>
  5
  6   |
```

```
1 ▾ .character-name {|
  2      font-family:'Monotype Corsiva';
  3      font-size:17px;
  4      padding-left:15px;
  5      padding-right:5px;
  6   }
  7
  8 ▾ p {
  9      font-size:14px;
 10   }
 11
```

Juliet. O Romeo, Romeo! wherefore art thou Romeo?
Deny thy father and refuse thy name;

Notice that above the word Juliet is enclosed in an <i> tag rather than a <span>. But the <i> tag continues to have the "character-name" class, so that it continues to have the CSS properties (like the Monotype Corsiva font) that we gave to this class.

In the CSS, I removed the "font-style:italic" property. The <i> tag has default italic styling, therefore this is no longer needed.

It is, however, better not to use the <i> and <b> tags for styling. It is best to use <span> tags and add the styling in the CSS. This allows us more leverage in the future. Maybe in the future we decide to change the appearance of the character names to bold instead of italic. If we had used <i> tags for all the character names, we would have had to go through thousands of lines of HTML to remove every <i> tag and change it to a <b> tag. But thanks to using <span> tags and CSS, changing one or two lines or CSS can change the appearance of every single character name in the text.

Now, we are ready to add two more lines of poetry:

```
1  <p><i class="character-name">Juliet.
2  </i><span class="text">O Romeo, Romeo!
3  wherefore art thou Romeo?<br>
4  Deny thy father and refuse thy name;<br>
5  Or, if thou wilt not, be but swon my love,<br>
6  And I'll no longer be a Capulet.</span></p>
7
8
```

```
1  .character-name {
2      font-family:'Monotype Corsiva';
3      font-size:17px;
4      padding-left:15px;
5      padding-right:5px;
6  }
7
8  p {
9      font-size:14px;
10 }
11
```

Juliet. O Romeo, Romeo! wherefore art thou Romeo?
Deny thy father and refuse thy name;
Or, if thou wilt not, be but swon my love,
And I'll no longer be a Capulet.

Since the two lines belong to the same passage, we add them inside the earlier <span> and <p> tags, rather than creating new ones for them.

As a reminder, here is the 1881 design again:

Juliet. O Romeo, Romeo! wherefore art thou Romeo?
Deny thy father and refuse thy name;
Or, if thou wilt not, be but sworn my love,
And I 'll no longer be a Capulet.
    Romeo. [*Aside*] Shall I hear more, or shall I speak at this?
    Juliet. 'T is but thy name that is my enemy;
Thou art thyself, though not a Montague.
What 's Montague? it is nor hand, nor foot,   40
Nor arm, nor face, nor any other part
Belonging to a man.   O, be some other name!
What 's in a name? that which we call a rose
By any other name would smell as sweet;

Let's now add Romeo's line:

```
1  <p><span class="character-name">Juliet.
2  </span><span class="text">O Romeo, Romeo!
3  wherefore art thou Romeo?<br>
4  Deny thy father and refuse thy name;<br>
5  Or, if thou wilt not, be but swon my love,<br>
6  And I'll no longer be a Capulet.</span></p>
7  <p><span class="character-name">Romeo.</span>
8  <span class="text">[Aside] Shall I hear more,
9  or shall I speak at this?</span></p>
```

```
1  .character-name {
2      font-style:italic;
3      font-family:'Monotype Corsiva';
4      font-size:17px;
5      padding-left:15px;
6      padding-right:5px;
7  }
8
9  p {
10     font-size:14px;
11 }
12
```

Juliet. O Romeo, Romeo! wherefore art thou Romeo?
Deny thy father and refuse thy name:
Or, if thou wilt not, be but swon my love,
And I'll no longer be a Capulet.

    Romeo. [Aside] Shall I hear more, or shall I speak at this?

I created a new <p> tag for Romeo's line. The <p> tag, as has already been mentioned, has a margin below it by default, as can be seen in the excessive amount of space between Juliet and Romeo's parts. We can undo the space by setting the "margin" CSS property to zero:

```
i 1▾ <p><span class="character-name">Juliet.
  2   </span><span class="text">O Romeo, Romeo!
  3   wherefore art thou Romeo?<br>
  4   Deny thy father and refuse thy name;<br>
  5   Or, if thou wilt not, be but swon my love,<br>
  6   And I'll no longer be a Capulet.</span></p>
  7▾ <p><span class="character-name">Romeo.</span>
  8▾ <span class="text">[Aside] Shall I hear more,
  9   or shall I speak at this?</span></p>
```

```
 1▾ .character-name {
  2       font-style:italic;
  3       font-family:'Monotype Corsiva';
  4       font-size:17px;
  5       padding-left:15px;
  6       padding-right:5px;
  7   }
  8
  9▾ p {
 10       font-size:14px;
 11       margin:0;
 12   }
 13
```

```
 1  
```

Juliet. O Romeo, Romeo! wherefore art thou Romeo?
Deny thy father and refuse thy name;
Or, if thou wilt not, be but swon my love,
And I'll no longer be a Capulet.
   Romeo. [Aside] Shall I hear more, or shall I speak at this?

Due to certain technicalities, if we had merely done "margin-bottom:0", this wouldn't have accomplished anything. We rather have to set the entire "margin" property to zero, then, if desired, we can add back some margin:

```
 9▾ p {
 10      font-size:14px;
 11      margin:0;
 12      margin-bottom:2px;
 13  }
 14
```

Juliet. O Romeo, Romeo! wherefore art thou Romeo?
Deny thy father and refuse thy name;
Or, if thou wilt not, be but swon my love,
And I'll no longer be a Capulet.
   Romeo. [Aside] Shall I hear more, or shall I speak at this?

The "margin:0" takes effect first, removing all margins. The "margin-bottom:2px" takes effect next, adding two pixels of margin underneath each paragraph. This is quite minimal and barely visible.

Below is the rest of the poem marked up in HTML:

```
i   1 ▾ <p><span class="character-name">Juliet.
    2   </span><span class="text">O Romeo, Romeo!
    3   wherefore art thou Romeo?<br>
    4   Deny thy father and refuse thy name;<br>
    5   Or, if thou wilt not, be but swon my love,<br>
    6   And I'll no longer be a Capulet.</span></p>
    7 ▾ <p><span class="character-name">Romeo.</span>
    8 ▾ <span class="text">[Aside] Shall I hear more,
    9   or shall I speak at this?</span></p>
   10 ▾ <p><span class="character-name">Juliet.
   11   </span><span class="text">'T is but thy name
   12   that is my enemy;<br>
   13   Thou art thyself, though not a Montague.<br>
   14   What's Montague? it is nor hand, nor foot,<br>
   15   Nor arm, nor face, nor any other part<br>
   16   Belonging to a man. O, be some other name!<br>
   17   What's in a name? that which we call a rose<br>
   18   By any other name would smell as sweet;
   19   </span></p>
```

You may note that the HTML is quite hard to read. We can't easily see where one thing begins and another ends. We can make it somewhat more readable by separating different sections:

```
i   1 ▾ <p>
    2 ▾     <span class="character-name">Juliet.
    3   </span>
    4
    5 ▾     <span class="text">O Romeo, Romeo!
    6   wherefore art thou Romeo?<br>
    7   Deny thy father and refuse thy name;<br>
    8   Or, if thou wilt not,
    9   be but swon my love,<br>
   10   And I'll no longer be a Capulet.</span>
   11   </p>
   12
   13 ▾ <p>
   14 ▾     <span class="character-name">Romeo.
   15   </span>
   16 ▾     <span class="text">[Aside] Shall I
   17       hear more, or shall I
   18       speak at this?</span>
   19   </p>
```

Tidying up code to make it easier to read is known as 'code formatting' and 'code styling' and has no effect on the final product.

> *Juliet.* O Romeo, Romeo! wherefore art thou Romeo?
> Deny thy father and refuse thy name;
> Or, if thou wilt not, be but swon my love,
> And I'll no longer be a Capulet.
> *Romeo.* [Aside] Shall I hear more, or shall I speak at this?
> *Juliet.* 'T is but thy name that is my enemy;
> Thou art thyself, though not a Montague.
> What's Montague? it is nor hand, nor foot,
> Nor arm, nor face, nor any other part
> Belonging to a man. O, be some other name!
> What's in a name? that which we call a rose
> By any other name would smell as sweet;

If you look at the 1881 original, you will notice that there is a somewhat large space in front of the "O" in "O, be some other name!". We can enclose the "O" in a new <span> and give it an "extra-space" class:

```
25   that is my enemy;<br>
26   Thou art thyself, though
27   not a Montague.<br>
28   What's Montague? it is
29   nor hand, nor foot,<br>
30   Nor arm, nor face, nor any other part<br>
31   Belonging to a man.
32   <span class="extra-space">O</span>,
33   be some other name!<br>
```

```
15   .extra-space {
16       padding-left:5px;
17   }
18   |
```

In the CSS, we gave the "extra-space" class a left padding of 5 pixels. The result is as follows:

> Nor arm, nor face, nor any other part
> Belonging to a man. O, be some other name!
> What's in a name? that which we call a rose
> By any other name would smell as sweet;

Another solution would be to use a non-breaking-space entity, as follows (line 32 of the HTML):

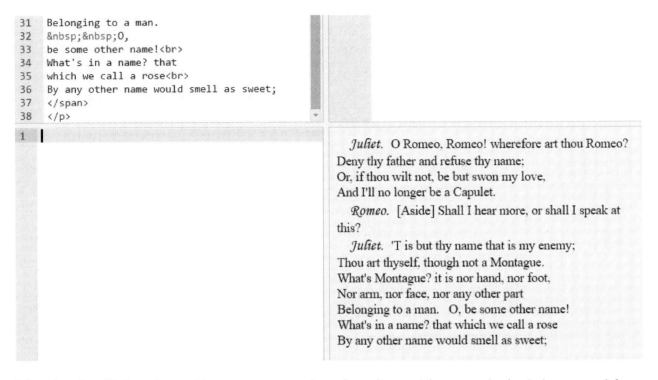

```
31  Belonging to a man.
32    O,
33  be some other name!<br>
34  What's in a name? that
35  which we call a rose<br>
36  By any other name would smell as sweet;
37  </span>
38  </p>
```

The " " (starting with an ampersand and ending with a semicolon) is a special instruction to the computer to create a space at this location.[5] Using two of them back-to-back tells the computer to add two spaces here. The end result is that the "O" now has more space to its left.

Using " " is not good practice because it reduces your leverage to make changes in the future. If, in the future, you wanted these extra spaces to be much larger or smaller, you would have to go through all of your HTML and make changes. If, however, you had used <span> and an "extra-space" class, you would have been able to change everything by making a few changes to the CSS.

---

[5] These special instructions are known as "HTML entities", and there are thousands of them, although you generally only have use for a few of them.

Divs

The <div> tag (standing for "division") enables us to divide an HTML document into multiple sections. <div> tags are often the starting point for any sophisticated design project. <div> tags are like <span> tags in that they do not carry any default styles. Their difference is that while <span> tags are *inline*, meaning that they can used in the middle of a paragraph to add some style to a word, a <div> tag is *blocking*, it is a block or rectangle that takes up a whole line of space, similar to a <p> tag. Unlike a <p> tag, it doesn't come with any pre-defined margins.

```
1    <div class="division-a"></div>
2    <div class="division-b"></div>
3
```

Above, we have defined two <div> tags with nothing inside them. If you run this code, you will get a blank output, because <div> tags by default have zero height and are therefore invisible. To explore what <div> tags are like, we will first give them a solid black border in the CSS and see what happens:

```
1    <div class="division-a"></div>           1 ▾ div {
2    <div class="division-b"></div>           2       border:1px solid black;
3                                              3   }
4    |                                         4
                                               5   |



1   |
```

The <div> tags show up as nothing but a black bar. This is because each <div> tag takes up a whole line. Since we have given each div a 1 pixel border, what ends up showing are two bars, each two pixels high. They are basically long borders with nothing inside them.

Let's now give the <div> tags some height:

```
i  1   <div class="division-a"></div>
   2   <div class="division-b"></div>
   3
   4   |
```

```
1 ▾  div {
⚠ 2      border:1px solid black;
   3      height:50px;
   4  }
   5
   6  |
```

```
1   |
```

Now the true appearance of the <div> tags becomes apparent. They are rectangles that take up whole lines. Below, I have given the <div> tag a margin of 20 pixels in the CSS definition. This margin applies to all sides of each div, adding 20 pixels of margin above, below and to the right and left of each div. The end result is that the <div> tags are separated and made smaller as 20 pixels of margin are added on all sides. Their height does not change because the CSS definition continues to force a height of 50 pixels.

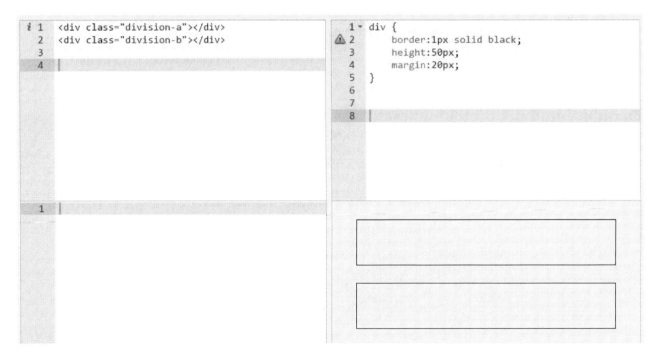

```
i  1   <div class="division-a"></div>
   2   <div class="division-b"></div>
   3
   4   |
```

```
1 ▾  div {
⚠ 2      border:1px solid black;
   3      height:50px;
   4      margin:20px;
   5  }
   6
   7
   8  |
```

```
1   |
```

We will now add some content to each <div> tag (lines 2-3 and 6-7 of the HTML):

```
1 ▾ <div class="division-a">
2       <h1>Main Title</h1>
3       <p>This is the main text.</p>
4   </div>
5 ▾ <div class="division-b">
6       <h2>Subsidiary Title</h2>
7       <p>Cautionary tale.</p>
8   </div>
9
10  |
```

```
1 ▾ div {
2       border:1px solid black;
3       height:50px;
4       margin:20px;
5   }
6
7
8   |
```

Main Title

This is the main text.
Subsidiary Title

Cautionary tale.

It can be seen that the content has a broken appearance. This is because in the CSS, we are forcing each <div> to have a height of 50 pixels, which is not high enough to contain the new content we added. The result is that the content "overflows", it pours out of the top <div> tag and spills over the next one. Using CSS, we can prevent overflow from taking place (line 5 of the CSS below):

```
1 ▾ <div class="division-a">
2       <h1>Main Title</h1>
3       <p>This is the main text.</p>
4   </div>
5 ▾ <div class="division-b">
6       <h2>Subsidiary Title</h2>
7       <p>Cautionary tale.</p>
8   </div>
9
10  |
```

```
1 ▾ div {
2       border:1px solid black;
3       height:50px;
4       margin:20px;
5       overflow:hidden;
6   }
7
8
9   |
```

Main Title

Subsidiary Title

Using "overflow:hidden", we cause the overflowed content to disappear. This is not ideal, since now the paragraphs cannot be seen.

Another thing we can do is use "overflow:scroll" (line 5 of the CSS below):

```
1 ▾ div {
2       border:1px solid black;
3       height:50px;
4       margin:20px;
5       overflow:scroll;
6   }
7
```

In this case, scroll bars appear to the left of the <div> tags if the content is too large, allowing the user to scroll through the content.

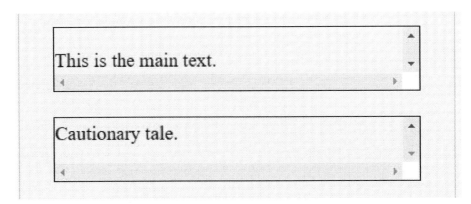

We can also spare ourselves all this trouble by simply removing the "height" property in the CSS. This will allow each <div> to expand in height so that all of the content can be seen:

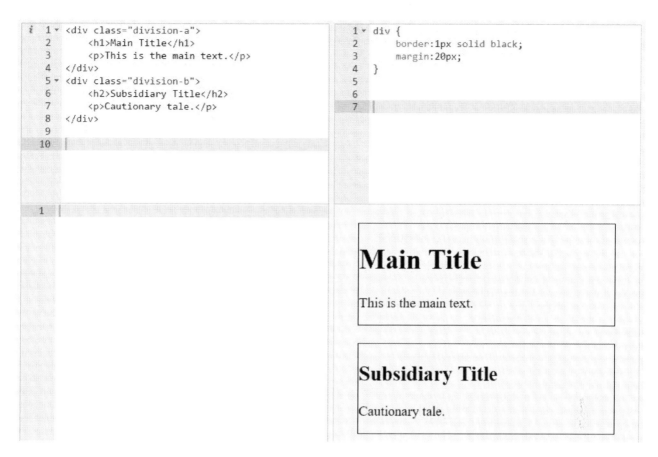

An empty <div> tag that does not have a height will be invisible. But if the <div> has visible content inside it, we can take away the height property and it will continue showing up.

We can now make use of the <div> tags' classes by making the second <div> tag's contents smaller (lines 6-8 of the CSS):

```css
1 ▾ div {
2       border:1px solid black;
3       margin:20px;
4  }
5
6 ▾ .division-b {
7       font-size:70%;
8  }
```

Here is the result:

Main Title

This is the main text.

Subsidiary Title

Cautionary tale.

Using <div> tags, I can give all the paragraphs in a specific part of an HTML document follow a certain style while leaving other paragraphs alone (lines 9-11 below):

```
 1   div {
 2       border:1px solid black;
 3       margin:20px;
 4   }
 5
 6   .division-b {
 7       font-size:70%;
 8   }
 9   .division-b p {
10       font-style:italic;
11   }
12
```

The CSS definition ".division-b p" (line 9 above) tells the web browser to apply the style that follows to every paragraph contained inside the class ".division-b". This has no effect on the paragraphs contained outside of it, such as the paragraph "This is the main text" inside division-a.

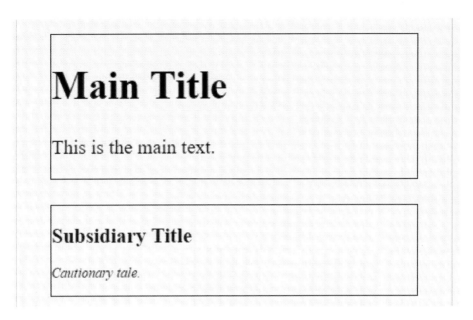

An important use of <div> tags is nesting, where we put one <div> inside another like Russian dolls. Below, I have moved division-b inside division-a

```
1   <div class="division-a">
2       <h1>Main Title</h1>
3       <p>This is the main text.</p>
4       <div class="division-b">
5           <h2>Subsidiary Title</h2>
6           <p>Cautionary tale.</p>
7       </div>
8   </div>
```

The result is as follows:

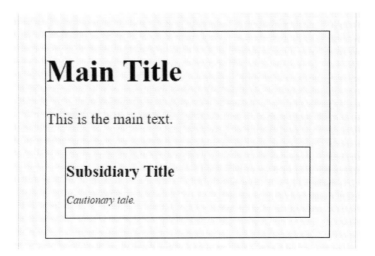

Thanks to the "cascading" nature of CSS (remember that CSS stands for Cascading Style Sheets), styles I add to division-a will also cascade down to the <div> tags contained inside

it. Below, I make division-a have an italic styling (line 7 of the CSS). Note the way the contents of division-b also become italic:

```
1 ▾ div {
2       border: 1px solid black;
3       margin: 20px;
4   }
5
6 ▾ .division-a {
7       font-style:italic;
8   }
```

Here is the result:

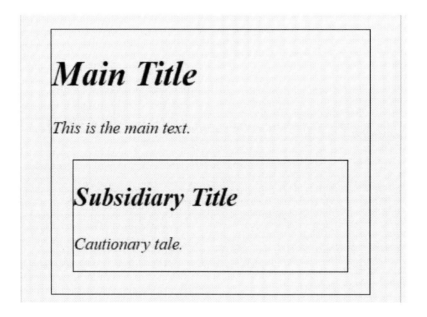

If we do not want the content of division-b to get the italic styling, we can cancel it out in this way (line 10 of the CSS):

```
 1 ▾ div {
 2       border: 1px solid black;
 3       margin: 20px;
 4   }
 5
 6 ▾ .division-a {
 7       font-style:italic;
 8   }
 9 ▾ .division-b {
10       font-style:normal;
11   }
```

Here is the result:

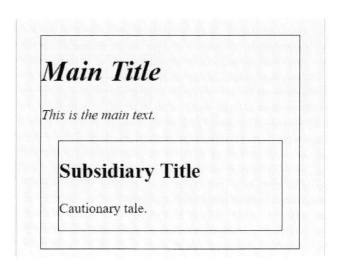

Above, on line 7 we declare that everything inside division-a should be italic. On line 10, we declare that everything inside division-b should be normal rather than italic. These two styles conflict, since now division-b is being told by line 7 to be italic and by line 10 to be normal. The normal style wins because it is *more specific*, since it applies directly to division-b. The italic styling only applies to division-b by chance, due to it being inside division-a. But the normal styling is specifically attached to division-b, therefore it takes precedence.

Styling Divs

We can now better study what padding is. Above, we added a margin of 20 pixels to each rectangle. You can see that the texts are uncomfortably close to the borders. What if we wanted to add space between the text and the borders that enclose them? We cannot do that with margin, since the margin is outside the borders. Padding allows us to do this. Padding is space *inside* the borders:

Below, I have added 10 pixels of padding to the CSS for the <div> tag (line 4 of the CSS), meaning it applies to both rectangles, since both of them are <div> elements.

```
1 ▾ div {
2       border: 1px solid black;
3       margin: 20px;
4       padding:10px;
5 }
```

Here is the result:

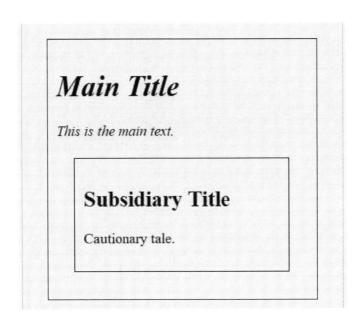

You can see that now the word "Main Title" has more space to its left. The same applies to the "Subsidiary Title".

Below, I have added some shadow to division-b using the "box-shadow" CSS property (line 12 of the CSS):

```
10 ▾  .division-b {
11         font-style:normal;
12         box-shadow:5px 5px 1px gray;
13    }
14    |
```

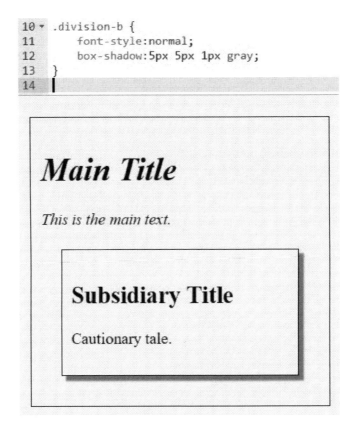

The pixels defined in the "box-shadow" property define the nature of the shadow. It is five pixels to the right, five pixels down, and larger by 1 pixel from the original rectangle, and its color is gray. You can play around with these numbers to produce various interesting effects (line 12 below):

```
10 ▾ .division-b {
11       font-style:normal;
12       box-shadow:15px 5px 21px gray;
13    }
14
```

The result is as follows:

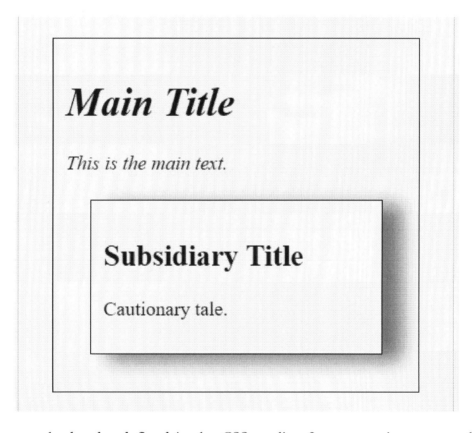

By taking away the border defined in the CSS on line 2, we can give a somewhat artistic appearance to the arrangement:

```
1 ▾ div {
2       margin: 20px;
3       padding:10px;
4    }
5
```

The result is as follows:

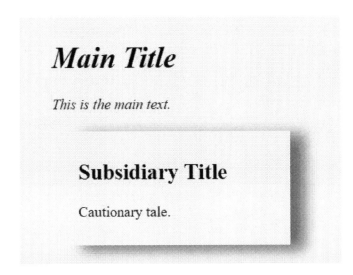

Below, I bring back the borders to show the border-radius CSS property (line 3 below), which allows us to create curved borders:

```
1 ▾ div {
2       border: 1px solid black;
3       border-radius:10px;
4       margin: 20px;
5       padding:10px;
6   }
```

The result is as follows:

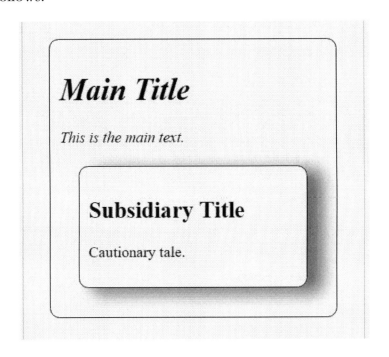

Even if we take the borders away again, the effect of the border-radius remains, as seen in the curvedness of the shadow below:

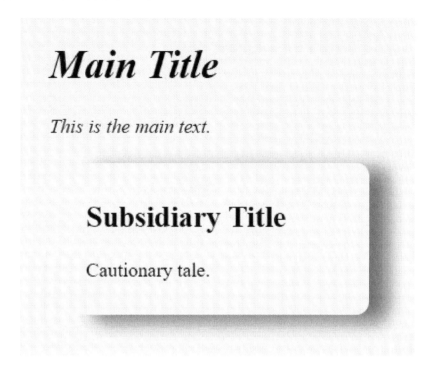

Below, I have given a gray background to division-a:

```
 7 ▾  .division-a {
 8         font-style:italic;
 9         background:#ccc;
10    }
```

The CSS property "background:#ccc" assigns a background to the division (and to any divisions contained inside it). The color code #ccc refers to a specific location on the RGB color spectrum that happens to be gray. In order to easily find out the code for a color, you can Google "CSS color chooser" and you will find many websites that let you pick colors and give you the RGB "hex" code for it.

By default, <div> elements have a transparent background.[6] Since division-b is transparent, the gray background of division-a shows through it. Below, I have given division-b a white background that overrides that gray background of division-a (line 14 of the CSS):

---

[6] The difference between a tag and an element is that the word "tag" refers to the HTML, while the word "element" refers to the *result* of the HTML that is displayed in a browser. When we see a <p>, this is a paragraph tag. But when we see that actual paragraph in an article, that is a paragraph element. Sometimes they are used interchangeably, especially when working with HTML. When working with CSS and JavaScript, usually the word "element" is used rather than tag, because CSS and JavaScript generally deal with the result of the HTML.

```
 7 ▾  .division-a {
 8         font-style:italic;
 9         background:#ccc;
10     }
11 ▾  .division-b {
12         font-style:normal;
13         box-shadow:15px 5px 21px gray;
14         background:white;
```

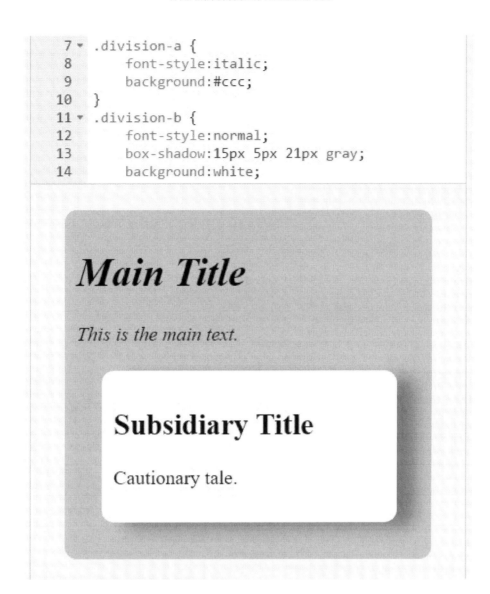

Instead of writing 'white' for the background, I could have written its RGB hex code, which is #fff.

This page intentionally left blank

2.
Understanding Lists

Lists are an important part of HTML with many uses. There are two types of lists, ordered and unordered.

```
1  <ol>
2      <li>First item.</li>
3      <li>Second item.</li>
4      <li>Third item.</li>
5  </ol>
6
```

1. First item.
2. Second item.
3. Third item.

Above is an ordered list, which is created using the <ol> tag. Ordered lists are automatically numbered by the browser, as can be seen in the output in the bottom right. Inside the <ol> tag, we use <li> ("list item") tags to add items to the list.

Using the "type" attribute, we can change the numbering system used by the <ol> tag, as follows (line 1 below):

```
i 1▾ <ol type="i">
  2        <li>First item.</li>
  3        <li>Second item.</li>
  4        <li>Third item.</li>
  5        <li>Fourth item.</li>
  6  </ol>
  7  |
```

Above, I have set the type to 'i', which means lower-case Roman numerals:

i. First item.
ii. Second item.
iii. Third item.
iv. Fourth item.

Changing the type to "A" makes the browser show the items given alphabetic 'numbering':

```
i 1▾ <ol type="A">
  2        <li>First item.</li>
  3        <li>Second item.</li>
  4        <li>Third item.</li>
  5        <li>Fourth item.</li>
  6  </ol>
  7  |
```

A. First item.
B. Second item.
C. Third item.
D. Fourth item.

We will introduce various of these numbering types throughout this chapter.

The <ol> tag, like a <div> tag, is *block* element that takes up the whole line, as can be seen below, where I have given the <ol> tag a border (line 2 of the CSS):

```
i 1 ▾ <ol type="A">
  2       <li>First item.</li>
  3       <li>Second item.</li>
  4       <li>Third item.</li>
  5       <li>Fourth item.</li>
  6  </ol>
  7  |
```

```
1 ▾ ol {
2       border:1px solid #000;
3  }
4  |
```

```
1  |
```

A. First item.
B. Second item.
C. Third item.
D. Fourth item.

The border color I have used is #000 (three zeroes), which is the same as "black". Beginners sometimes mistakenly type capital letter O's ("O" as in "Oscar") instead of zeroes. Coding programs like JSTinker help us distinguish between zeroes and capital O's by adding a diagonal slash inside zeroes, as seen below:

```
Three zeroes:
000
Three capital O's:
OOO
```

To continue our analysis, below I have given a dashed border to the <li> tags (lines 4-6 of the CSS).

```
1 ▾ ol {
2       border:1px solid #000;
3  }
4 ▾ li {
5       border:1px dashed #000;
6  }
7  |
```

See what happens:

59

```
A. First item.
B. Second item.
C. Third item.
D. Fourth item.
```

The numbering (the A, B, C and D) are part of the <ol> tag, but they are outside the <li> tags. Yet, they are attached to the <li> tags. Let's give the <li> tag a left margin of 20 pixels (line 6 of the CSS below):

```
1   <ol type="A">
2       <li>First item.</li>
3       <li>Second item.</li>
4       <li>Third item.</li>
5       <li>Fourth item.</li>
6   </ol>
7
```

```
1   ol {
2       border:1px solid #000;
3   }
4   li {
5       border:1px dashed #000;
6       margin-left:20px;
7   }
8
```

```
A. First item.
B. Second item.
C. Third item.
D. Fourth item.
```

We have now increased the distance between the <li> tags and the <ol> tag that contains them. Yet the numbering has moved right along with the <li> tags.

In order to increase the distance between the list items and their numbering, we will have to use left padding (line 6 of the CSS below):

```
i 1▾ <ol type="A">
  2      <li>First item.</li>
  3      <li>Second item.</li>
  4      <li>Third item.</li>
  5      <li>Fourth item.</li>
  6  </ol>
  7  |
```

```
1▾ ol {
2      border:1px solid #000;
3  }
4▾ li {
5      border:1px dashed #000;
6      padding-left:20px;
7  }
8  |
```

```
A.   First item.
B.   Second item.
C.   Third item.
D.   Fourth item.
```

Taking away the borders by setting them to zero (lines 2 and 5 of the CSS), the list now appears as follows:

```
i 1▾ <ol type="A">
  2      <li>First item.</li>
  3      <li>Second item.</li>
  4      <li>Third item.</li>
  5      <li>Fourth item.</li>
  6  </ol>
  7  |
```

```
1▾ ol {
i 2      border:0px solid #000;
3  }
4▾ li {
i 5      border:0px dashed #000;
6      padding-left:20px;
7  }
8  |
```

```
A.   First item.
B.   Second item.
C.   Third item.
D.   Fourth item.
```

Instead of deleting the border definitions in the CSS, I have set the borders to zero pixels, which means that they will not show up. It is the same as deleting the definitions, except that now I can bring the borders back more easily, merely by changing the zero again to 1 or some other number, instead of having to type the border definitions again.

If we give a specific style to the <li> tags, this also affects the style of their numbering. Below, I have made the list items italic (line 7 of the CSS):

```
1▾ ol {
2      border:0px solid #000;
3  }
4▾ li {
5      border:0px dashed #000;
6      padding-left:20px;
7      font-style:italic;
8  }
9  |
```

This makes their numbering also italic:

```
A.    First item.
B.    Second item.
C.    Third item.
D.    Fourth item.
```

This is not always ideal. Sometimes you want the numbering to have one style and the text itself another style. We can create our own custom numbering to get around this issue and create our own self-styled numbering.

To do that, first we hide the existing numbering by adding a line of CSS to the <ol> tag (line 3 below):

```
1▾ <ol type="A">
2      <li>First item.</li>
3      <li>Second item.</li>
4      <li>Third item.</li>
5      <li>Fourth item.</li>
6  </ol>
7  |
```

```
1▾ ol {
2      border:0px solid #000;
3      list-style:none;
4  }
5▾ li {
6      border:0px dashed #000;
7      padding-left:20px;
8      font-style:italic;
9  }
10 |
```

```
First item.
Second item.
Third item.
Fourth item.
```

The CSS property "list-style:none" tells the browser not to show any numbering. Next, using some advanced features of CSS, we create our own "counter" (lines 5, 11 and 15 of the CSS):

```
 1
 2 ▾  ol {
 3         border:0px solid #000;
 4         list-style:none;
 5         counter-reset:mylist;
 6    }
 7 ▾  li {
 8         border:0px dashed #000;
 9         padding-left:20px;
10         font-style:italic;
11         counter-increment: mylist;
12    }
13
14 ▾  li:before {
15      content: counter(mylist);
16    }
17
```

At the top of the CSS, we have added a new CSS counter, "counter-reset:mylist" creates a 'variable' called 'mylist'. CSS gives this variable a default value of zero. In the <li> tag's CSS, we have added "counter-increment: mylist". This tells the browser to increase the "mylist" counter for every <li> tag that it creates. Finally, we have created an entirely new definition, which starts with "li:before". This is known as a CSS pseudo-selector, and it is a way of adding content before a particular element.[7] Here, we are saying that before every <li> tag, we want to add the content "counter(mylist)". This tells the browser that before every <li> tag, the value of a CSS counter named "mylist" should be printed.

1First item.
2Second item.
3Third item.
4Fourth item.

The end result, as seen, is that certain numbers are printed before each list item. They don't look good, but now we have great power to change their appearance.

If you found the idea of a variable and a counter confusing, there is no need to worry. Most people learn CSS by copying code from other people on the Internet, often while only half understanding what they are doing. It is sufficient to be able to copy the code above and use

---

[7] Anything we declare inside CSS in order to give a style to a specific element (such as ".division-a" which we used in the past) is known as a "selector". In the CSS above, the word "ol" on line 2, the word "li" on line 7 and the word "li:before" on line 14 are all selectors. A selector that has a colon inside it is known as a pseudo-selector.

it in your own project. It will work even if you do not understand it. You need to add a "counter-reset" property to the <ol> tag, a "counter-increment" property to the <li> tag, and create a new CSS definition (li:before), in which you add a "content" property, and its content is "counter(mylist)". Instead of using the word "mylist", we could have used any word we wanted. It could have been "Jakes_list" or "cat". Whatever name you choose, you must stick with it on lines 5, 11 and 15.

Now, we are ready to add some nifty styling to our numbering (line 16 below):

```
14 ▾  li:before {
15         content: counter(mylist);
16         border:1px solid #000;
17     }
18
19
20     |
```

```
1 First item.
2 Second item.
3 Third item.
4 Fourth item.
```

Our styling efforts will focus on the "li:before" selector. Above, I have added a 1 pixel border to the numbering.

Notice how the numbering is in italics. I can now cancel this out (line 18 below):

```
 8 ▾  li {
 9        border:0px dashed #000;
10        padding-left:20px;
11        font-style:italic;
12        counter-increment: mylist;
13    }
14
15 ▾  li:before {
16        content: counter(mylist);
17        border:1px solid #000;
18        font-style:normal;
19    }
20    |
```

> 1 *First item.*
> 2 *Second item.*
> 3 *Third item.*
> 4 *Fourth item.*

In the <li> tag's definition, we added "font-style:italic" to make the list items italic, which also affected the list items' numbering. In the "li:before" selector, we add "font-style:normal" to overrule this style, forcing the numbering to not be italic.

Let's now increase the space between the numbering and the list items. Even though there is a "padding-left:20px" definition on the <li> tag (line 10 above), the new numbering we created is not affected by it.

Below, I have removed the padding on the <li> definition, while adding a right margin of five pixels on "li:before" (line 18). Now the numbering is separated from the items.

```
 8 ▾ li {
 9      border:0px dashed #000;
10      font-style:italic;
11      counter-increment: mylist;
12 }
13
14 ▾ li:before {
15      content: counter(mylist);
16      border:1px solid #000;
17      font-style:normal;
18      margin-right:5px;
19 }
20 |
```

1 *First item.*
2 *Second item.*
3 *Third item.*
4 *Fourth item.*

Below, I have added a "border-radius" of 100%, meaning to make the borders as circular as possible (line 19):

```
14 ▾ li:before {
15      content: counter(mylist);
16      border:1px solid #000;
17      font-style:normal;
18      margin-right:5px;
19      border-radius:100%;
20 }
```

① *First item.*
② *Second item.*
③ *Third item.*
④ *Fourth item.*

To make the numbers look better, we can make the numbering wider, so that the borders look less like eggs and more like circles.

```
14 ▾ li:before {
15       content: counter(mylist);
⚠ 16       border:1px solid #000;
17       font-style:normal;
18       margin-right:5px;
19       border-radius:100%;
20       width:10px;
21    }
22
23    |
24
25
26
27
28
29
```

① *First item.*
② *Second item.*
③ *Third item.*
④ *Fourth item.*

Above, I have added a "width:10px" definition (line 20), but it is not having any effect. The reason is that the numbering that we artificially created are "inline" elements (similar to <span> tags), so that they cannot take a width. Inline elements have their width decided for them by the browser.

To get around this, we need to make the numbering stop being inline (line 21 below):

```
14 ▾ li:before {
15       content: counter(mylist);
⚠ 16       border:1px solid #000;
17       font-style:normal;
18       margin-right:5px;
19       border-radius:100%;
20       width:10px;
21       display:block;
22    }
```

Above, I have used the "display" property to turn the numbering into "block" elements, meaning they can now take widths.

① First item.

② Second item.

③ Third item.

④ Fourth item.

You can see that the numbers have more space inside their egg-shaped borders. The problem is that a block takes up a whole line, forcing the list items to appear on the next line. What we need is for the numbers to act like block elements so that they can take a width, but we also do not want them to take up a whole line. The solution is to use the "inline-block" value for the "display" property, creating a hybrid element that has the properties we desire:

```
14 ▾  li:before {
15         content: counter(mylist);
16         border:1px solid #000;
17         font-style:normal;
18         margin-right:5px;
19         border-radius:100%;
20         width:10px;
21         display:inline-block;
22     }
23
24     |
```

① First item.
② Second item.
③ Third item.
④ Fourth item.

An inline-block element has some of the properties of a block element (it can take a width, for example), but it does not take up a whole line.

Now that that problem is out of the way, we can focus on the width of the numbering. Instead of using pixels for the width, we can use another unit known as an "em" (line 20 below).

```
14 ▾  li:before {
15         content: counter(mylist);
⚠ 16        border:1px solid #000;
17         font-style:normal;
18         margin-right:5px;
19         border-radius:100%;
20         width:1em;
21         display:inline-block;
22     }
23     |
24
```

① First item.
② Second item.
③ Third item.
④ Fourth item.

An "em" refers to the "point" size of a specific font. If I give the numbering a width of 1 em, it means the width of the numbering will be equal to the average size of a letter (or number) in the present font that is being used. Think of "em" as "size of a capital M". 1 em means "as wide as a capital M".[8]

You can see that the eggs are more like circles now. They have expanded to the size of 1 em, meaning the size of an average letter or number. That' still not exactly like a circle, so we will increase it to 1.2 ems (line 20 below):

```
14 ▾  li:before {
15         content: counter(mylist);
⚠ 16        border:1px solid #000;
17         font-style:normal;
18         margin-right:5px;
19         border-radius:100%;
20         width:1.2em;
21         display:inline-block;
22     }
```

Here is the result:

---

[8] This is not absolutely accurate. For more information see the Wikipedia article about the em:
https://en.wikipedia.org/wiki/Em_(typography)

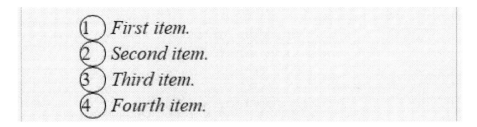

The cool thing about an em is that it expands and shrinks with the font size. If I reduce the font size to 10 pixels as follows (line 12 below), the circles shrink with the font size.

```
 8 ▾  li {
i 9         border:0px dashed #000;
 10         font-style:italic;
 11         counter-increment: mylist;
 12         font-size:10px;
 13    }
 14
 15 ▾  li:before {
 16         content: counter(mylist);
⚠ 17        border:1px solid #000;
 18         font-style:normal;
 19         margin-right:5px;
 20         border-radius:100%;
 21         width:1.2em;
 22         display:inline-block;
 23    }
 24
```

① First item.
② Second item.
③ Third item.
④ Fourth item.

Above, I have added a "font-size:10px" definition to the <li> tag. As can be seen, the numbering and the circle around it have also shrunk.

If instead of using an em, we had used pixels, the result would have been as follows:

① First item.
② Second item.
③ Third item.
④ Fourth item.

The circles have become deformed. To see this better, let's increase the font size to 30 pixels (line 12 below):

```
 8 ▾ li {
 9       border:0px dashed #000;
10       font-style:italic;
11       counter-increment: mylist;
12       font-size:30px;
13 }
14
15 ▾ li:before {
16       content: counter(mylist);
17       border:1px solid #000;
18       font-style:normal;
19       margin-right:5px;
20       border-radius:100%;
21       width:10px;
22       display:inline-block;
23 }
24
```

1*First item.*
2*Second item.*
3*Third item.*
4*Fourth item.*

Above, the font size of the list items and the numbering has increased. But the "width" of the numbers remains 10 pixels, so that the numbering starts to overflow outside the borders. Changing the width to 1.2 ems again (line 21 below), the circles come back again in their proper shape:

```
15 ▾  li:before {
16         content: counter(mylist);
⚠ 17       border:1px solid #000;
18         font-style:normal;
19         margin-right:5px;
20         border-radius:100%;
21         width:1.2em;
22         display:inline-block;
23     }
24
```

① *First item.*

② *Second item.*

③ *Third item.*

④ *Fourth item.*

If this talk of ems and pixels has confused you, it is sufficient to know that ems are a unit of size that shrink and grow according to the font size currently in effect. Changing the font size makes the size of an "em" change.

Now that the text is larger, the space between the numbering and the list items has shrunk. They are again uncomfortably close. This is because we used a margin of 5 pixels between the numbering and the list items (line 19 above). As you make the font size larger, the 5 pixels remain 5 pixels, meaning that visually the space appears smaller, similar to the way a truck appears small when it is standing next to one of those massive mining trucks. We can fix this too by using ems for the margin (line 19 below):

```
15 ▾  li:before {
16         content: counter(mylist);
⚠17        border:1px solid #000;
18         font-style:normal;
19         margin-right:0.6em;
20         border-radius:100%;
21         width:1.2em;
22         display:inline-block;
23
24     }
```

Above, I have changed the "margin-right" property's value to "0.6em". This tells the browser to keep a space between the numbering and the list items that equals a little over half the size of an average letter. As the size of the letters grows and shrinks, this margin will grow and shrink with it.

Let's now center the numbers inside their circular borders. To do so, we use the "text-align" property (line 23 below):

```
15 ▾  li:before {
16         content: counter(mylist);
⚠17        border:1px solid #000;
18         font-style:normal;
19         margin-right:0.6em;
20         border-radius:100%;
21         width:1.2em;
22         display:inline-block;
23         text-align:center;
24     }
```

Here is the result:

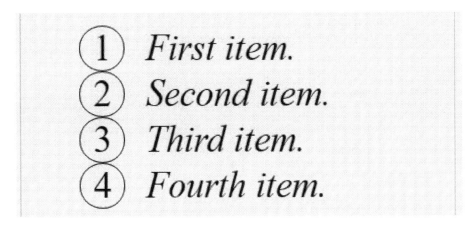

The "text-align" property takes the values of "left", "right" and "center".

To make the circles stop touching each other, we will give the "li:before" selector a bottom margin (line 24 below):

```
15 ▾ li:before {
16       content: counter(mylist);
⚠17      border:1px solid #000;
18       font-style:normal;
19       margin-right:0.6em;
20       border-radius:100%;
21       width:1.2em;
22       display:inline-block;
23       text-align:center;
24       margin-bottom:0.1em;
25   }
26   |
```

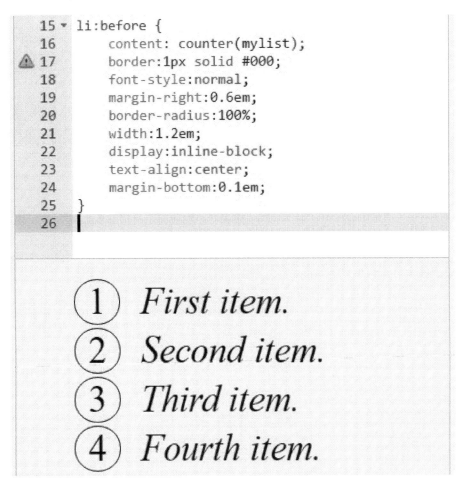

Going on with our styling efforts, below I will make the text white and its background dark gray (lines 25 and 26 below):

```
15 ▾ li:before {
16        content: counter(mylist);
⚠ 17      border:1px solid #000;
18        font-style:normal;
19        margin-right:0.6em;
20        border-radius:100%;
21        width:1.2em;
22        display:inline-block;
23        text-align:center;
24        margin-bottom:0.1em;
25        color:#fff;
26        background:#666;
27 }
28 |
```

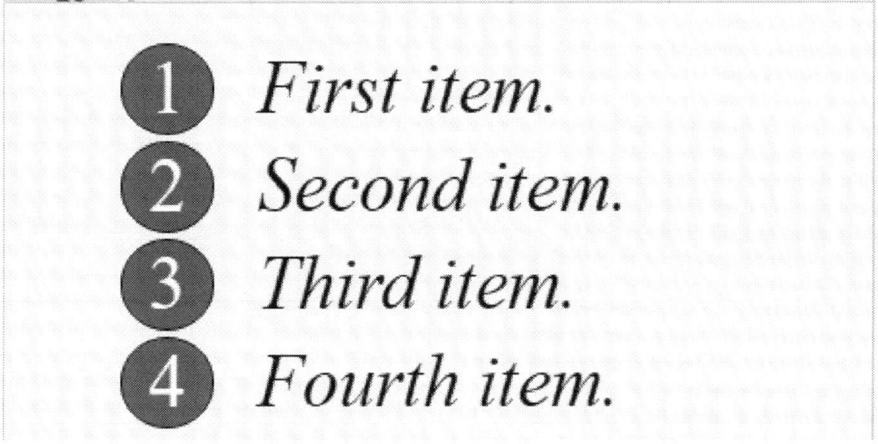

1 *First item.*

2 *Second item.*

3 *Third item.*

4 *Fourth item.*

We can now change the font size of the <li> tag back to default by removing the "font-size:30px" definition that we added earlier on line 12 of the CSS:

```
8 ▾ li {
i 9      border:0px dashed #000;
10       font-style:italic;
11       counter-increment: mylist;
12 }
```

As can be seen below, everything shrinks appropriately thanks to our use of ems rather than pixels:

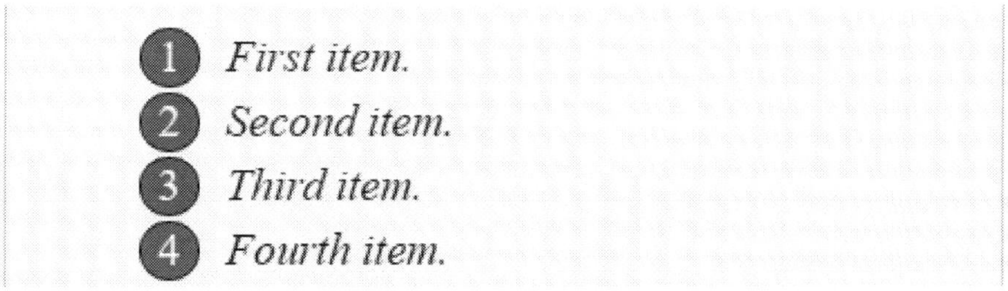

1 *First item.*

2 *Second item.*

3 *Third item.*

4 *Fourth item.*

To show the interplay between our new numbers and the list tags, below I have made the fourth item longer (lines 5 and 6 of the HTML) and I have brought back the borders I hid a while back (lines 3 and 9 of the CSS):

```
1  <ol type="A">
2      <li>First item.</li>
3      <li>Second item.</li>
4      <li>Third item.</li>
5      <li>Roses are red, violets are blue.<br>
6      The fourth item is relatively long.</li>
7  </ol>
8
```

```
1
2  ol {
3      border:1px solid #000;
4      list-style:none;
5      counter-reset:mylist;
6  }
7
8  li {
9      border:1px dashed #000;
10     font-style:italic;
11     counter-increment: mylist;
12 }
13
14 li:before {
15     content: counter(mylist);
16     border:1px solid #000;
17     font-style:normal;
18     margin-right:0.6em;
19     border-radius:100%;
20     width:1.2em;
21     display:inline-block;
```

> ① *First item.*
> ② *Second item.*
> ③ *Third item.*
> ④ *Roses are red, violets are blue.*
> *The fourth item is relatively long.*

You may note how the <ol> tag is now wasting space on the left, since the numbers are no longer inside that space but are inside the <li> tags. To prevent this waste, we set the left-padding of the <ol> tag to zero on line 6 of the CSS:

```
2  ol {
3      border:1px solid #000;
4      list-style:none;
5      counter-reset:mylist;
6      padding-left:0;
7  }
```

Here is the result:

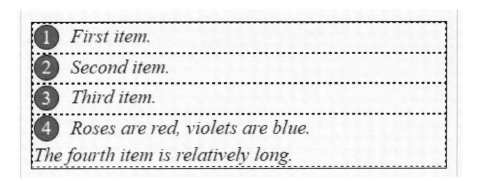

Now, the list items take up the whole of the <ol> tag.

In the HTML, the <ol> tag continues to have the type="A" attribute, which means that its numbering should be made of ABCs rather than decimals. This is no longer having an effect because we hid the default numbering on line 4 above in the CSS. Our new numbering is custom-made on line 16.

In order to create Roman numbering, we have to make a change to line 16 of the CSS:

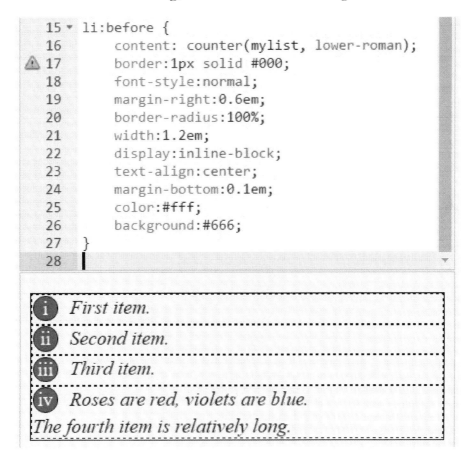

We have changed the value of the "content" property on line 16 so that it now has the word "lower-roman" in it. Note the comma separating "mylist" from "lower-roman", this is necessary.

Instead of Roman numbering, we can use Greek (line 16 below):

```
15 ▾ li:before {
16        content: counter(mylist, lower-greek);
17        border:1px solid #000;
18        font-style:normal;
```

The result is as follows:

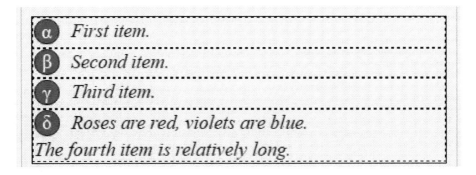

Other possible number formats to use are decimal, decimal-leading-zero, lower-roman, upper-roman, lower-greek, lower-latin, upper-latin, armenian, georgian, lower-alpha and upper-alpha.

Instead of using a number format, we can also use 'static' content to turn the list into a bullet list (line 16 below):

```
15 ▾ li:before {
16        content: '*';
⚠ 17       border:1px solid #000;
18        font-style:normal;
19        margin-right:0.6em;
20        border-radius:100%;
21        width:1.2em;
22        display:inline-block;
23        text-align:center;
24        margin-bottom:0.1em;
25        color:#fff;
26        background:#666;
27 }
28
```

- *First item.*
- *Second item.*
- *Third item.*
- *Roses are red, violets are blue. The fourth item is relatively long.*

On line 16 above, I have changed the 'content' property to '*', meaning to use an asterisk as the content. We can also use one of many thousands of Unicode symbols[9], such as the snowman symbol on line 16 below:

```
15 ▾ li:before {
16        content: '☃';
⚠ 17       border:1px solid #000;
```

The result is as follows:

---

[9] Google "Unicode symbols" to find one of many sites that let you find all kinds of symbols and copy paste them into your code. Your HTML document must be formatted as a Unicode document. This is the default format on most modern systems.

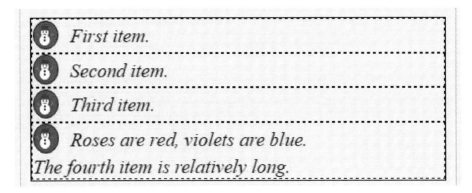

To make the snowmen more visible, I have removed the dark gray background, the circular border and the dashed border on the list items and increased the font size on the list items:

```
 9 ▾ li {
10      font-style:italic;
11      counter-increment: mylist;
12      font-size:20px;
13 }
14
15 ▾ li:before {
16      content: '☃';
17      font-style:normal;
18      margin-right:0.6em;
19      border-radius:100%;
20      width:1.2em;
21      display:inline-block;
22      text-align:center;
23      margin-bottom:0.1em;
24      color:#fff;
25 }
26 |
```

Here is the result:

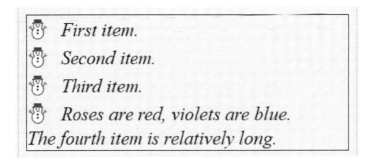

Since we are no longer using a CSS counter, we can remove the 'counter-reset' and 'counter-increment' properties from the <ol> and the <li> tags respectively in the CSS:

```
 2 ▾  ol {
 3        border:1px solid #000;
 4        list-style:none;
 5        padding-left:0;
 6    }
 7    |
 8 ▾  li {
 9        font-style:italic;
10        font-size:20px;
11    }
12
13 ▾  li:before {
14        content: '☃';
15        font-style:normal;
16        margin-right:0.6em;
17        border-radius:100%;
18        width:1.2em;
19        display:inline-block;
20        text-align:center;
21        margin-bottom:0.1em;
```

> ☃ *First item.*
> ☃ *Second item.*
> ☃ *Third item.*
> ☃ *Roses are red, violets are blue.*
> *The fourth item is relatively long.*

Counters are only useful if you want the browser to automatically number your list items for you. If no numbering is involved, if the content is static as in the snowman above, you no longer have a need for counters.

Unordered Lists

Unordered lists are very much like the ordered lists covered above, except that they do not use numbers, they use bullet points instead. Unordered lists are created using the <ul> tag (instead of the <ol> tag):

```
i 1▾  <ul>
  2       <li>First item.</li>
  3       <li>Second item.</li>
  4       <li>Third item.</li>
  5▾      <li>Roses are red, violets are blue.<br>
  6       The fourth item is relatively long.</li>
  7    </ul>
  8
```

```
1
```

```
1
```

- First item.
- Second item.
- Third item.
- Roses are red, violets are blue.
  The fourth item is relatively long.

Note how we are not using any CSS. The browser automatically adds the bullets to the list items. Adding borders to the <ul> and <li> tags, we can see the interplay between the list items and the bullets:

```
i 1▾  <ul>
  2       <li>First item.</li>
  3       <li>Second item.</li>
  4       <li>Third item.</li>
  5▾      <li>Roses are red, violets are blue.<br>
  6       The fourth item is relatively long.</li>
  7    </ul>
  8
```

```
1▾  ul {
 2      border:1px solid #000;
 3  }
 4▾  li {
 5      border:1px dashed #000;
 6  }
 7
```

```
1
```

- First item.
- Second item.
- Third item.
- Roses are red, violets are blue.
  The fourth item is relatively long.

We can make the bullets part of the list items using "list-style:inside" (line 6 below):

```
4 ▾ li {
5       border:1px dashed #000;
6       list-style:inside;
7  }
8  |
```

- First item.
- Second item.
- Third item.
- Roses are red, violets are blue.
The fourth item is relatively long.

Using "list-style", we can also determine the shape of the bullets (line 6 below):

```
4 ▾ li {
5       border:1px dashed #000;
6       list-style:circle;
7  }
8  |
```

○ First item.
○ Second item.
○ Third item.
○ Roses are red, violets are blue.
The fourth item is relatively long.

To make the circles go inside the list items, we can do as follows (line 6 below):

```
4 ▾ li {
5        border:1px dashed #000;
6        list-style:circle inside;
7 }
8 |
```

○   First item.
○   Second item.
○   Third item.
○   Roses are red, violets are blue.
The fourth item is relatively long.

Note that there is a space (but no comma) between "circle" and "inside".

We can also turn the bullet list into a numbered list, although there is no good reason for doing so, by giving the "list-style" property the name of a numbering format:

```
4 ▾ li {
5        border:1px dashed #000;
6        list-style: decimal inside;
7 }
8 |
```

1. First item.
2. Second item.
3. Third item.
4. Roses are red, violets are blue.
The fourth item is relatively long.

We can also use an image file to use it as a bullet, as follows:

```
4 ▾  li {
5        border:1px dashed #000;
6        list-style: url("flower_small.png");
7    }
8    |
```

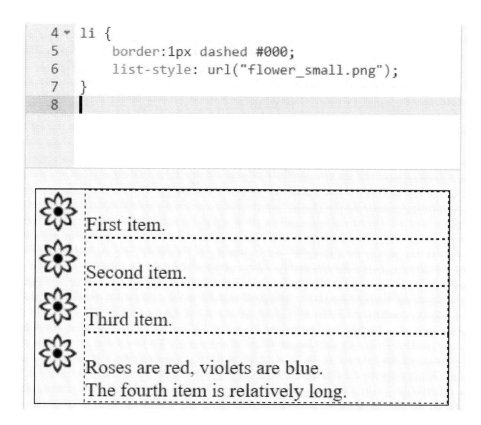

The property definition "url('flower_small.png')" tells the browser to look for an image file named "flower_small.png", located inside the JSTinker folder, and to use that image for the bullet point. If the image we wanted to use was an internet image, we'd have to spell out the image's full URL. For example this is the URL of an image on my personal website:

http://hawramani.com/wp-content/uploads/2018/02/flower_small.png

The full CSS would be as follows:

```
list-style: url("http://hawramani.com/wp-content/uploads/2018/02/flower_small.png");
```

If you are not sure what all of this means, there is no need to worry. The details of URLs, links and images will be covered in detail later.

Back to the list, you can see how the flowers are too large. Unfortunately, CSS doesn't allow us much control over the appearance of stuff we add through "list-style".

In order to change the size of the flowers so that they show up properly, we need to get creative like we did with the snowman.

First, we have to set the "list-style" property to none (line 6 of the CSS below):

```
 i  1 ▾  <ul>
    2          <li>First item.</li>
    3          <li>Second item.</li>
    4          <li>Third item.</li>
    5 ▾        <li>Roses are red, violets are blue.<br>
    6          The fourth item is relatively long.</li>
    7      </ul>
    8      |

    1      |
```

```
    1 ▾  ul {
    2          border:1px solid #000;
    3      }
    4 ▾  li {
    5          border:1px dashed #000;
    6          list-style: none;
    7      }
    8      |
```

```
First item.
Second item.
Third item.
Roses are red, violets are blue.
The fourth item is relatively long.
```

Next, we add back the flowers using a new selector, the "li:before" that we used for the snowman (lines 8-10 below):

```
    4 ▾  li {
    5          border:1px dashed #000;
    6          list-style: none;
    7      }
    8 ▾  li:before {
    9          content:url('flower_small.png');
   10      }
   11      |
```

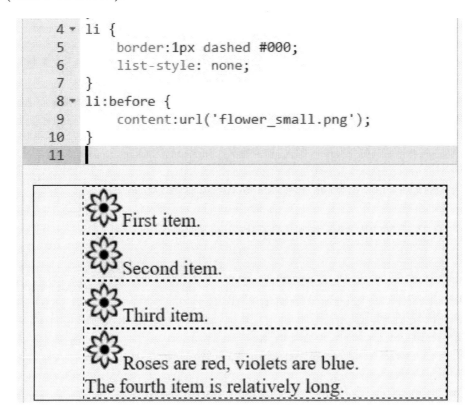

Note that in the "li:before" definition, we are not using a "list-style" property, we are using a "content" property (line 9 above). This gives us some control over the flowers, but it does not let us change their size.

Instead, we set the 'content' property to a blank string, then make use of the 'background-image' property:

```
 8 ▾ li:before {
 9       background-image:url('flower_small.png');
10       content:'';
11   }
12
13   |
```

```
First item.
Second item.
Third item.
Roses are red, violets are blue.
The fourth item is relatively long.
```

A blank string is what you get when you take out the stuff enclosed in quotes. For example if you have the string 'word', if you delete *word*, what remains are the quotes. In computer parlance, we call that a blank string. Above, I have added the flower as a "background-image". Nothing shows up because the "li:before" has a size of zero at the moment, since the content specified on line 10 is empty. This is similar to the way that a <div> shows up as nothing unless we give it a size and border or put some stuff inside it.

Below, I will give the "li:before" selector a height and width of 1 em (lines 10 and 11), and I will also switch its "display" property to the hybrid "inline-block" value (line 12):

```
 8 ▾ li:before {
 9       background-image:url('flower_small.png');
10       height:1em;
11       width:1em;
12       display:inline-block;
13       content:'';
14   }
15
16
```

```
First item.
Second item.
Third item.
Roses are red, violets are blue.
The fourth item is relatively long.
```

87

Above, everything is working perfectly now, except not. The problem is that the image is still too large. The "li:before" is small, but the image underneath is large, similar to a large flower being seen through a small window. We can visualize this more clearly by giving the "li:before" a border (line 14 below):

```
 8 ▼ li:before {
 9        background-image:url('flower_small.png');
10        height:1em;
11        width:1em;
12        display:inline-block;
13        content:'';
14        border:3px solid #000;
15 }
16 |
```

We need to make the image itself smaller. In computer speak, we call this "scaling" an image. To do so, we use the "background-size" CSS property (line 10 below):

```
 8 ▾ li:before {
 9       background-image:url('flower_small.png');
10       background-size:1em 1em;
11       height:1em;
12       width:1em;
13       display:inline-block;
14       content:'';
⚠15       border:3px solid #000;
16   }
```

❀First item.
❀Second item.
❀Third item.
❀Roses are red, violets are blue.
The fourth item is relatively long.

Now, both the window through which we see the flower, and the image of the flower, are both 1em high and wide. This allows us to see the full flowers. Below, I have removed the border from line 15 above so that only the flowers can be seen:

```
 8 ▾ li:before {
 9       background-image:url('flower_small.png');
10       background-size:1em 1em;
11       height:1em;
12       width:1em;
13       display:inline-block;
14       content:'';
15   }
16
```

❀First item.
❀Second item.
❀Third item.
❀Roses are red, violets are blue.
The fourth item is relatively long.

Below, I have given the "li:before" a right margin of 0.6 ems (line 15 below). I have also hidden the borders on the <ul> and <li> tags by setting them to zero (on lines 2 and 5 below) in order to see the result of our work:

```
 1 ▾ ul {
 i  2       border:0px solid #000;
 3   }
 4 ▾ li {
 i  5       border:0px dashed #000;
 6       list-style: none;
 7   }
 8 ▾ li:before {
 9       background-image:url('flower_small.png');
10       background-size:1em 1em;
11       height:1em;
12       width:1em;
13       display:inline-block;
14       content:'';
15       margin-right:0.6em;
16   }
```

❀ First item.
❀ Second item.
❀ Third item.
❀ Roses are red, violets are blue.
The fourth item is relatively long.

Thanks to using ems for the "background-size" and "height" and "width" properties on the "li:before", if we increase the font size on the <li> tag (line 7 below), the flowers will grow larger too:

```
 4 ▾  li {
 5        border:0px dashed #000;
 6        list-style: none;
 7        font-size:30px;
 8    }
 9 ▾  li:before {
10        background-image:url('flower_small.png');
11        background-size:1em 1em;
12        height:1em;
13        width:1em;
14        display:inline-block;
15        content:'';
16        margin-right:0.6em;
```

❀ First item.
❀ Second item.
❀ Third item.
❀ Roses are red,
violets are blue.
The fourth item is
relatively long.

Since the flowers are from an image, if we make the font too large (as above), the flowers get blurry. This is due to the nature of images on computers and there is no cure for it. To avoid it, one should either make sure the font is always at the right size for the image, or they should use non-image glyphs, such as the Unicode snowman earlier.[10]

---

[10] Using Unicode comes with its own issues, as some systems may not be able to display the Unicode glyphs properly. The solution to that is to use a web font that comes with its own glyphs. Web fonts will be covered later.

This page intentionally left blank

3.
The Art of Floating

Using the CSS mechanism of 'floating', we can make a blocking element stop taking up a whole line. This enables us to have multiple <div> or <li> tags show up side-by-side.

Let's look at the unordered list from the last chapter:

```
1   <ul>
2       <li>First item.</li>
3       <li>Second item.</li>
4       <li>Third item.</li>
5       <li>Roses are red, violets are blue.<br>
6       The fourth item is relatively long.</li>
7   </ul>
8
```

```
1   ul {
2       border:0px solid #000;
3   }
4   li {
5       border:1px dashed #000;
6       list-style: none;
7   }
8   li:before {
9       background-image:url('flower_small.png');
10      background-size:1em 1em;
11      height:1em;
12      width:1em;
13      display:inline-block;
14      content:'';
15      margin-right:0.6em;
16  }
17
18
19
```

❀ First item.
❀ Second item.
❀ Third item.
❀ Roses are red, violets are blue.
The fourth item is relatively long.

Below, on line 7, I add the "float" property and give it a value of "left":

```
4 ▾ li {
5       border:1px dashed #000;
6       list-style: none;
7       float:left;
8 }
```

Here is the result:

❀ First item. ❀ Second item.
❀ Third item.
❀ Roses are red, violets are blue.
The fourth item is relatively long.

Now, each list item, instead of taking up the whole line, only takes up as much space as its contents require. This makes the first and the second list item show up side-by-side, because the first list item shrinks so much that sufficient space is left on its right to allow the second list item to show up there.

If we make the font size really small (line 8 below), all of the list items will show up side-by-side:

```
4 ▾ li {
5       border:1px dashed #000;
6       list-style: none;
7       float:left;
8       font-size:8px;
9 }
10 ▾ li:before {
11       background-image:url('flower_small.png');
12       background-size:1em 1em;
13       height:1em;
14       width:1em;
15       display:inline-block;
16       content:'';
17       margin-right:0.6em;
18 }
19 |
```

❀ First item. ❀ Second item. ❀ Third item. ❀ Roses are red, violets are blue.
The fourth item is relatively long.

We can now use margins (line 8 below) to space out the list items so that they are not all mashed together:

```
4 ▾  li {
5        border:1px dashed #000;
6        list-style: none;
7        float:left;
8        margin:5px;
```

The result is as follows:

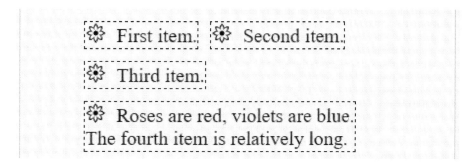

To make the list items look less disorganized, we can give them all a certain width (line 9 below):

```
4 ▾  li {
⚠ 5      border:1px dashed #000;
6        list-style: none;
7        float:left;
8        margin:5px;
9        width:40%;
```

The result is as follows:

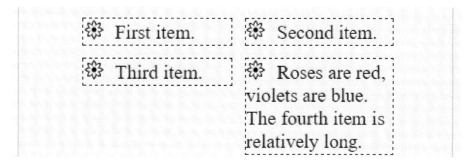

The 40% width means that each list item should take up 40% of the available horizontal space. This "available" space changes depending on the outer context. For example, if we give the <ul> tag a width of 200 pixels (line 3 below), the list items will shrink to each take up 40% of the available 200 pixels:

```
1 ▾ ul {
2       border:0px solid #000;
3       width:200px;
4 }
5 ▾ li {
6       border:1px dashed #000;
7       list-style: none;
8       float:left;
9       margin:5px;
10      width:40%;
```

The result is as follows:

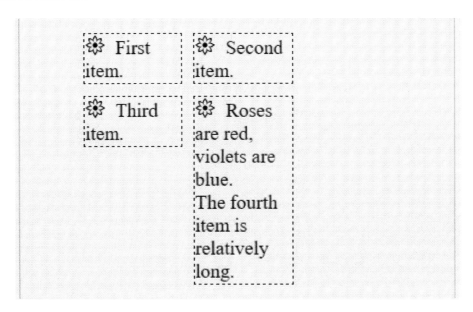

To give our list items a uniform height, we have to specify the height too (line 10 below):

```
8       margin:5px;
9       width:40%;
10      height:5em;
```

Here is the result:

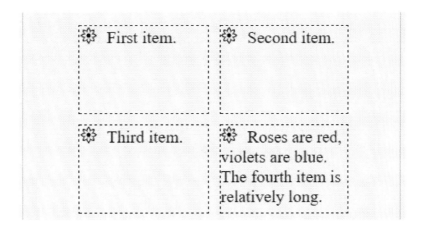

We cannot give floating things heights in percentages because an HTML document technically has infinite height.[11] The height must always be in some absolute or relative unit, like pixels or ems.

When setting a height, you must ensure that it provides sufficient space for the content. If we set the height to 3.5em (line 10 below), the first three items have no issue with it, but the fourth item overflows:

```
 4 ▾  li {
 5        border:1px dashed #000;
 6        list-style: none;
 7        float:left;
 8        margin:5px;
 9        width:40%;
10        height:3.5em;
```

The result is as follows:

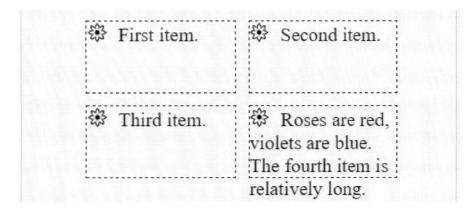

Even if we set the height to 5 ems (line 10 below), a change in font size (line 11 below) can cause the content to spill:

---

[11] Unless the container has a specific height, in which case a percentage height works. This will be seen later.

```
 9        width:40%;
10        height:5em;
11        font-size:17px;
```

Here is the result:

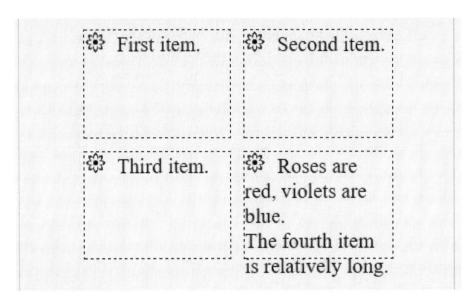

Perhaps you may think spilling wouldn't be an issue if we hide the borders. But if there were more items below the fourth item, the spillage would cause the text of the fourth item to merge with the text of the item below it, causing a broken appearance.

Below, I have removed the flower bullet point in order to simplify the example:

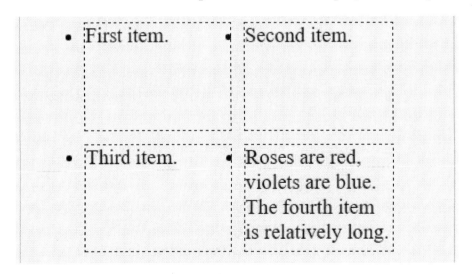

It can be seen that the bullets for the list items on the right are overflowing onto the items on the left. One way to fix this is to make the bullets appear inside the list items using "list-style:inside" (line 11 below):

```
 4 ▾  li {
 5        border:1px dashed #000;
 6        float:left;
 7        margin:5px;
 8        width:40%;
 9        height:5em;
10        font-size:17px;
11        list-style:inside;
```

The result is as follows:

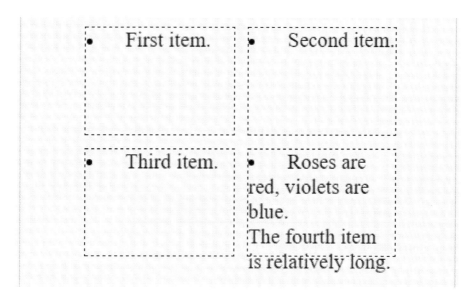

Another way is to prevent the bullets from intruding on their neighbors is to increase the left margin (line 8 below, I have removed the "list-style:inside" definition from earlier):

```
 4 ▾  li {
 5        border:1px dashed #000;
 6        float:left;
 7        margin:5px;
 8        margin-left:1em;
 9        width:40%;
10        height:5em;
11        font-size:17px;
```

Above, on line 7, we give the list items a margin of 5 pixels all round. On the next line, we modify the left margin, which overwrites the 5 pixels on line 7 with the "1em" on line 8. The 1 em of space is sufficient to prevent the bullets from merging into the items on the left.

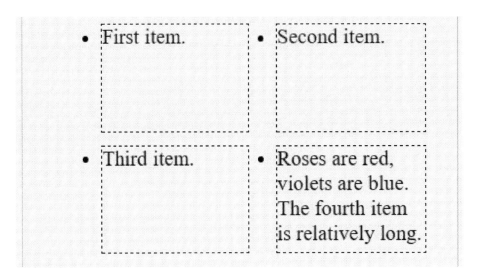

Instead of floating the items to the left, we could have floated them to the right as follows (line 6):

```
 1 ▾ ul {
 2       border:0px solid #000;
 3   }
 4 ▾ li {
 5       border:1px dashed #000;
 6       float:right;
 7       margin:5px;
 8       margin-left:1em;
 9       width:40%;
10       height:5em;
11       font-size:17px;
12   }
13   |
```

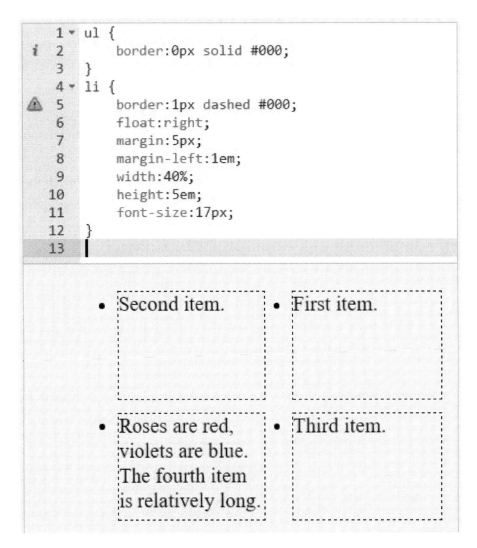

Floating items to the right causes the first item to appear on the top right, the next one on the top left, the third on the bottom right, and so on. Due to the fact that English-speakers are used to a left-to-right language, floating items to the right feels unnatural and is rarely used on a collection of items. It is, however, common to use it on individual elements, as follows:

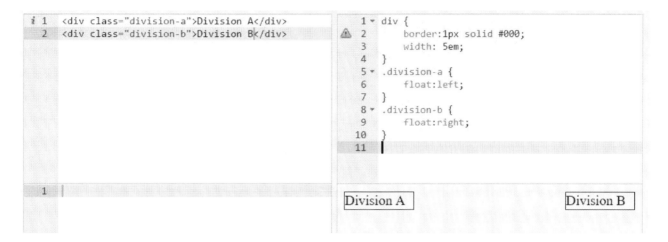

Above, division-a is floated to the left (line 6) while division-b is floated to the right (line 9).

Below, I have put the two <div> tags inside another <div> tag with the class "container":

There is a problem, however. The container <div> tag is too small, because in the CSS we have declared that all <div> tags should have a width of 5 ems (CSS line 3 above). In order to fix this, we will cause the width to only apply to the two inner <div> tags:

```
i 1▾ <div class="container">
  2      <div class="division-a">Division A</div>
  3      <div class="division-b">Division B</div>
  4  </div>
  5  |
```

```
1  1▾ div {
  2      border:1px solid #000;
  3  }
  4▾ .division-a, .division-b {
  5      width:5em;
  6  }
  7▾ .division-a {
  8      float:left;
  9  }
 10▾ .division-b {
 11      float:right;
 12  }
 13  |
```

Division A			Division B

Above, I have created a new CSS selector (line 4 of the CSS), which applies equally to both division-a and division-b (note the way their names are separated by a comma). Now, only division-a and division-b have a width of 5 ems, meaning the container <div> retains its default width (which is to take up the whole line).

You may notice the black bar on top of the texts "Division A" and "Division B". That is the container <div>'s borders. The issue is that since the container <div> tag is not floating (only division-a and division-b are floating, as determined by the CSS on lines 8 and 11), it does not have any content that can give it a height. CSS ignores the height of contained elements if they are floating, *unless* the container element is floating too.

Below, I have added a new CSS selector for the container <div> tag to make it float (line 14 below):

```
 1 ▾ div {
 2        border:1px solid #000;
 3   }
 4 ▾ .division-a, .division-b {
 5        width:5em;
 6   }
 7 ▾ .division-a {
 8        float:left;
 9   }
10 ▾ .division-b {
11        float:right;
12   }
13 ▾ .container {
14        float:left;
15   }
16   |
```

| Division A | Division B |

Above, due to the fact that floating elements do not take up a whole line, the container <div> tag is now as small as it can possibly get. Its width is decided by the width of the stuff inside it, which means the width of division-a and division-b. This makes division-a and division-b touch, because the space between them is shrunk as much as possible. They are still floating apart, but the container div is too small to let them separate.

We can change this by giving the container <div> tag a width (CSS line 15 below):

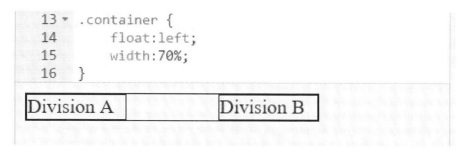

```
13 ▾ .container {
14        float:left;
15        width:70%;
16   }
```

| Division A | | Division B |

The container <div> tag now has a width of 70%, meaning that it takes up 70% of the available horizontal space. This increased space allows the right-floating division-b to separate from the left-floating division-a. We can also give the container <div> tag a width of 100% to make it take up the whole line:

```
13 ▾  .container {
14         float:left;
15         width:100%;
16     }
```

| Division A | | Division B |

Let's now give the container <div> tag a padding, in order to separate its border from the borders of the elements inside it (CSS line 16 below):

```
13 ▾  .container {
14         float:left;
15         width:100%;
16     padding:1em;
17     }
```

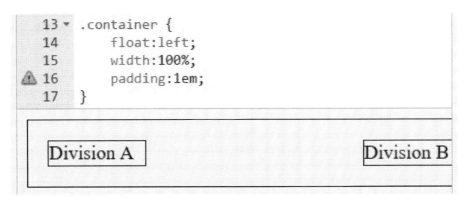

Notice how the right border of the container <div> element and division-b is "clipped". That's because the container <div> element is too large to be contained in its line, so it spills outside of it. The reason for this is that the padding we added on line 16 is added onto the 100% width on line 15, increasing the width beyond 100%, meaning the container div is now too large to show up on one line. This is fixed by reducing the width of the container <div> element as follows (line 15 below):

```
13 ▾  .container {
14         float:left;
15         width:91%;
16     padding:1em;
17     }
```

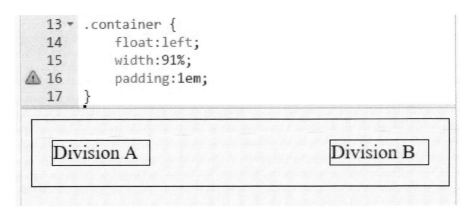

The width is now 91%, which, along with the container <div> element's padding, does not take up the whole line, allowing us to properly see the whole <div>.

Now, let's add a new division, named division-c (line 4 of the HTML below):

```
 1 ▾ <div class="container">
 2        <div class="division-a">Division A</div>
 3        <div class="division-b">Division B</div>
 4        <div class="division-c">Division C</div>
 5    </div>
 6    |
```

The result is as follows:

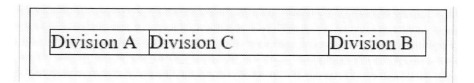

This new division is *not* floating, therefore it will have a strange relationship with the other <div> tags. It will try to take up the whole of the available horizontal space, so that it appears to the right of division-a and takes up everything until the left of division-b.

```
 1 ▾ <div class="container">
 2        <div class="division-a">Division A</div>
 3        <div class="division-b">Division B</div>
 4 ▾      <div class="division-c">Division C
 5        contains more text than the other
 6        divisions. Roses are red, violets are
 7        blue.
 8        </div>
 9    </div>
10    |
```

Above, I have added more text inside division-c. The result is as follows:

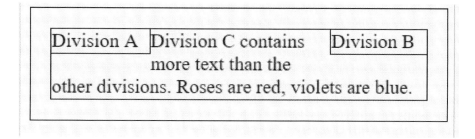

Notice how the content of division-c expands to take up all the available horizontal space Notice also that now the border of division-c appears to contain both divisions a and b, although in reality it does not contain them. This is merely the browser's best effort to make sense of the HTML and CSS that we have given it.

Making division-c also float will change everything. Below, I have added division-c to line 7, so that the left float will also apply to it:

```
 4 ▾ .division-a, .division-b {
 5        width:5em;
 6   }
 7 ▾ .division-a, .division-c {
 8        float:left;
 9   }
10 ▾ .division-b {
11        float:right;
12   }
```

The result is as follows:

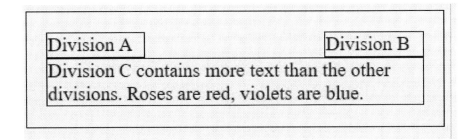

Now, division-c is on an equal footing with divisions a and b. Its width is determined by its contents, therefore it is so wide that it cannot fit between divisions a and b, so it is shown below them.

Below, I have added division-c to line 4, giving it a width of 5 ems similar to divisions a and b:

```
 4 ▾ .division-a, .division-b, .division-c {
 5        width:5em;
 6   }
 7 ▾ .division-a, .division-c {
 8        float:left;
 9   }
```

Here is the result:

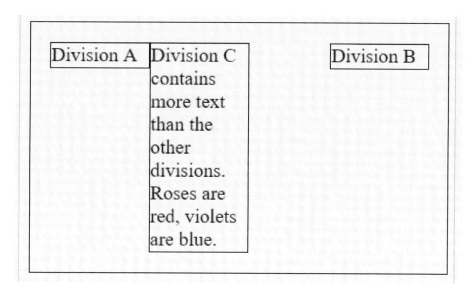

Now, since all three <div> tags have the same same width of 5 ems, there is sufficient space to show them all on the same line, so the browser does that. But since the contents of division-c are long, they automatically expand downwards.

There is no space between division-a and division-c. Since they are both floating left, they touch and stick together. We can change this by giving division-a a right margin (CSS line 11 below):

```
10 ▼ .division-a {
11       margin-right:1em;
12   }
```

Now, the space between divisions-a and division-c is controlled by our CSS, while the space between divisions b and c is automatic., determined by the width of the container <div>.

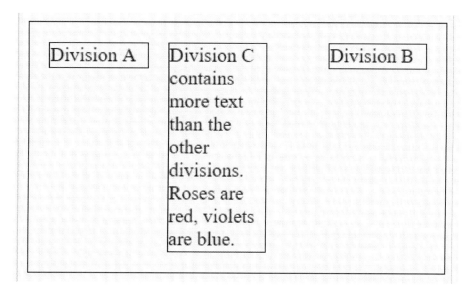

If the width of the container is reduced, the space is reduced or eliminated (CSS line 18 below):

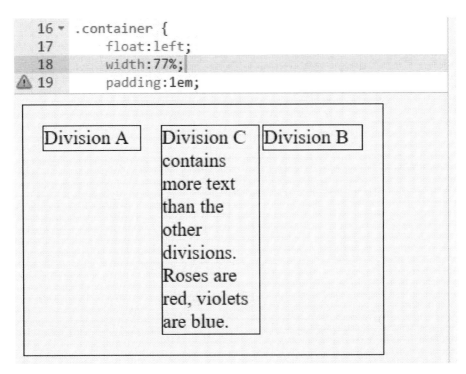

If we reduce the space too much, division-c is forced onto the next line because there is no longer sufficient space to show it side-by-side with divisions a and b (CSS line 18 below):

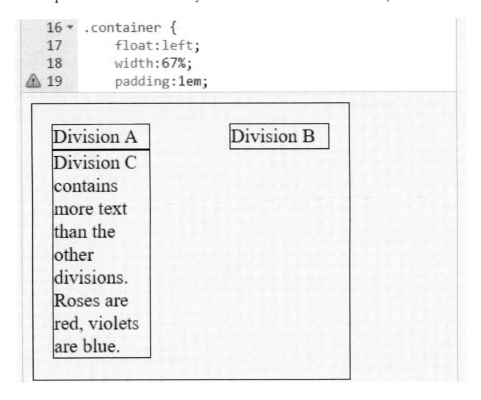

If we wanted to make divisions a, b and c to always have the same amount of space between them regardless of the width of the container <div> tag, this can only be accomplished by giving them all the same float. Below, I have removed all the CSS that applied to floating and have moved the float property to line 3, so that it applies to all four <div> tags (the container <div> tag and the other three):

```
1 ▾ div {
2       border:1px solid #000;
3       float:left;
4 }
5 ▾ .division-a, .division-b, .division-c {
6       width:5em;
7 }
8
9 ▾ .division-a {
10      margin-right:1em;
11 }
```

Now, all divisions are floating left. Since division-a has a right margin of 1 ems (line 10 above), the result is that there is some space between divisions a and b, but no space between divisions b and c:

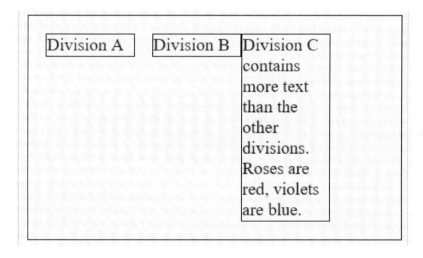

Below, I have moved the margin definition that used to be on line 10 onto line 7, so that it applies to all three <div> tags:

```
1 ▾ div {
2       border:1px solid #000;
3       float:left;
4 }
5 ▾ .division-a, .division-b, .division-c {
6       width:5em;
7       margin-right:1em;
8 }
9 ▾ .container {
10      float:left;
11      width:91%;
12      padding:1em;
13 }
```

The result is as follows:

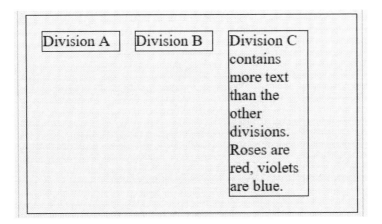

We could prevent the <div> tags from being forced onto new lines when the container <div> tag's width is shrunk by giving everything widths and margins in percentages, as follows:

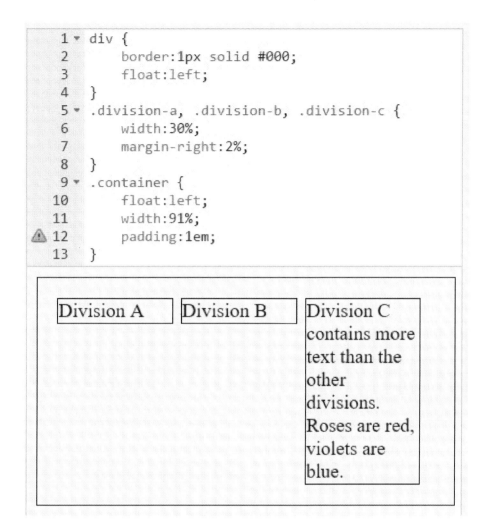

```
 1 ▾ div {
 2        border:1px solid #000;
 3        float:left;
 4 }
 5 ▾ .division-a, .division-b, .division-c {
 6        width:30%;
 7        margin-right:2%;
 8 }
 9 ▾ .container {
10        float:left;
11        width:91%;
12        padding:1em;
13 }
```

Above, on lines 6 and 7, I have changed the widths and margins to percentages. This means that each <div> tag will take up 30% of the available space regardless of how large or small that space is, and that each <div> will have a right margin that amounts to 2% of the available space.

Now, if I were to shrink the container <div> element's width, the rest of the <div> elements will shrink with it (line 11 below):

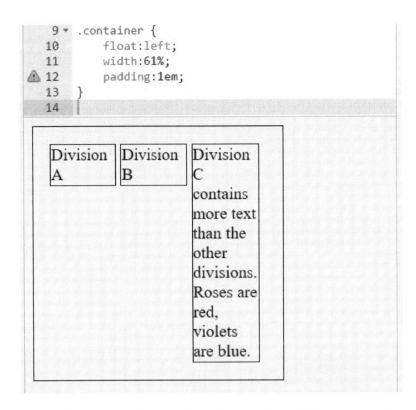

Below, I have increased the container <div> element's width again and given it a border-radius:

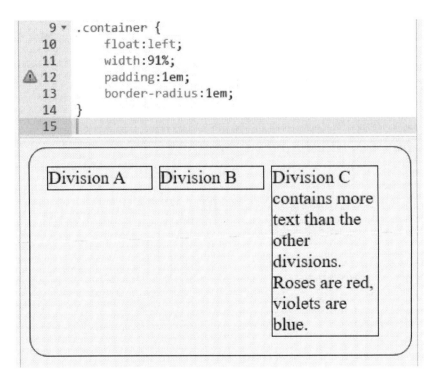

The border-radius property is purely aesthetic and does not affect the contained elements, but it can clip them. This is best illustrated by giving the border-radius a value of 100% (line 13 below):

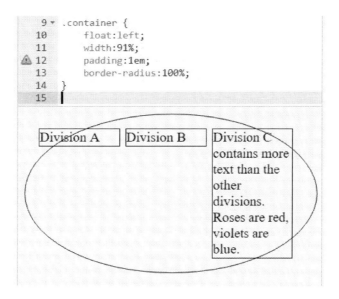

Below, I have given the three divisions a white background (line 8) in order to illustrate their relationship with the border-radius:

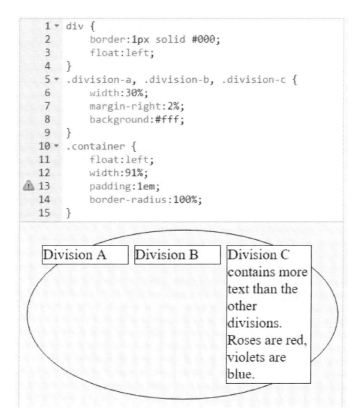

By giving the container <div> an "overflow:hidden" property (line 12 below), we can cause the border radius to clip the contained <div> elements (I have changed the border-radius and the width and padding of the three <div> elements for decorative reasons):

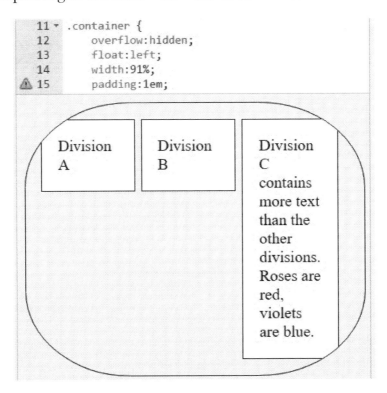

Moving on, below I have removed the border radius and the new styling I added to divisions a, b and c (but I have kept the white background). I have also added a new division-d element (line 9 of the HTML). Here is the new HTML:

```
1    <div class="container">
2        <div class="division-a">Division A</div>
3        <div class="division-b">Division B</div>
4        <div class="division-c">Division C
5        contains more text than the other
6        divisions. Roses are red, violets are
7        blue.
8        </div>
9        <div class="division-d">Division D</div>
10   </div>
```

I have made division-d have the same styling as the rest of the divisions a, b and c by adding it to the selector on line 6 of the CSS:

```
 1 ▾ div {
 2       border:1px solid #000;
 3       float:left;
 4   }
 5   .division-a, .division-b, .division-c,
 6 ▾ .division-d {
 7       width:20%;
 8       margin-right:2%;
 9       background:#fff;
10   }
11 ▾ .container {
12       float:left;
13       width:91%;
14       padding:1em;
15   }
```

Division A	Division B	Division C contains more text than the other divisions. Roses are red, violets are blue.	Division D

If we increase the width of the <div> elements (line 7 below), division-d will be forced onto a new line:

```
 5   .division-a, .division-b, .division-c,
 6 ▾ .division-d {
 7       width:25%;
 8       margin-right:2%;
 9       background:#fff;
10   }
```

Here is the result:

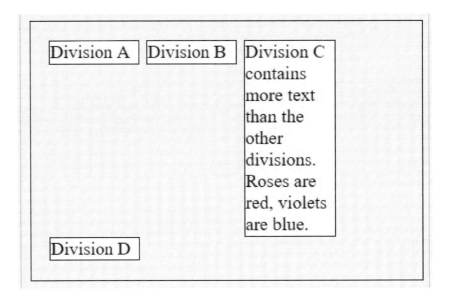

Above, notice that division-d is below the lowest point of division-c. Division-c is forcing its own line to expand vertically due to its large amount of content. There is, unfortunately, no way to avoid this and make the browser understand that we want division-d to show up right below division-a. We can, however, achieve this by making division-c float on the right:

```
 5    .division-a, .division-b, .division-c,
 6 ▾  .division-d {
 7        width:25%;
 8        margin-right:2%;
 9        background:#fff;
10    }
11 ▾  .division-c {
12        float:right;
13    }
```

The result is as follows:

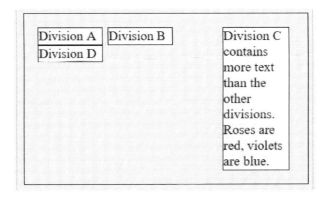

Above, now that division-c is floating on the right, it acquires its own "context" that is independent from divisions existing on the left. We can now add any number of left-floating divisions without them being affected by division-c. Below, I have added division-e and division-f, and I have added them to the CSS on line 6 so that they have the same styles as the other left-floating divisions:

```
 1   <div class="container">
 2       <div class="division-a">Division A</div>
 3       <div class="division-b">Division B</div>
 4       <div class="division-c">Division C
 5   contains more text than the other
 6   divisions. Roses are red, violets are
 7   blue.
 8       </div>
 9       <div class="division-d">Division D</div>
10       <div class="division-e">Division E</div>
11       <div class="division-f">Division F</div>
12   </div>
13
```

```
 1   div {
 2       border:1px solid #000;
 3       float:left;
 4   }
 5   .division-a, .division-b, .division-c,
 6   .division-d, .division-e, .division-f {
 7       width:25%;
 8       margin-right:2%;
 9       background:#fff;
10   }
11   .division-c {
12       float:right;
13   }
14   .container {
15       float:left;
```

Division A	Division B		Division C
Division D	Division E		contains
Division F			more text
			than the
			other
			divisions.
			Roses are
			red, violets
			are blue.

Below I have added a new paragraph (<p> tag) underneath the <div> tags with some Shakespeare lines:

```
11       <div class="division-f">Division F</div>
12       <p>'Tis but thy name that is my enemy;<br>
13   Thou art thyself, though not a Montague.<br>
14   What's Montague? It is nor hand, nor foot,<br>
15   Nor arm, nor face, nor any other part</p>
16   </div>
```

Here is the result:

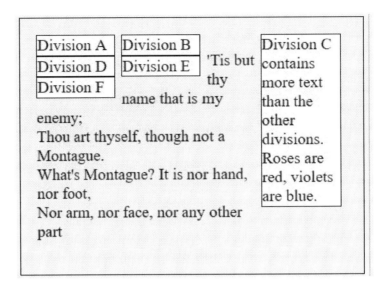

Since the new paragraph is not floating, the browser tries to make it fill the available space wherever that space may be.

To pin down the real location of the <p> element, below I have given it a 3-pixel dashed border (line 20 of the CSS):

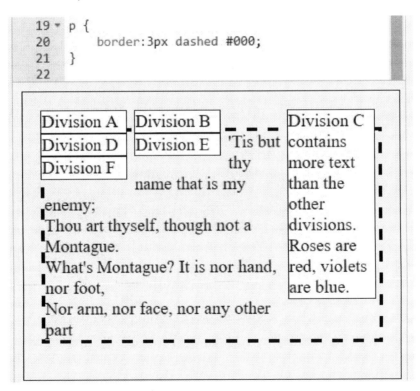

Even if we give the <p> tag a width of 100% (line 21 below), it will not get on its own line, because the floating <div> elements exist in their own parallel reality, they are "floating", they hover over the <p> element, except that they change the <p> element's appearance.

The browser makes sure none of the text of the <p> element gets underneath the floating elements.

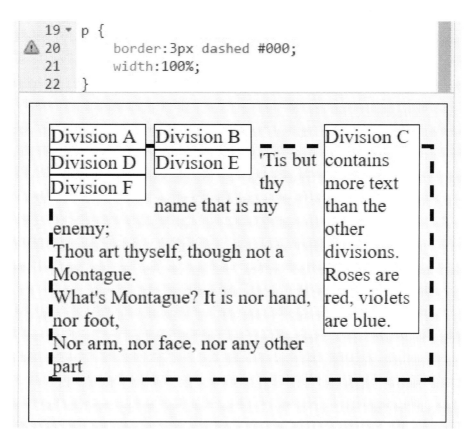

We can now introduce the "clear" property. Below, I have given the <p> element a "clear:left" property (CSS line 22):

```
19 ▾ p {
20       border:3px dashed #000;
21       width:100%;
22       clear:left;
```

The result is as follows:

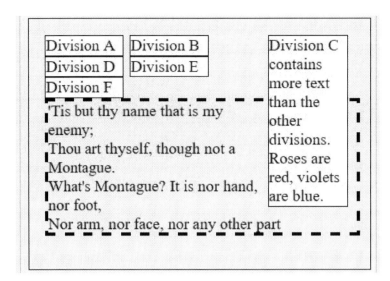

The "clear:left" property tells the browser that we do not want anything on the left of our paragraph. If there is something on the left, as there was earlier, the browser forces the <p> element onto a new line so that its left remains empty of all other elements. Note how the paragraph has not cleared division-c, since we have only instructed the left side to be cleared, the right side remains open for elements like division-c.

We can change this by also giving the <p> element a "clear:right" property (line 23 below):

```
19 ▾ p {
20      border:3px dashed #000;
21      width:100%;
22      clear:left;
23      clear:right;
```

Here is the result:

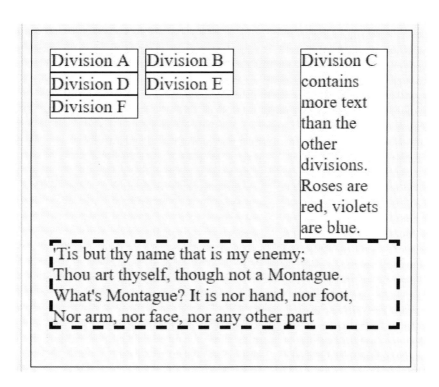

Above, both the left and right sides of the <p> element are not cleared. We can shorten the CSS by using the "clear:both" shorthand (line 22 below):

```
19 ▾ p {
⚠ 20        border:3px dashed #000;
21        width:100%;
22        clear:both;
23   }
24
```

Rules of Nesting and Inheritance

Below, I have switched things up by removing most of the <div> tags. I have placed a <div> element inside the paragraph, causing a broken appearance:

```
i 1 ▾ <div class="container">
  2 ▾      <p>'Tis but thy name that is my enemy;<br>
  3    Thou art thyself, though not a Montague.<br>
  4    <div class="division-a">Division A</div>
  5    What's Montague? It is nor hand, nor foot,<br>
❌ 6    Nor arm, nor face, nor any other part</p>
  7    </div>
```

Here is the result:

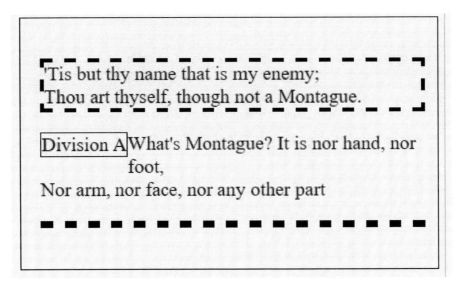

The reason for the broken appearance is that putting a <div> element inside a <p> element breaks the laws of HTML. A <p> element is only allowed to contain *inline* elements (such as <span> and <b>), it is not allowed to contain block elements like a <div>. To fix things, I change the <p> element to a <div> element with a class of "poem":

```
i 1 ▾  <div class="container">
  2 ▾      <div class="poem">'Tis but thy name
  3          that is my enemy;<br>
  4      Thou art thyself, though not a Montague.<br>
  5      <div class="division-a">Division A</div>
  6      What's Montague? It is nor hand, nor foot,<br>
  7      Nor arm, nor face, nor any other part</div>
  8      </div>
  9      |
```

In the CSS, I change the "p" selector to ".poem" (line 11):

```
 11 ▾  .poem {
⚠ 12        border:3px dashed #000;
 13        width:100%;
 14  }
```

Now, the broken appearance is fixed:

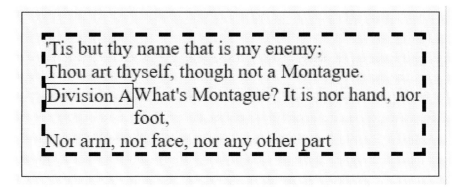

Below, I have given division-a a margin and padding of 1 em (lines 12 and 13):

```
 6 ▾ .container {
 7       float:left;
 8       width:91%;
 9       padding:1em;
10   }
11 ▾ .division-a {
12       padding:1em;
13       margin:1em;
14   }
15 ▾ .poem {
16       border:3px dashed #000;
```

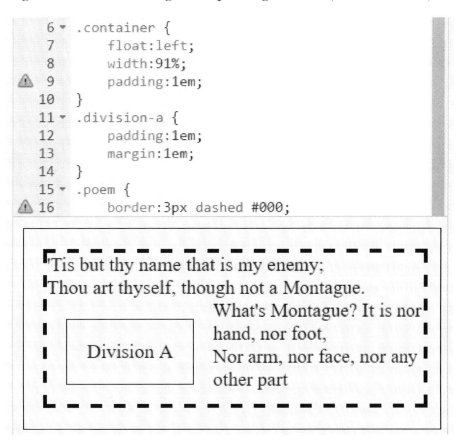

The browser rearranges the text so that it makes room for division-a's increased size.

Below, I add some more lines of poetry:

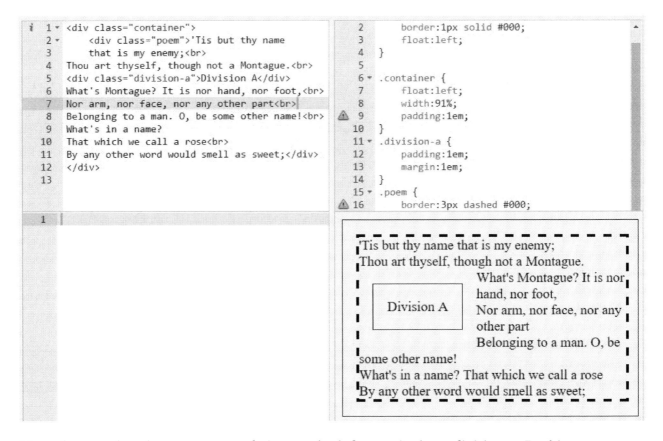

Note the way that the text resumes being on the left once it clears division-a. In this way, we can add side notes or images to a main text, useful for many purposes. Below, I have made division-a float on the right (line 14 of the CSS) instead of left:

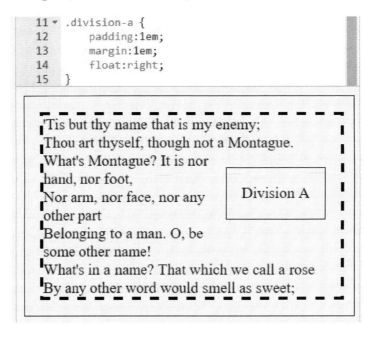

Since division-a is inside the poem, any styling we add to the poem class will also affect division-a. Above, I have added italic styling on line 19 to the poem class:

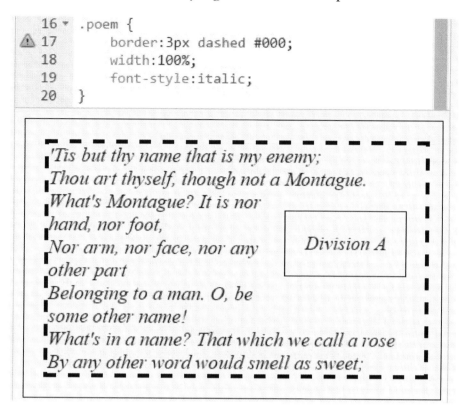

However, only some CSS properties are inheritable. Even if we remove the solid border of the <div> element, division-a will not get the poem class's dashed border. Below, I have deleted the "border:1px solid #000" property that used to be on line 2. The result is that division-a loses its border. But it does not end inheriting the border of the poem class (defined on line 16), despite being contained inside it and inheriting its italic styling. Margins and padding are also not inheritable.

```
1 ▾ div {
2       float:left;
3   }
4
5 ▾ .container {
6       float:left;
7       width:91%;
8       padding:1em;
9   }
10 ▾ .division-a {
11      padding:1em;
12      margin:1em;
13      float:right;
14  }
15 ▾ .poem {
16      border:3px dashed #000;
17      width:100%;
18      font-style:italic;
19  }
```

'Tis but thy name that is my enemy;
Thou art thyself, though not a Montague.
What's Montague? It is nor
hand, nor foot,
Nor arm, nor face, nor any   *Division A*
other part
Belonging to a man. O, be
some other name!
What's in a name? That which we call a rose
By any other word would smell as sweet;

When a <div> is inside another <div>, we call the outer <div> the "parent" element and the inner <div> a "child" element. In the above example, the <div> that has the "poem" class is the parent of division-a, and division-a is the child of "poem". And both of them are "descendants" of "container", and "container" is their "ancestor".

To clarify these concepts further, below I have created a situation where we have three <div> elements, one inside another:

```
i 1▾ <div class="division-a">Division A
  2▾     <div class="division-b">Division B
  3▾         <div class="division-c">Division C
  4             </div>
  5         </div>
  6 </div>
  7
  1
```

```
1▾ div {
  2     border:1px solid #000;
  3     padding:1em;
  4 }
  5
  6
  7
  8
  9
```

```
Division A
    Division B
        Division C
```

The parent-child relationship only applies to elements that are directly related. The element division-a is the parent of division-b, but it is not the parent of division-c, because division-c's parent is division-b. Instead, division-a is the *grandparent* or *ancestor* of division-c. Using the parent-child metaphor is useful when talking about HTML elements.

Note the way that the border and padding we defined on lines 2 and 3 affected all three <div> elements. This is because on line 1 we have declared that this styling should apply to *all* <div> elements. No inheritance is involved here, regardless of where a particular <div> is located, the styling will apply to it.

If, instead of applying the styling to the <div> selector we had applied it to division-a, the styling wouldn't have affected the other <div> elements, as seen below:

```
i 1▾ <div class="division-a">Division A
  2▾     <div class="division-b">Division B
  3▾         <div class="division-c">Division C
  4             </div>
  5         </div>
  6 </div>
  7
  1
```

```
1▾ .division-a {
  2     border:1px solid #000;
  3     padding:1em;
  4 }
  5
  6
  7
  8
  9
```

```
Division A
Division B
Division C
```

The border and padding affect division-a but do not affect division-b and c. This is because, as mentioned, border and padding are not inheritable. If, instead, we add a font family or some other property, this ends up affecting all the <div> elements, even though this is only added to the division-a selector:

```
1 ▼ .division-a {
2       border:1px solid #000;
3       padding:1em;
4       font-size:25px;
5       font-family:'Monotype Corsiva';
6       text-decoration:underline;
7 }
```

Here is the result:

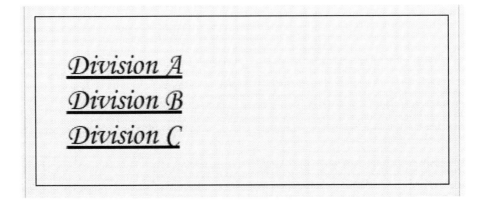

Learning which CSS properties are inheritable and which ones are not happens with practice and trial and error. There is no need to worry about memorizing them.

If we give the <div> tag a left padding of 1 em (line 2 below), the following situation is created:

```
1 ▾ div {
2       padding-left:1em;
3   }
4 ▾ .division-a {
5       border:1px solid #000;
6       padding:1em;
7       font-size:25px;
8       font-family:'Monotype Corsiva';
9       text-decoration:underline;
```

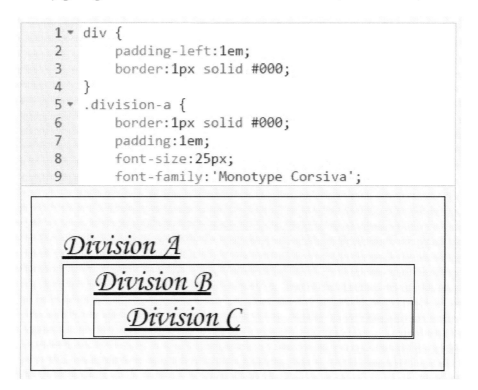

This happens because each <div> element's padding affects the ones inside it. This can be clarified further by giving all of the <div> elements a border (line 3 below):

```
1 ▾ div {
2       padding-left:1em;
3       border:1px solid #000;
4   }
5 ▾ .division-a {
6       border:1px solid #000;
7       padding:1em;
8       font-size:25px;
9       font-family:'Monotype Corsiva';
```

The padding on division-a forces everything inside it to move rightward by 1em. The same process repeats between divisions b and c. If you feel somewhat confused by this, there is no need to worry. Even skilled web designers get confused by the complex relationships that sometimes get created inside HTML documents. Sometimes they happen on the correct design without fully understanding how it works.

4.
The Joys of Positioning

Besides floating, there is another way of making HTML elements appear where we want them, and that way is known as positioning, which uses the "position" CSS property.

Below, we have two <div> elements:

```
i 1   <div class="division-a">Division A</div>
  2   <div class="division-b">Division B</div>
  3   |
  4
```

```
1 ▾ div {
2       border:1px solid #000;
3       margin:1em;
4   }
5   |
```

```
Division A
Division B
```

Below, I give division-a the CSS property "position:absolute" (line 6 below):

```
1 ▾ div {
2       border:1px solid #000;
3       margin:1em;
4   }
5 ▾ .division-a {
6       position:absolute;
7   }
```

Here is the result:

131

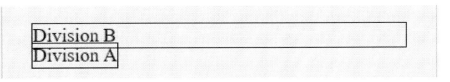

Absolute positioning causes the element to "hover" over the document. Unlike in floating, the element stops having any relationship whatsoever with the stuff underneath it. The broken appearance above is due to division-a hovering, causing the browser to put division-b up where division-a used to be.

Now that we have given division-a absolute positioning, we can move it wherever we want using CSS, as follows (lines 7 and 8):

```
1 ▾ div {
2       border:1px solid #000;
3       margin:1em;
4   }
5 ▾ .division-a {
6       position:absolute;
7       top:2em;
8       left:2em;
9   }
```

Division B

Division A

The "top" property determines the distance of division-a from the top edge, and the "left" property determines its distance from the left edge.

Below, I have reduced the top distance while increasing the left distance:

```
1 ▾ div {
2       border:1px solid #000;
3       margin:1em;
4   }
5 ▾ .division-a {
6       position:absolute;
7       top:1em;
8       left:7em;
9   }
```

Division B

Division A

We can also determine these distances in percentages, as follows:

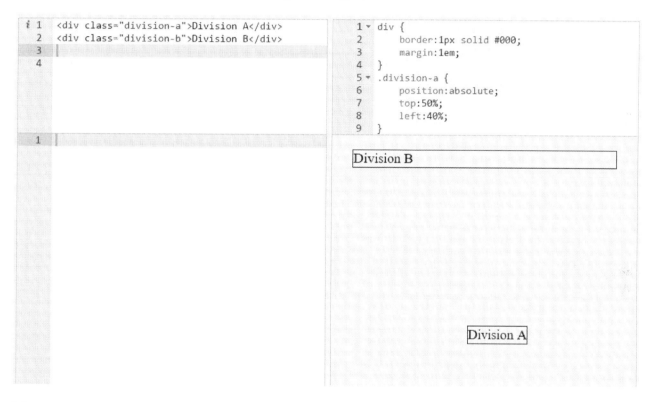

The property "top:50%" tells the browser to show division-a at or near the middle of its containing element. If there isn't a container, it refers to the browser window. To illustrate this, below I have created a new file on my computer called test.html:

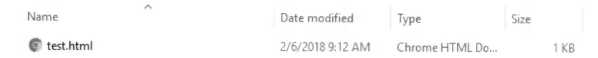

Name	Date modified	Type	Size
test.html	2/6/2018 9:12 AM	Chrome HTML Do...	1 KB

Opening this file in Notepad, I paste into it the HTML and CSS from above:

```
test.html - Notepad                    —    □    ×
File   Edit   Format   View   Help
<style>
div {
    border:1px solid #000;
    margin:1em;
}
.division-a {
    position:absolute;
    top:50%;
    left:40%;
}
</style>

<div class="division-a">Division A</div>
<div class="division-b">Division B</div>
```

Note that I had to create a new <style> tag which now contains the CSS. Without this, the browser does not know that this is CSS and interprets it as text. To illustrate, below I have removed the <style> tag:

```
test.html - Notepad                    —    □    ×
File   Edit   Format   View   Help

div {
    border:1px solid #000;
    margin:1em;
}
.division-a {
    position:absolute;
    top:50%;
    left:40%;
}


<div class="division-a">Division A</div>
<div class="division-b">Division B</div>
```

Now, if I were to open this test.html document in a browser, this is what I get:

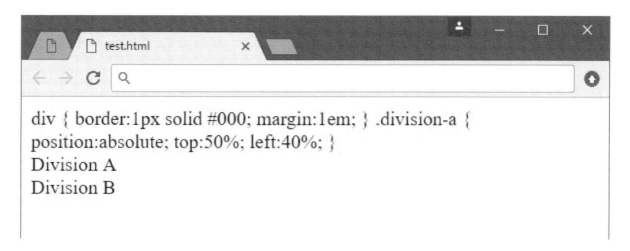

Below, I have added the <style> tag back, getting the following result:

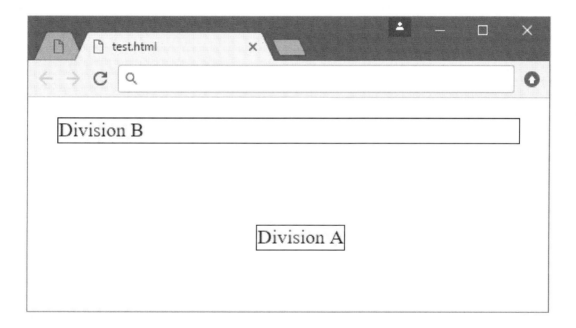

If I increase the height of the browser window (by using my mouse to drag its bottom border), division-a goes down with it:

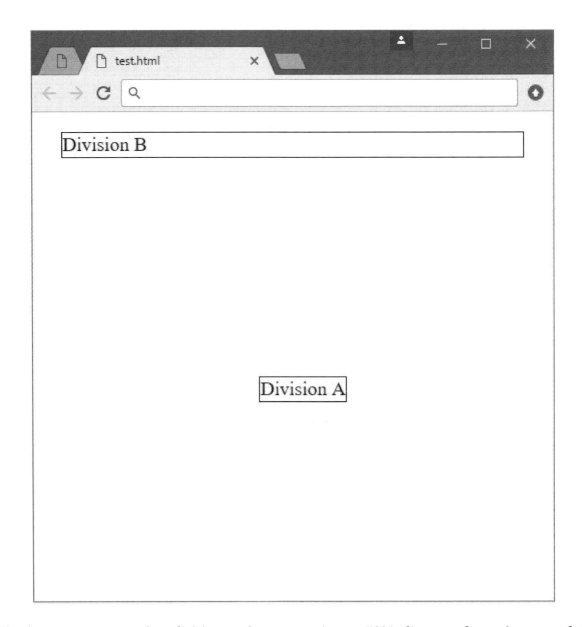

The browser ensures that division-a always remains at 50% distance from the top of the window. If the window is made larger, that 50% distance also becomes larger, so that division-a moves downward. If I shrink the window, division a moves up:

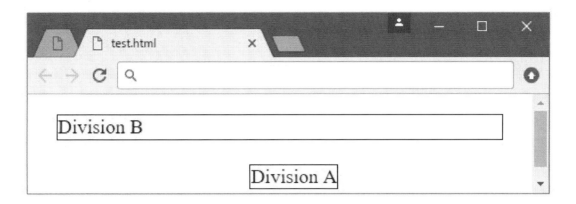

Going back to JSTinker, below I have given division-b absolute positioning by adding it to division-a's CSS selector on line 5. I have also changed the "top" and "left" properties to ems rather than percentages (lines 7 and 8):

```
 1 ▼ div {
 2       border:1px solid #000;
 3       margin:1em;
 4   }
 5 ▼ .division-a, .division-b {
 6       position:absolute;
 7       top:2em;
 8       left:2em;
 9   }
10
```

Division B

Something strange takes place because we have declared that both divisions should appear at the exact same location, which forces them to get overlaid on each other. It is like having a piece of glass with text written on it and putting another piece of glass on it that also has text on it. The two texts get merged.

If, however, we give the <div> elements a background (currently their background is transparent), one of the elements ends up occluding the other (line 9 below):

```
 1 ▾ div {
 2        border:1px solid #000;
 3        margin:1em;
 4   }
 5 ▾ .division-a, .division-b {
 6        position:absolute;
 7        top:2em;
 8        left:2em;
 9        background:#fff;
10   }
```

Division B

Above, the white background of division-b causes division-a (which is exactly underneath it) to hide. We can check this by moving division-b slightly down (line 12 below):

```
 5 ▾ .division-a, .division-b {
 6        position:absolute;
 7        top:2em;
 8        left:2em;
 9        background:#fff;
10   }
11 ▾ .division-b {
12        top:2.5em;
13   }
14
```

Division B

On line 11, I have added a new CSS selector specifically for division-b. On line 12, I have given division-b a top distance of 2.5 ems (rather than the 2 ems declared on line 7). The result is that we see division-a peeking from under division-b.

Instead of using "top" and "left", we can also use "right" and "bottom", as follows (lines 14 and 15):

```
 9 ▾ .division-a {
10       top:2em;
11       left:2em;
12 }
13 ▾ .division-b {
14       bottom:2em;
15       right:2em;
16 }
```

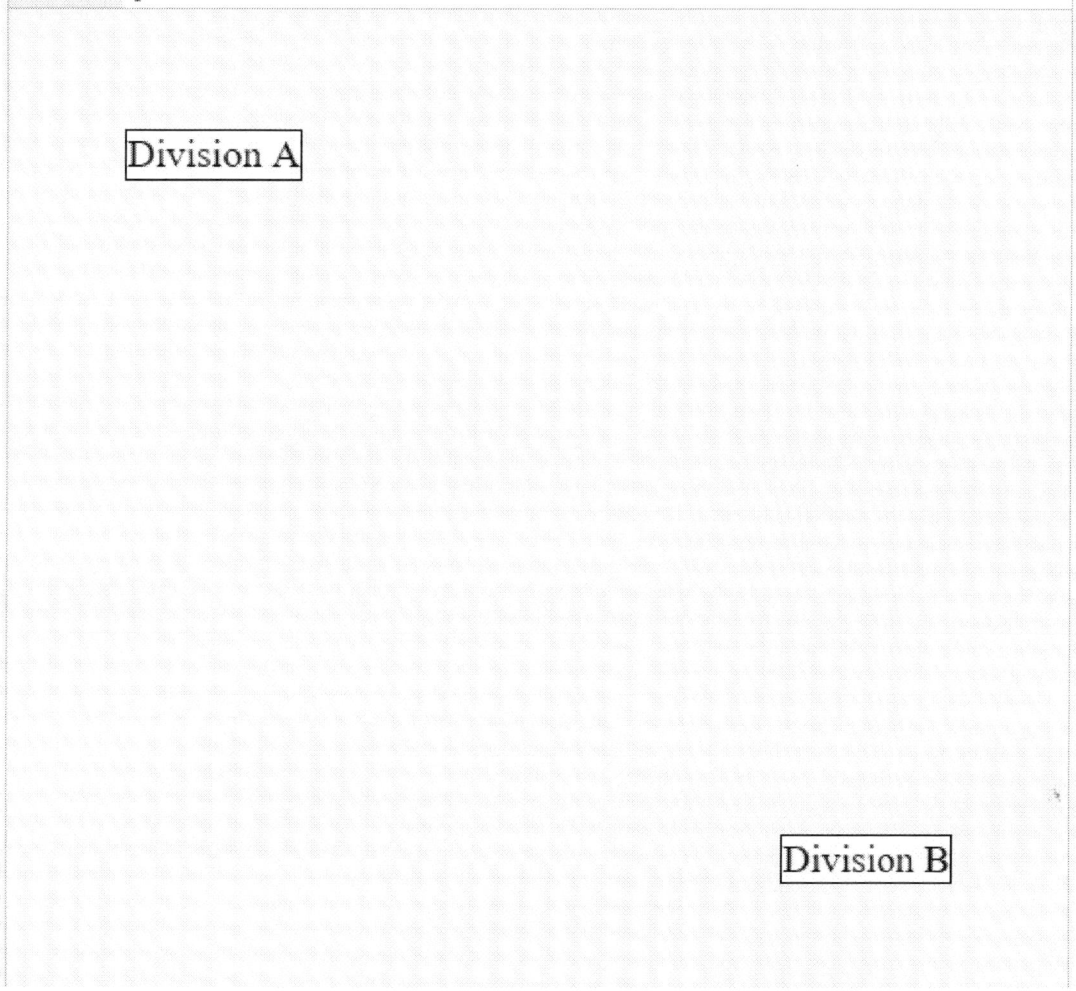

Division A

Division B

Above, division-a is 2 ems distant from the left and top, while division-b is 2 ems distant from the right and bottom.

Below, I have changed division-b's CSS so that it is now 2 ems distant from the top rather than bottom (lines 14 and 15):

```
 5 ▾  .division-a, .division-b {
 6        position:absolute;
 7        background:#fff;
 8    }
 9 ▾  .division-a {
10        top:2em;
11        left:2em;
12    }
13 ▾  .division-b {
14        top:2em;
15        right:2em;
16    }
```

Division A   Division B

Above, both elements are 2 ems distant from the top, but division-a is 2 ems distant from the left while division-b is 2 ems distant from the right, causing them to be at the same position vertically.

Below, I have increased the left distance of division-a and the right distance of division-b:

```
 9 ▾  .division-a {
10        top:2em;
11        left:8em;
12    }
13 ▾  .division-b {
14        top:2em;
15        right:8em;
16    }
```

Division A Division B

If I keep increasing both of these distances, the two divisions run into each other:

```
 9 ▾ .division-a {
10       top:2em;
11       left:9em;
12   }
13 ▾ .division-b {
14       top:2em;
15       right:9em;
16   }
```

DivisioDivision B

Above, division-b wins out and division-a goes underneath it. This is because division-b is declared further down in the HTML, causing it to have precedence. We can, however, declare that one division should be in front of another using the "z-index" property (lines 12 and 17):

```
 9 ▾ .division-a {
10       top:2em;
11       left:9em;
12       z-index:2;
13   }
14 ▾ .division-b {
15       top:2em;
16       right:9em;
17       z-index:1;
18   }
```

Division Aision B

The "z-index" property determines at what "depth" the element should appear compared to other elements. The higher the value, the less depth the element will have, meaning the higher it will be. Above, division-a has a z-index of 2, while division-b has a z-index of 1. This makes division-a "higher", so that it shows on top of division-b.

The values we give to the "z-index" property are arbitrary. We could have given division-a a z-index of 999 and division-b a z-index of 998 and the result would be the same:

141

```
 9 ▾ .division-a {
10       top:2em;
11       left:9em;
12       z-index:999;
13   }
14 ▾ .division-b {
15       top:2em;
16       right:9em;
17       z-index:998;
18   }
```

Division A|sion B

Playing with Coins

At this point, we can use our knowledge to create some interesting though crude drawings. Below, I have created five divisions:

```
1  <div class="division-a"></div>
2  <div class="division-b"></div>
3  <div class="division-c"></div>
4  <div class="division-d"></div>
5  <div class="division-e"></div>
6  
```

Below, I give the <div>s a height, width and border using CSS:

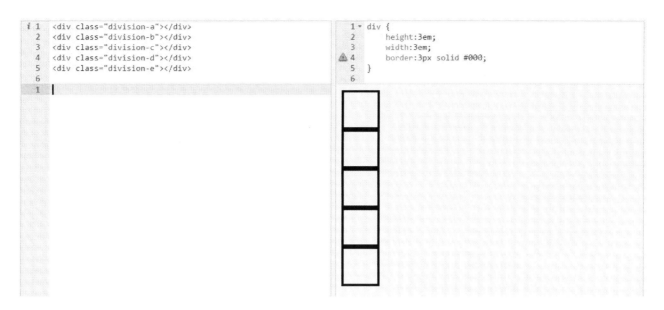

By giving the <div> elements a border-radius of 100%, I turn the rectangles into circles. I have also given them a yellow background (which will not show up if you are reading this in black and white):

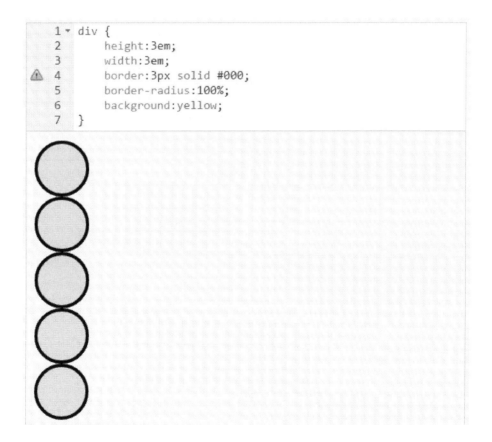

Below, I give the <div> elements absolute positioning (line 7), which makes them all pile on each other due to the fact that they all have the same distance from the top and left by default:

```
1 ▾ div {
2       height:3em;
3       width:3em;
4       border:3px solid #000;
5       border-radius:100%;
6       background:yellow;
7       position:absolute;
8   }
```

Below, I give each <div> its own top and left distance (lines 9 to 13):

```
1 ▾ div {
2       height:3em;
3       width:3em;
4       border:3px solid #000;
5       border-radius:100%;
6       background:yellow;
7       position:absolute;
8   }
9   .division-a {top:1em;left:1em}
10  .division-b {top:1em;left:1.5em}
11  .division-c {top:1em;left:2em}
12  .division-d {top:1em;left:2.5em}
13  .division-e {top:1em;left:3em}
14
```

Above, I have formatted my CSS differently to make it take up less space. The <div> elements appear like a pile of coins, with division-e appearing at the top due to being declared last in the HTML.

By fiddling with the CSS, we can create various designs:

```
 1 ▾ div {
 2       height:3em;
 3       width:3em;
⚠ 4       border:3px solid #000;
 5       border-radius:100%;
 6       background:yellow;
 7       position:absolute;
 8   }
 9   .division-a {top:1em;left:1em}
10   .division-b {top:2.5em;left:3em}
11   .division-c {top:1em;left:5em}
12   .division-d {top:2.5em;left:7em}
13   .division-e {top:1em;left:9em}
14
```

Below, using "z-index", I have forced divisions b and d to appear on top of the rest:

```
 9   .division-a {top:1em;left:1em;z-index:1;}
10   .division-b {top:2.5em;left:3em;z-index:2;}
11   .division-c {top:1em;left:5em;z-index:1;}
12   .division-d {top:2.5em;left:7em;z-index:2;}
13   .division-e {top:1em;left:9em;z-index:1;}
14
```

Above, divisions a, c and e have a "z-index" of 1, while divisions b and d have a "z-index" of 2. This means divisions a, c and e appear on a lower "plane" than divisions b and d.

Using scaling, we can make the discs above have varying sizes:

```
 9 ▾  .division-a {top:1em;left:1em;z-index:1;
10        transform:scale(0.5);}
11    .division-b {top:2.5em;left:3em;z-index:2;}
12    .division-c {top:1em;left:5em;z-index:1;}
13    .division-d {top:2.5em;left:7em;z-index:2;}
14    .division-e {top:1em;left:9em;z-index:1;}
15
16
17
```

Above, on line 10, I have made division-a appear smaller using the "transform" property, which is used for applying transformations to an element. The value of the property is "scale(0.5)", meaning to *scale* (i.e. change the size of) the element to 0.5 times its original size. The result is that division-a is now half as large as before.

Below, I have given division-b a scaling of 1.5 (line 12), meaning that it is now one and a half times larger than before:

```
 9 ▾  .division-a {top:1em;left:1em;z-index:1;
10        transform:scale(0.5);}
11 ▾  .division-b {top:2.5em;left:3em;z-index:2;
12        transform:scale(1.5);}
13    .division-c {top:1em;left:5em;z-index:1;}
14    .division-d {top:2.5em;left:7em;z-index:2;}
15    .division-e {top:1em;left:9em;z-index:1;}
```

Scaling an element causes everything about it to change in size, for example any text contained inside it, and the thickness of its border.

Relative Positioning

We have covered the "position:absolute" property, which allows us to give an element an "absolute" position, meaning that its location is unaffected by anything around it.[12] Instead of that, we can also use *relative* positioning. This allows us to have some control over the position of something while also having it be affected by things around it.

```
1  <div>
2      "Power attracts the corruptible.
3      Suspect all those who seek it."
4  </div>
5  <div>Frank Herbert</div>
6
```

```
1  div {
2      font-size:20px;
3  }
4
```

"Power attracts the corruptible. Suspect all those who seek it."
Frank Herbert

Above, we have a quotation from Frank Herbert, writer of the *Dune* series of sci-fi books. We will go about improving the appearance of this quotation and through this process, learn the use of relative positioning.

First, I will give the quote author's name a class so that I can give it a style (line 5 below):

```
1  <div>
2      "Power attracts the corruptible.
3      Suspect all those who seek it."
4  </div>
5  <div class="author">Frank Herbert</div>
6
```

I will make the author's name appear on the right using the "text-align" property on line 5 of the CSS:

---

[12] There are caveats to this, as will be made clear.

```
1 ▾  div {
2        font-size:20px;
3    }
4 ▾  .author {
5        text-align:right;
6    }
7    |
```

"Power attracts the corruptible. Suspect all those
who seek it."

Frank Herbert

Instead of using plain double quotes, I will use curly double quotes which have a better appearance. This is done through using the "“" and "”" HTML entities, as follows:

```
i 1 ▾  <div>
  2        &ldquo;Power attracts the corruptible.
  3        Suspect all those who seek it.&rdquo;
  4    </div>
  5    <div class="author">Frank Herbert</div>
  6    |
```

The result is as follows:

"Power attracts the corruptible. Suspect all those
who seek it."

Frank Herbert

I will give the quotation its own class and make its text larger (line 1 of the HTML, lines 7-9 of the CSS):

```
 1  <div class="quote-text">
 2      &ldquo;Power attracts the corruptible.
 3      Suspect all those who seek it.&rdquo;
 4  </div>
 5  <div class="author">Frank Herbert</div>
 6  |
```

```
 1  div {
 2      font-size:20px;
 3  }
 4  .author {
 5      text-align:right;
 6  }
 7  .quote-text {
 8      font-size:150%;
 9  }
10  |
```

"Power attracts the corruptible. Suspect all
those who seek it."

Frank Herbert

I will style the quotation marks by placing them inside <span> tags with the class "qmark",
meaning "quotation mark" (lines 2 and 5):

```
 1  <div class="quote-text">
 2      <span class="qmark">&ldquo;</span>Power
 3      attracts the corruptible.
 4      Suspect all those
 5      who seek it.<span class="qmark">&rdquo;</span>
 6  </div>
 7  <div class="author">Frank Herbert</div>
 8  |
```

Below, we will give the quotation marks a font-size of 250% (lines 10-12 of the CSS):

```
 1  div {
 2      font-size:20px;
 3  }
 4  .author {
 5      text-align:right;
 6  }
 7  .quote-text {
 8      font-size:150%;
 9  }
10  .qmark {
11      font-size:250%;
```

The result is as follows:

149

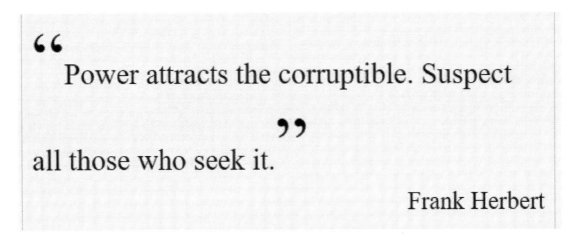

Above, notice how the second line of the quotation has a broken appearance. That's because the end quotation mark is so large that it pushes the whole of the second line down. We can verify this by giving the quotation marks a border (line 12 below):

```
10 ▾  .qmark {
11        font-size:250%;
12        border:1px solid #000;
13  }
14
```

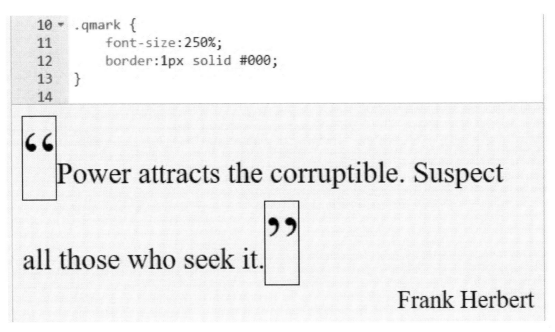

To fix this, we will give the whole quote a "line-height" property. This controls the spacing between lines, as follows (line 9 below):

```
 7 ▼  .quote-text {
 8         font-size:150%;
 9         line-height:1em;
10    }
11 ▼  .qmark {
12         font-size:250%;
13         border:1px solid #000;
14    }
```

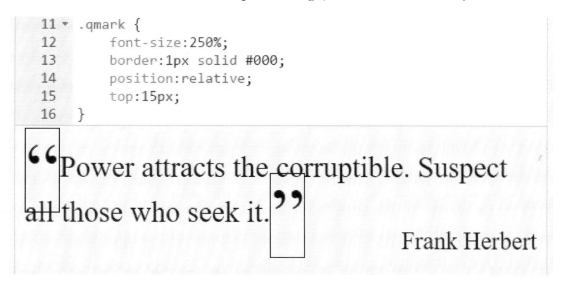

Above, the spacing between the first and second lines of the quote is now appropriate, but the quotation marks are not showing up properly because their larger font size makes not fit properly inside the small font size of the text. We have to force the quotation marks downward, and to do so we use relative positioning (lines 14 and 15 below):

```
11 ▼  .qmark {
12         font-size:250%;
13         border:1px solid #000;
14         position:relative;
15         top:15px;
16    }
```

Above, we are declaring that the quotation marks should be 15 pixels distant from the top of their previous position. The quotation marks move down 15 pixels *relative* to their original position. This makes them adaptable to their environment. For example, below I delete the second sentence of the quotation:

```
1 ▾ <div class="quote-text">
2       <span class="qmark">&ldquo;</span>Power
3       attracts the
4       corruptible.<span class="qmark">&rdquo;</span>
5   </div>
6   <div class="author">Frank Herbert</div>
7   |
```

```
1 ▾ div {
2       font-size:20px;
3   }
4 ▾ .author {
5       text-align:right;
6   }
7 ▾ .quote-text {
8       font-size:150%;
9       line-height:1em;
10  }
11 ▾ .qmark {
12      font-size:250%;
13      border:1px solid #000;
14      position:relative;
15      top:15px;
16  }
```

> **"**Power attracts the corruptible.**"**
> Frank Herbert

Above, notice the way the ending quotation mark has now moved. Its relative positioning means that it is always 15 pixels below where it would be if we hadn't given it positioning.

Below, I bring back the second sentence while hiding the borders by setting the border to zero on line 13 of the CSS:

```
11 ▾ .qmark {
12      font-size:250%;
13      border:0px solid #000;
14      position:relative;
15      top:15px;
16  }
```

"Power attracts the corruptible. Suspect all those who seek it.**"**

Frank Herbert

The quotations are a little too close to the text, we can change this with padding (line 16 below):

```
11 ▼  .qmark {
12        font-size:250%;
i 13        border:0px solid #000;
14        position:relative;
15        top:15px;
16        padding:5px;
17    }
```

❝ Power attracts the corruptible. Suspect all those who seek it. ❞

Frank Herbert

The styling we create in one font can appear less appealing in another font. For example, below I change the font of the quotation (including the quotation marks) to Monotype Corsiva (line 10 below):

```
7 ▼  .quote-text {
8        font-size:150%;
9        line-height:1em;
10        font-family:'Monotype Corsiva';
11    }
12 ▼  .qmark {
13        font-size:250%;
i 14        border:0px solid #000;
15        position:relative;
16        top:15px;
17        padding:5px;
```

❝ Power attracts the corruptible. Suspect all those who seek it. ❞

Frank Herbert

Now, the ending quotation mark is too far away from the text. To fix this, we give the ending quotation mark a new class while letting it keep the qmark class (line 5 below):

```
i 1 ▾  <div class="quote-text">
  2        <span class="qmark">&ldquo;</span>Power
  3        attracts the corruptible.
  4        Suspect all those
  5        who seek it.<span class="qmark end">&rdquo;</span>
  6    </div>
  7    <div class="author">Frank Herbert</div>
  8    |
```

You can add any number of classes to an element by separating them with spaces (not commas).

Below, I have fixed the appearance of the ending quotation mark on lines 19 to 21:

```
 12 ▾  .qmark {
 13        font-size:250%;
i 14       border:0px solid #000;
 15        position:relative;
 16        top:15px;
 17        padding:5px;
 18    }
 19 ▾  .end {
 20        right:13px;
 21    }
```

> **"** *Power attracts the corruptible. Suspect all those who seek it.* **"**
>
> Frank Herbert

Above, the ending quotation mark takes its styling from both classes (qmark and end). On the end class, I declare that it should be 13 pixels distant from its previous *right* position, which causes the quotation mark to move leftwards by 13 pixels, making it closer to the text.

Another way of achieving the same would be to give it a *negative* left distance, as follows (line 20 below):

```
19 ▾  .end {
20        left:-13px;
21    }
```

> " *Power attracts the corruptible. Suspect all those who seek it.* "
>
> Frank Herbert

Above, the end result is exactly the same as the "right:13px" property. This is because negative distance causes the element to move in the opposite direction.

Absolutes within Relatives

A common usage of relative position is to help us have more control over a certain part of an HTML document. Below, we have a quotation from Shakespeare inside one division, and a Shakespeare portrait inside the other division:

```
1 ▾ <div class="division-a">
2        Cowards die many times before their deaths;<br>
3    The valiant never taste of death but once.<br>
4    Of all the wonders that I yet have heard,<br>
5    It seems to me most strange that men should fear;<br>
6    Seeing that death, a necessary end,<br>
7    Will come when it will come.
8
9    </div>
10 ▾ <div class="division-b">
11        <img src="shakespeare_portrait.gif" />
12    </div>
13    |
```

```
1 ▾ .division-a, .division-b {
2        float:left;
3        border:1px solid #000;
4        height:200px;
5
6    }
7 ▾ .division-a {
8        width:60%;
9        font-size:90%;
10   }
11 ▾ .division-b {
12       width:35%;
13       margin-left:4%;
14   }
15   |
```

Cowards die many times before their deaths;
The valiant never taste of death but once.
Of all the wonders that I yet have heard,
It seems to me most strange that men should fear;
Seeing that death, a necessary end,
Will come when it will come.

Inside division-b, we have an <img> tag, which is how we include images inside an HTML document.

When it comes to <div> tags and most other tags, we have an opening and a closing tag. But the <img> tag, similar to the <br> tag, does not have a closing tag, because it has no content besides the image. The "src" attribute on the <img> tag tells the browser where the image is located on your computer or on the Internet.

To illustrate further, below I have a picture (goats_and_girl.jpg) and an html file (test.html) inside the same folder on my computer:

If I open test.html in Notepad, this is what it contains:

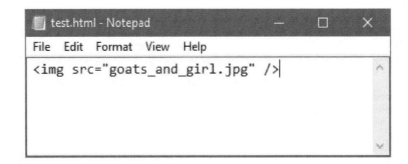

And if I open it in a web browser, I will see this:

When you give only a file name in the "src" tag, the browser will look for the image inside the folder where the html file is.

Below, I have created a new folder and placed the image inside it:

Name	Date modified
my_new_folder	2/7/2018 8:34 AM
test.html	2/7/2018 8:32 AM

Now, if I open "test.html" in a browser, I will only get an icon that tells me the image could not be found:

This is because the "src" tag tells the browser to look for the image inside the same folder as test.html. The browser does just that, but finds nothing. It is not smart enough to look elsewhere for the image. It will only look exactly where we tell it to look. I can tell the browser to look for the image inside the new folder I created that actually contains the image, by modifying "test.html" inside Notepad as follows:

Above, you see what we call a path. "my_new_folder" *slash* "goats_and_girls.jpg" means there is a folder called "my_new_folder", and inside it there is an image file called "goats_and_girl.jpg". If we save the file and open it again in the browser, we will see the image again:

Let us now go back to JSTinker and Shakespeare:

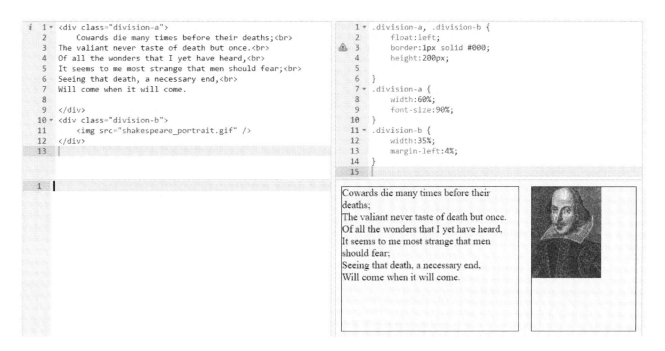

Now, if I give the `<img>` tag absolute positioning and a left distance of 2 ems, the following takes place:

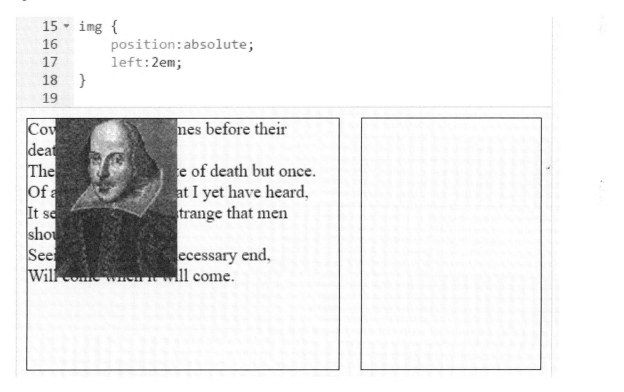

Intuitively, we'd expect the image to stay inside its own box. But the browser interprets the "left" distance as having to do with the whole browser screen, so the image is shown 2 ems distant from the left edge of the whole HTML document. By putting relative positioning on division-b (the box on the right) we can change things (line 14 below):

```
11 ▾  .division-b {
12        width:35%;
13        margin-left:4%;
14        position:relative;
15    }
16 ▾  img {
17        position:absolute;
18        left:2em;
```

Here is the result:

Cowards die many times before their
deaths;
The valiant never taste of death but once.
Of all the wonders that I yet have heard,
It seems to me most strange that men
should fear;
Seeing that death, a necessary end,
Will come when it will come.

Above, since division-b has *relative* positioning, the browser interprets the absolute positioning of the <img> element as restricted to division-b. The "left" distance of 2 ems now is calculated from the left edge of division-b rather than the left edge of the whole document.

By giving division-b relative positioning, its appearance or position does not change (unless we give it a "left" property or some other such property). What changes is its authority. Anything inside it that has absolute positioning will now have their position calculated with respect to division-b rather than with respect to the whole document. This allows us to create different zones of authority, i.e. different contexts, within a particular document, helping us create complex designs.

In short, if you give an element absolute positioning, its position is not always calculated with respect to the whole document. If the element is contained inside a <div> that has relative positioning, this forces the absolute position to be calculated with respect to this parent <div>.

To clarify things further, below I have placed Shakespeare's portrait inside three <div> elements:

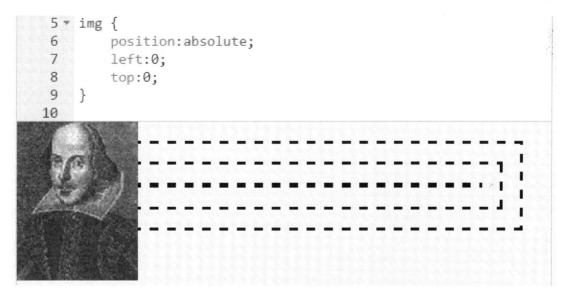

```
1  <div class="a">
2      <div class="b">
3          <div class="c">
4              <img src="shakespeare_portrait.gif" />
5          </div>
6      </div>
7  </div>
8
```

```
1  div {
2      border: 2px dashed #000;
3      margin:15px;
4  }
5
```

If I give the portrait absolute positioning and a left and top distance of zero, this takes place:

```
5  img {
6      position:absolute;
7      left:0;
8      top:0;
9  }
10
```

Above, the image's distance is calculated from the left and top of the whole document, without any respect for the <div> elements, since none of these elements have absolute or relative positioning. The innermost <div> (division "c") appears as collapsed onto itself because we have given its content (the image) absolute positioning, which makes it "hover" over the document without having any influence on other elements. As far as the appearance of division "c" is concerned, it might as well have no contents.

Below, I have given division "a" relative positioning (line 6). The image now changes position, because its top and left distances are now calculated with respect to division "a":

```
5 ▾  .a {
6        position:relative;
7    }
```

Here is the result:

Below, I change things so that now division "b" has relative positioning rather than division "a" (line 5):

```
5 ▾  .b {
6        position:relative;
7    }
8 ▾  img {
9        position:absolute;
10       left:0;
11       top:0;
12   }
13
14   |
```

Above, the image's position is calculated with respect to division "b". If we change "b" to "c" (line 5 below), as would be expected, the image moves again:

```
 5 ▾ .c {
 6       position:relative;
 7 }
 8 ▾ img {
 9       position:absolute;
10       left:0;
11       top:0;
12 }
13
14  |
```

What if two ancestors have relative positioning? Below I have given both divisions "b" and "c" relative positioning. The image's position does not change, because its position is calculated with respect to the *nearest* relative that has relative or absolute positioning, and in this case, that relative happens to be division "c":

```
 5 ▾ .b, .c {
 6       position:relative;
 7 }
 8 ▾ img {
 9       position:absolute;
10       left:0;
11       top:0;
12 }
13  |
14
```

Absolutes within Absolutes

To clarify the issue of absolutes within absolutes, below I have a single division (division "a") containing Shakespeare's portrait:

```
1 ▾ <div class="a">
2              <img src="shakespeare_portrait.gif" />
3    </div>
```

Here is the CSS:

```
1 ▾ div {
2       border: 2px dashed #000;
3       margin:15px;
4    }
5 ▾ img {
6       position:absolute;
7       left:0;
8       top:0;
9    }
```

And here is the result:

The division is collapsed onto itself because the image has absolute positioning, meaning it hovers in a way that takes up no height of its parent element. Division "a" is taking up a whole line, which is why it appears as a dashed black bar.

If we give division "a" absolute positioning (line 6 below), something strange takes place:

```
 1 ▾ div {
 2       border: 2px dashed #000;
 3       margin:15px;
 4   }
 5 ▾ .a {
 6       position:absolute;
 7   }
 8 ▾ img {
 9       position:absolute;
10       left:0;
11       top:0;
12   }
13
14
```

Above, division "a" seems to disappear. This is because the absolute positioning makes it collapse horizontally. It stops taking up a whole line, because it is now hovering over the document. The result is that the division becomes as small as it can get. Above, you can actually see it on the top left of Shakespeare's portrait. It looks like a very small square. That is the division's border. It is now a division that is wholly made up of borders, with nothing inside it.

Now, wherever we move division "a", that image will also move there with it, because division "a" is an ancestor of the image and has absolute positioning, so that the image's position is calculated with respect to it. Below, I have given division "a" a left distance of 5 ems and a top distance of 1 em (lines 7 and 8):

```
 1 ▾ div {
 2        border: 2px dashed #000;
 3        margin:15px;
 4   }
 5 ▾ .a {
 6        position:absolute;
 7        top:1em;
 8        left:5em;
 9   }
10 ▾ img {
11        position:absolute;
12        left:0;
13        top:0;
14   }
```

Below, I have given division "a' a width and height, so that it expands in order to appear as if it is the border of the image:

```
 5 ▾ .a {
 6        position:absolute;
 7        top:1em;
 8        left:5em;
 9        height:8em;
10        width:7em;
11   }
```

The result is as follows:

It is difficult to make the image and the border line up perfectly because they are hovering at different planes (as if they are drawn on separate pieces of clear glass that are placed on each other). If we wanted division "a" to properly encapsulate the image, we'd have to make the image relative so that it starts to take up height again.

Below, I have removed the height and width of division "a" and changed the image's positioning to relative:

```
5 ▾ .a {
6       position:absolute;
7       top:1em;
8       left:5em;
9   }
10 ▾ img {
11      position:relative;
12      left:0;
13      top:0;
```

Here is the result:

Above, the <div>'s positioning is absolute. But since the image's positioning is relative, it is properly contained inside the <div>, it forces the div to expand around it, creating the effect of a frame.

You may notice, however, that there is some space underneath the image, between the image and the frame. This is caused by the fact that an image is an inline element. I will not go into the details of why this happens, as it gets technical. We can solve it by giving the image a "display:block" property (line 14 below):

```
 5 ▾   .a {
 6         position:absolute;
 7         top:1em;
 8         left:5em;
 9     }
10 ▾   img {
11         position:relative;
12         left:0;
13         top:0;
14         display:block;
15     }
```

We can make the image escape its border by giving its "left" and "top" properties some value, as follows:

```
 5 ▾  .a {
 6        position:absolute;
 7        top:1em;
 8        left:5em;
 9    }
10 ▾  img {
11        position:relative;
12        left:1em;
13        top:1em;
14        display:block;
15    }
```

Note that the "left" and "top" properties of the image are calculated with respect to its place inside the <div>, rather than with respect to the edge of the <div>. To illustrate this, below I have added a <p> element inside the <div> but above the image (HTML line 2):

```
1  <div class="a">
2      <p>Test</p>
3      <img src="shakespeare_portrait.gif" />
4  </div>
5
```

```
1  div {
2      border: 2px dashed #000;
3      margin:15px;
4  }
5  .a {
6      position:absolute;
7      top:1em;
8      left:5em;
9  }
10 img {
11     position:relative;
12     left:1em;
13     top:1em;
14     display:block;
15 }
```

The image moves down because its "left" and "top" distances of 1em are calculated from its natural position inside the <div>. That natural position is somewhere below the <p> element.

If, however, we change the image back to "absolute" (line 11), its position will be calculated with respect to the edge of its parent <div>, without any respect for its natural position inside the <div>:

```
1  <div class="a">
2      <p>Test test test test test</p>
3      <p>Test test test test test</p>
4      <p>Test test test test test</p>
5      <p>Test test test test test</p>
6      <p>Test test test test test</p>
7      <img src="shakespeare_portrait.gif" />
8  </div>
9
```

```
1  div {
2      border: 2px dashed #000;
3      margin:15px;
4  }
5  .a {
6      position:absolute;
7      top:1em;
8      left:5em;
9  }
10 img {
11     position:absolute;
12     left:1em;
13     top:1em;
14     display:block;
15 }
```

Above, I have added a number of additional <p> elements (see the HTML), while giving the image absolute positioning (line 11 of the CSS). The image's position is now calculated with respect to the edges of division "a", without respect for what it contains, so that it hovers over the contents.

Below, I change the image's positioning back to relative (line 11):

```
10 ▾ img {
11        position:relative;
12        left:1em;
13        top:1em;
14        display:block;
15   }
```

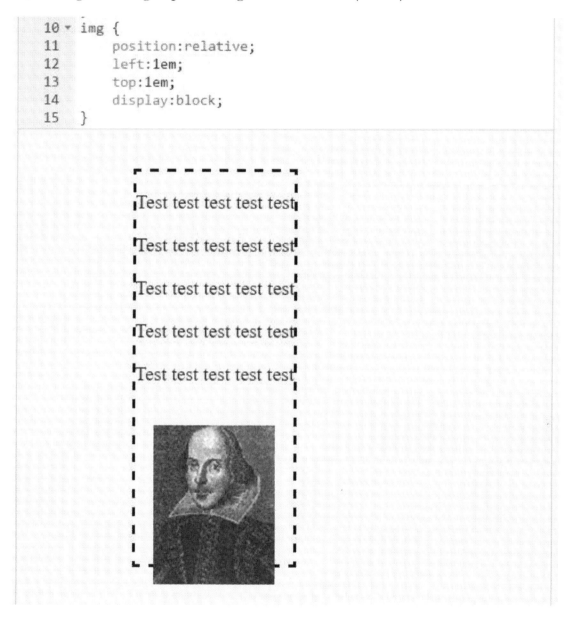

Above, the image jumps back down to the bottom. The relative positioning makes the image appear where it would without positioning.

Below, I have moved the <img> tag to the middle of the HTML (line 5 of the HTML):

```
1 ▾  <div class="a">
2        <p>Test test test test test</p>
3        <p>Test test test test test</p>
4        <p>Test test test test test</p>
5        <img src="shakespeare_portrait.gif" />
6        <p>Test test test test test</p>
7        <p>Test test test test test</p>
8    </div>
9    |
```

This causes the image to appear in the middle of the document:

Above, the image's relative positioning continues to exert influence. The image is still 1 em distant from the left and 1 em distant from the top of the image's original position, which is one reason why there is so much space at the top of the image.

In CSS, all elements have 'static' positioning by default. We can disable the effects of positioning by changing the value of the 'position' property to 'static', as follows (line 11 of the CSS):

```
10 ▾ img {
11        position:static;
12        left:1em;
13        top:1em;
14        display:block;
15    }
```

Test test test test test

Test test test test test

Test test test test test

Test test test test test

Above, the image now appears exactly where it would appear without positioning. The "top" and "left" properties no longer exert any influence, because 'static' positioning disables the effects of positioning. Now, if we were to take away all the positioning-related CSS, the image will continue to be exactly where it is above:

```
10 ▾  img {
11        display:block;
12    }
13
14    |
15
```

Above, the image stays where it is because if we do not specify any positioning, CSS assumes 'static' positioning by default.

Fixed Positioning

The final type of positioning to talk about is 'fixed' positioning. One of the main tasks of a web designer is to create annoyances for their users, as directed by their bosses. Fixed positioning is one of the main tools for achieving this. Let's say you have a page with an image that people really want to see, but you want to display a reminder that seriously annoys people. We begin with the reminder at the top and the image below it:

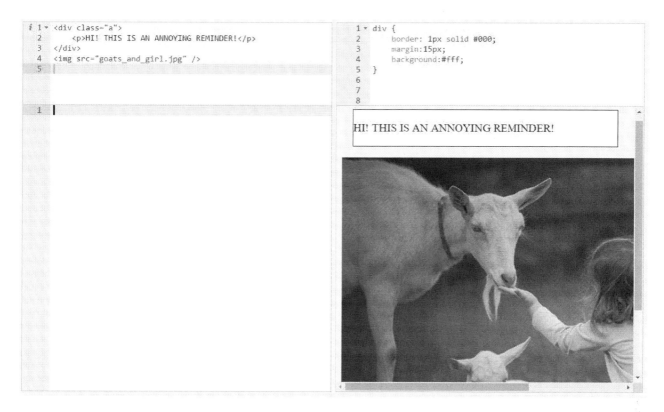

Above, we have a <div> with a paragraph inside it. Below that we have an <img> tag. If the user scrolls down, they will no longer see the reminder, as follows. This will allow them to enjoy the image without having to see the reminder:

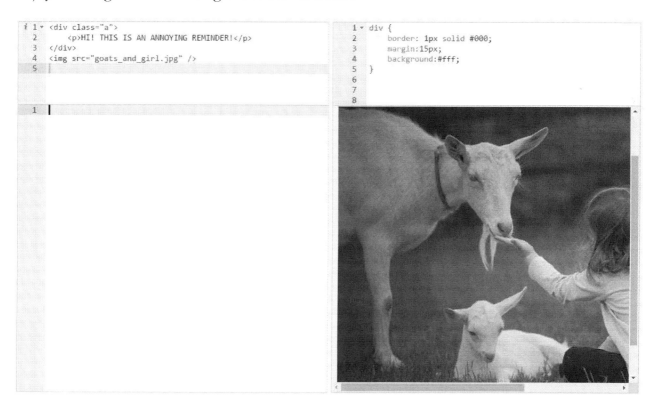

Below, we use CSS to give division "a" fixed positioning (lines 6-10):

```
1 ▾ div {
2       border: 1px solid #000;
3       margin:15px;
4       background:#fff;
5 }
6 ▾ .a {
7       position:fixed;
8       top:0;
9       left:0;
10 }
11
```

HI! THIS IS AN ANNOYING REMINDER!

So far, this appears similar to absolute positioning. What's special about it is that if the user scrolls down, the reminder keeps in view:

To further illustrate, below I have added a new image underneath the image shown earlier (HTML line 5):

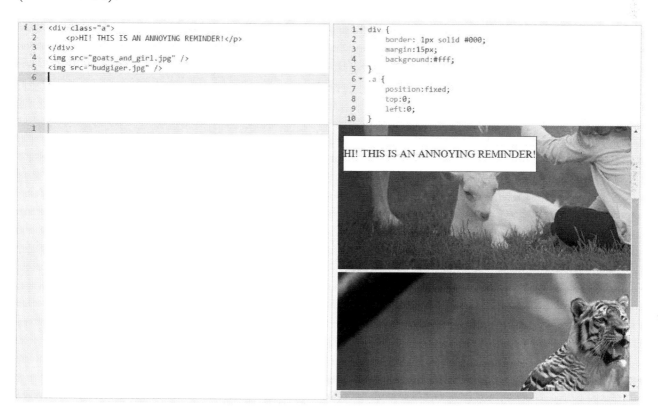

Above, I have scrolled down the document further but the reminder keeps in view.

Instead of top positioning, we can give it bottom positioning to plaster the reminder to the bottom of the screen:

```
1 ▾ div {
2       border: 1px solid #000;
3       margin:15px;
4       background:#fff;
5   }
6 ▾ .a {
7       position:fixed;
8       bottom:0;
9       left:0;
10  }
```

If you have browsed the web on your phone, you have probably run into websites that use fixed positioning to show you an ad at the bottom of the screen which does not go away even if you scroll down.

Below is a picture of a Vietnamese news website that uses fixed positioning to show a 'jump back to top' button on the bottom right of their articles:

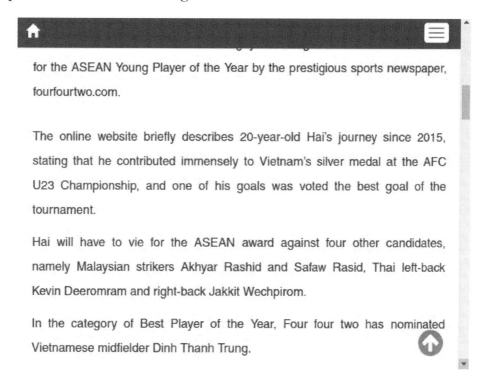

Above, notice the top-facing arrow on the bottom-right. As you scroll down the article, this arrow continues to remain where it is. If you click on it, it takes you back to the top of the page.

This page intentionally left blank

5.
Playing with Tables

Tables are an important part of HTML. Below I have created a table with two rows and two columns:

```
1  <table>
2      <tr>
3          <td>Row 1 Item 1</td>
4          <td>Row 1 Item 2</td>
5      </tr>
6      <tr>
7          <td>Row 2 Item 1</td>
8          <td>Row 2 Item 2</td>
9      </tr>
10 </table>
```

Row 1 Item 1 Row 1 Item 2
Row 2 Item 1 Row 2 Item 2

We can make it look more like a table by using borders. Below, I have given the <td> tag a border:

```
1  td {
2      border:1px solid #000;
3  }
4
```

| Row 1 Item 1 | Row 1 Item 2 |
| Row 2 Item 1 | Row 2 Item 2 |

In HTML, we create tables using the <table> tag. Inside them, we create rows using the <tr> tag (which stands for "table row"), and inside that we use the <td> tag to create individual "cells" of the row.

Below, I have given the <table> element a border (line 5):

```
1 ▾ td {
2        border:1px solid #000;
3   }
4 ▾ table {
5        border:1px solid #000;
6   }
7   |
```

| Row 1 Item 1 | Row 1 Item 2 |
| Row 2 Item 1 | Row 2 Item 2 |

While it looks more like a table now, the double border looks a bit strange. We can fix this using the table-specific property "border-collapse" (line 6):

```
1 ▾ td {
2        border:1px solid #000;
3   }
4 ▾ table {
5        border:1px solid #000;
6        border-collapse:collapse;
7   }
8   |
```

| Row 1 Item 1 | Row 1 Item 2 |
| Row 2 Item 1 | Row 2 Item 2 |

Now, no one can say this is not a proper table. The "border-collapse" property causes the borders on the <td> element to become the borders of the whole table. We can verify this by giving the table a dashed border (line 5 below):

```
1 ▾ td {
2       border:1px solid #000;
3   }
4 ▾ table {
5       border:1px dashed #000;
6       border-collapse:collapse;
7   }
8   |
```

Row 1 Item 1	Row 1 Item 2
Row 2 Item 1	Row 2 Item 2

Above, nothing happens because that table's border is hidden behind the <td> border. If, however, we make the table's border thicker, the table's border takes precedence. Below, I have increased the border on the <table> element to 2 pixels:

```
1 ▾ td {
2       border:1px solid #000;
3   }
4 ▾ table {
5       border:2px dashed #000;
6       border-collapse:collapse;
7   }
8   |
```

Row 1 Item 1	Row 1 Item 2
Row 2 Item 1	Row 2 Item 2

Above, note the way the inner borders between the cells are not dashed, that is because they are continuing to show the 1 pixel border on the <td> element. If we increase the border on the <td> element so that its thickness equals the border on <table> element, it takes precedence (line 2 below):

```
1 ▼ td {
2       border:2px solid #000;
3 }
4 ▼ table {
5       border:2px dashed #000;
6       border-collapse:collapse;
7 }
8 |
```

Row 1 Item 1	Row 1 Item 2
Row 2 Item 1	Row 2 Item 2

Instead of giving a border to the <td> element, we can give it to the <tr> element, as follows (I've changed the selector on line 1 to "tr" instead of "td"):

```
1 ▼ tr {
2       border:2px solid #000;
3 }
4 ▼ table {
5       border:2px dashed #000;
6       border-collapse:collapse;
7 }
8 |
```

Row 1 Item 1	Row 1 Item 2
Row 2 Item 1	Row 2 Item 2

Above, there is no border between the cells, since the border is on the rows. The border on the <tr> element will not show up unless we are using the "border-collapse:collapse" property on the <table> element. Below, I have deleted the "border-collapse" property from line 6:

```
1 ▾ tr {
2       border:2px solid #000;
3 }
4 ▾ table {
5       border:2px dashed #000;
6 }
7 |
```

Row 1 Item 1 Row 1 Item 2
Row 2 Item 1 Row 2 Item 2

Due to the finicky nature of styling the <tr> element, it is best not to use it unless you really have to. Stick to styling the <td> element.

Below, I have changed the "tr" selector back to "td" (line 1):

```
1 ▾ td {
2       border:2px solid #000;
3 }
4 ▾ table {
5       border:2px dashed #000;
6 }
7 |
```

Row 1 Item 1 Row 1 Item 2
Row 2 Item 1 Row 2 Item 2

Above, the dashed border on the <table> element and the solid border on the <td> element both show up, since there is no "border-collapse" property to force them to merge.

Below, I have brought back the "border-collapse" property (line 6 of the CSS). I have also added a new cell to the first row (line 5 of the HTML):

```
 1 ▾ <table>
 2 ▾     <tr>
 3             <td>Row 1 Item 1</td>
 4             <td>Row 1 Item 2</td>
 5             <td>Row 1 Item 3</td>
 6         </tr>
 7 ▾     <tr>
 8             <td>Row 2 Item 1</td>
 9             <td>Row 2 Item 2</td>
10         </tr>
11 </table>
 1
```

```
 1 ▾ td {
 2         border:2px solid #000;
 3 }
 4 ▾ table {
 5         border:2px dashed #000;
 6         border-collapse:collapse;
 7 }
 8
```

Row 1 Item 1	Row 1 Item 2	Row 1 Item 3
Row 2 Item 1	Row 2 Item 2	

Above, since there is no corresponding cell on the second row, it shows up empty. We can fix this by adding a new <td> element on line 10 of the HTML (even if we have no text to put inside it):

```
 1 ▾ <table>
 2 ▾     <tr>
 3             <td>Row 1 Item 1</td>
 4             <td>Row 1 Item 2</td>
 5             <td>Row 1 Item 3</td>
 6         </tr>
 7 ▾     <tr>
 8             <td>Row 2 Item 1</td>
 9             <td>Row 2 Item 2</td>
10             <td></td>
11         </tr>
12 </table>
 1
```

```
 1 ▾ td {
 2         border:2px solid #000;
 3 }
 4 ▾ table {
 5         border:2px dashed #000;
 6         border-collapse:collapse;
 7 }
 8
```

Row 1 Item 1	Row 1 Item 2	Row 1 Item 3
Row 2 Item 1	Row 2 Item 2	

Failing to have the same number of cells on each row (i.e. the same number of <td> elements) can cause all kinds of glitches, therefore it is important to make sure to create the same number of <td> elements inside every <tr> element, even if you have nothing to put inside them. This way they show up as empty cells as they should.

Below, I have given the top left cell a class of "a" (line 3 of the HTML). I have also given this class a width of 200 pixels (line 9 of the CSS):

```
 1 ▾ <table>
 2 ▾     <tr>
 3             <td class="a">Row 1 Item 1</td>
 4             <td>Row 1 Item 2</td>
 5             <td>Row 1 Item 3</td>
 6         </tr>
 7 ▾     <tr>
 8             <td>Row 2 Item 1</td>
 9             <td>Row 2 Item 2</td>
10             <td></td>
11         </tr>
12 </table>
 1
```

```
 1 ▾ td {
 2         border:2px solid #000;
 3 }
 4 ▾ table {
 5         border:2px dashed #000;
 6         border-collapse:collapse;
 7 }
 8 ▾ .a {
 9         width:200px;
10 }
11
```

Row 1 Item 1	Row 1 Item 2	Row 1 Item 3
Row 2 Item 1	Row 2 Item 2	

By giving the top cell in a column a particular width, all the cells underneath it end up getting the same width (notice how the bottom left cell is now as wide as the top left cell).

Instead of giving a cell a particular width, we can give the whole table a certain width, as follows (line 7 of the CSS):

```
1 ▾ td {
2       border:2px solid #000;
3   }
4 ▾ table {
5       border:2px dashed #000;
6       border-collapse:collapse;
7       width:50%;
8   }
```

The result is as follows:

Row 1 Item 1	Row 1 Item 2	Row 1 Item 3
Row 2 Item 1	Row 2 Item 2	

Above, the browser automatically shrinks all the cells so that the table as a whole takes up 50% of the available horizontal space. All the cells retain the same shrunken width. We can still give some cells different widths compared to others, as follows (line 10 of the CSS):

```
 9 ▾ .a {
10       width:100px;
11   }
12   |
```

Row 1 Item 1	Row 1 Item 2	Row 1 Item 3
Row 2 Item 1	Row 2 Item 2	

Above, the first column has expanded, but the table as a whole continues to take up 50% of the available horizontal space. The result is that the second and third columns are squeezed. Below, I have given the first column a width of 200 pixels (line 10):

```
 9 ▾  .a {
10        width:200px;
11   }
12   |
```

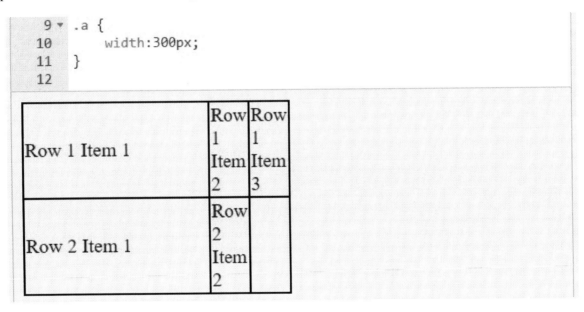

Above, the first column has expanded as much as it can. To put it another way, the second and third columns have shrunk as much as they can. Now, if I tried to further increase the width of the first column nothing will happen, because the second and third columns cannot squeeze further. Below, I have given the first column a width of 300 pixels (line 10):

```
 9 ▾  .a {
10        width:300px;
11   }
12
```

Above, the width of the first column is exactly the same as it was earlier. We cannot stretch a cell indefinitely because the width of the table and the width of the other cells limit its expansion. Table cells cannot shrink more than their contents.

Mr. Batchelor's Expenses

Below, we have the top part of a table of expenses (expressed in pounds, shillings and pennies) found in Thomas Batchelor's *General View of the Agriculture of the County of Bedford. Drawn Up by Order of the Board of Agriculture, and Internal Improvement*, published in the year 1808. We will now use HTML and CSS to recreate this top part of the table. Throughout this section, we will introduce many new and interesting concepts.

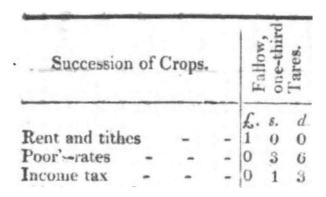

The table has two columns and five rows (there is a row above "Rent and tithes", but it's first cell is empty, while the second cell has the pound, shilling and penny symbols. Below, we have created the table in HTML and added the five rows, but no cells yet:

```
1    <table>
2        <tr></tr>
3        <tr></tr>
4        <tr></tr>
5        <tr></tr>
6        <tr></tr>
7    </table>
8    
```

We now add the first row's contents:

```
 i  1 ▾  <table>
    2 ▾      <tr>
    3 ▾          <td>
    4                  Succession of Crops.
    5              </td>
    6 ▾          <td>
    7                  Fallow, one-third Tares.
    8              </td>
    9          </tr>
   10          <tr></tr>
```

Here is the result:

Succession of Crops. Fallow, one-third Tares.

We now add the thick border at the top of the table present in the original:

```
 1 ▾  table {
 2        border-collapse:collapse;
 3        border-top:4px solid #000;
 4    }
 5    
```

The result is as follows:

Succession of Crops. Fallow, one-third Tares.

We now add a class of "first-row" to the <td> tags on the first row (lines 3 and 6 below):

```
 i   1 ▾  <table>
     2 ▾      <tr>
     3 ▾          <td class="first-row">
     4                  Succession of Crops.
     5              </td>
     6 ▾          <td class="first-row">
     7                  Fallow, one-third Tares.
     8              </td>
     9          </tr>
    10          <tr></tr>
    11          <tr></tr>
    12          <tr></tr>
    13          <tr></tr>
    14      </table>
```

Using CSS, we give the first row's cells a bottom border (line 6 below):

```
 1 ▾  table {
 2        border-collapse:collapse;
 3        border-top:4px solid #000;
 4      }
 5 ▾  .first-row {
 6        border-bottom:2px solid #000;
 7      }
 8
```

Succession of Crops. Fallow, one-third Tares.

Let's now take another look at the original table:

Notice how "Succession of Crops" is centered and has a lot of space around it. We recreate this using "text-align" and padding. But first, we need to give the top left cell a new class so that we can target it specifically for padding. Below, we give the top left cell a class of "first-cell" (line 3):

```
 1   <table>
 2       <tr>
 3           <td class="first-row first-cell">
 4               Succession of Crops.
 5           </td>
 6           <td class="first-row">
 7               Fallow, one-third Tares.
```

In the CSS, we add a "text-align" property to the "first-row" class:

```
 5   .first-row {
 6       border-bottom:2px solid #000;
 7       text-align:center;
 8   }
 9
10   |
11
```

Succession of Crops. Fallow, one-third Tares.

Above, the text of both the left and right cells is now center-aligned, but we cannot see it yet due to the small width of their cells.

Next, inside our CSS, we create a brand new selector ".first-row.first-cell":

```
 8   }
 9   .first-row.first-cell {
10       padding:1em;
11   }
12
```

Succession of Crops.   Fallow, one-third Tares.

Note that there is no space between the two class names. This selector is something we haven't seen before. This syntax allows us to target an element that has two classes using both classes. It means "give a padding of 1 em to any element that has a class of first-row *and* a class of first-cell". If there was a space between ".first-row" and ".first-cell", the meaning would change. The browser looks at the cells to see if any of them has a class of "first-row" and "first-cell", and finds just such a cell in the top left cell.

The padding we added to the top left cell also affects the top right cell (the cell containing "Fallow…"). This is because the padding expands the top left cell, which forces its whole row to expand, and this expansion affects any other cell on the same row.

Below, I give the top right cell a class of "second-cell" to enable me to target it specifically (line 6):

```
1 ▾  <table>
2 ▾      <tr>
3 ▾          <td class="first-row first-cell">
4                  Succession of Crops.
5          </td>
6 ▾          <td class="first-row second-cell">
7                  Fallow, one-third Tares.
8          </td>
9      </tr>
```

Now, we use the "transform" property to rotate the second cell 270 degrees (line 13 below):

```
12 ▾  .first-row.second-cell {
13         transform:rotate(270deg);
14
15  }
```

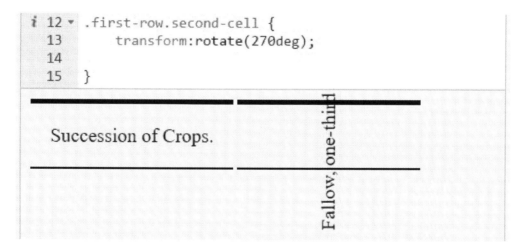

Above, even though we rotated the cell, its borders do not rotate with it. This is because a cell is not allowed to escape the limits of the row and table that contain it. Therefore while the contents rotate, the borders remain in place.

Let's look again at the original table:

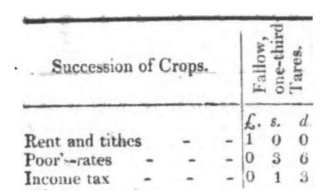

We will now add <br> tags to break up the top right cell's words so that they fit better inside the cell (lines 7-9 below):

```
 i   1 ▼ <table>
     2 ▼     <tr>
     3 ▼         <td class="first-row first-cell">
     4               Succession of Crops.
     5           </td>
     6 ▼         <td class="first-row second-cell">
     7 ▼             <div>Fallow,<br>
     8               one-third<br>
     9               Tares.</div>
    10           </td>
    11       </tr>
```

The result is as follows:

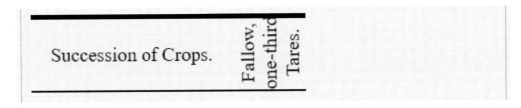

Let's add some padding to make the text stop touching the borders (lines 14 and 15):

```
 9 ▾  .first-row.first-cell {
10        padding:1em;
11    }
12 ▾  .first-row.second-cell {
13        transform:rotate(270deg);
14        padding-top:0.5em;
15        padding-bottom:0.5em;
16    }
```

Succession of Crops.   Fallow, one-third Tares.

Above, even though the cell has been rotated, we still use "padding-top" and "padding-bottom" to add space on the top and bottom, because the rotation does not affect the cell's padding due to the peculiarities of table cells.

Notice that in the original the top right cell's contents are left-aligned (the letter "F" in "Fallow" is directly in line with the "o" in "one"). We recreate this by giving the cell a left alignment (line 16 below):

```
12 ▾  .first-row.second-cell {
13        transform:rotate(270deg);
14        padding-top:0.5em;
15        padding-bottom:0.5em;
16        text-align:left;
17    }
```

Succession of Crops.   Fallow, one-third Tares.

In the original, there is a border between the first and second cells. We recreate this using the CSS on line 11 below:

```
 9   .first-row.first-cell {
10        padding:1em;
11        border-right:2px solid #000;
12   }
13   .first-row.second-cell {
14        transform:rotate(270deg);
15        padding-top:0.5em;
16        padding-bottom:0.5em;
17        text-align:left;
```

Above, we add a border to the right of the top left cell. The border falls between the two cells, appearing as if it is there to separate the two cells, even though in reality the border belongs to the top left cell.

Let's now work on the second row. We add an empty cell to this second row on line 13 of the HTML. The next cell contains a brand new table of its own:

```
12     <tr>
13         <td></td>
14         <td>
15             <table>
16                 <tr>
17                     <td>£</td>
18                     <td>s.</td>
19                     <td>d.</td>
20                 </tr>
21             </table>
22         </td>
23     </tr>
```

The result is as follows:

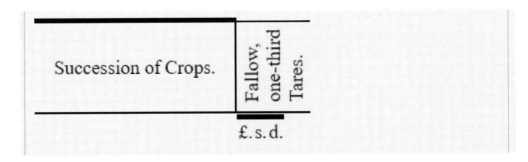

The reason we create a new table to contain the pound, shilling and penny signs is that there is some distance between them in the original, and the best way to create that distance and align the contents properly is to put them in their own table-within-a-table.

This is further clarified when we add the third row (which contains the word "Rent and tithes"):

```
24   <tr>
25       <td>Rent and tithes</td>
26       <td>
27           <table>
28               <tr>
29                   <td>1</td>
30                   <td>0</td>
31                   <td>0</td>
32               </tr>
33           </table>
34       </td>
35   </tr>
```

The result is as follows:

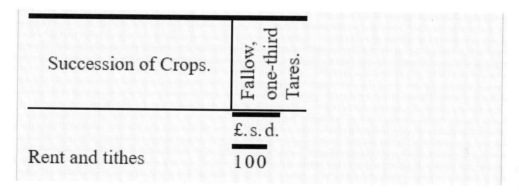

The values for rent and tithes are 1, 0, 0. Together they appear as the number 100, which can confuse people. And they do not line up properly with the symbols above them. The reason we added them to a table within a table is that doing things this way gives us the control necessary to make them line up properly with the stuff above them.

We now have three tables. The "outer" table and two tables on the second column. One inner table contains the symbols, the other contains numbers.

Notice how the new tables have a thick black border at the top. They get this because we declared in the CSS that all tables should have a thick top black border (line 3 below):

```
1 ▾ table {
2       border-collapse:collapse;
3       border-top:4px solid #000;
4 }
```

In order to stop the inner tables from having a border, we create a new selector (line 19 below):

```
19 ▾ table table {
20       border: 0;
21 }
22
23  |
```

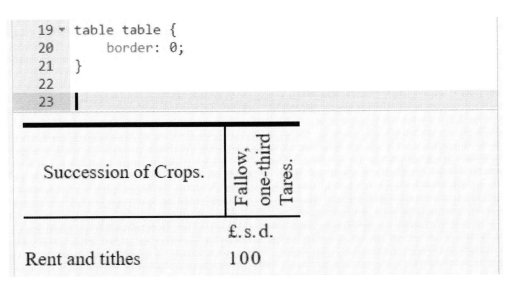

The "table table" selector means "a table contained inside another table". We declare that tables that are inside tables should have no border. The result is that the thick black border on the inner tables disappears.

Next, we need to make the symbols and numbers line up properly even though they are in different cells and tables. We do this by giving the "table table" selector a width of 100% (line 21 below):

```
19 ▾ table table {
20       border: 0;
21       width:100%;
22 }
23  |
```

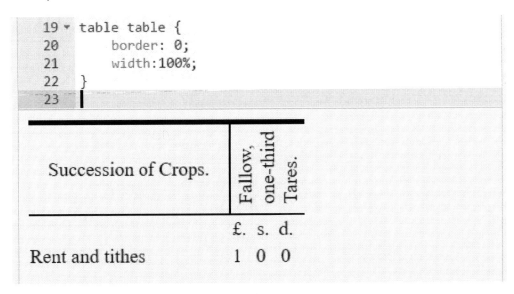

Above, thanks to the fact that all cells belonging to the same column get the same width, when we give the two tables a width of 100%, it means they should expand until they fill all the available horizontal space, and that horizontal space in both cells is exactly the same.

To further clarify things, below we give the cells of the inner tables a dashed border (lines 24-26):

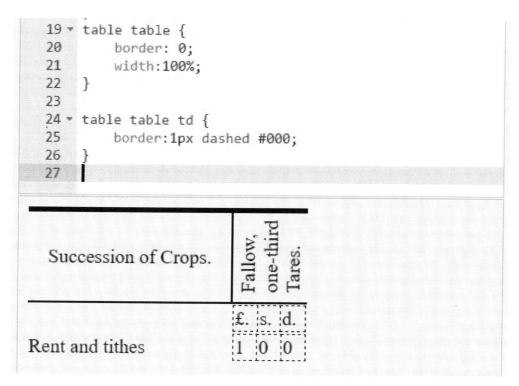

The selector "table table td" means "a cell that is inside a table that is inside a table". The dashed border helps us see the inner tables clearly. We have a table on the second row which contains the symbols. This table has only one row and three cells. The table on the third row (the "Rent and tithes" row) has one row and three cells, each cell contains a number.

Let's now add the rest of the rows:

```
36 ▾        <tr>
37              <td>Poor-rates</td>
38 ▾            <td>
39 ▾                <table>
40 ▾                    <tr>
41                          <td>0</td>
42                          <td>3</td>
43                          <td>6</td>
44                      </tr>
45                  </table>
46              </td>
47          </tr>
48 ▾        <tr>
49              <td>Income tax</td>
50 ▾            <td>
51 ▾                <table>
52 ▾                    <tr>
53                          <td>0</td>
54                          <td>1</td>
55                          <td>3</td>
56                      </tr>
57                  </table>
58              </td>
59          </tr>
```

And here is the result:

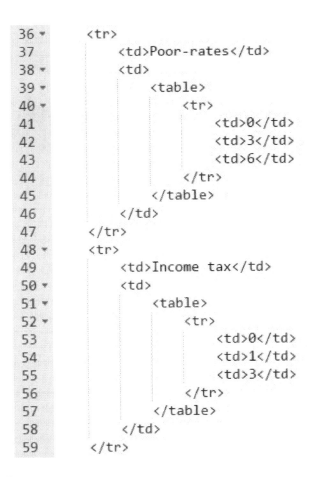

In the original table, the numbers corresponding to pounds are left-aligned, those corresponding to shillings are center-aligned, and those corresponding to pennies are right-aligned. Let's now recreate this. There are all kinds of ways of achieving this. We could, for example, give every left cell of the inner tables a class of "left", every middle cell a class of "middle", and so on (lines 17-19 of the HTML and lines 26-34 of the CSS):

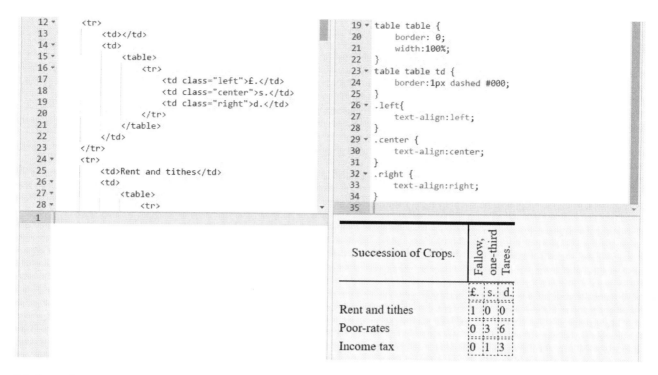

If the table contains hundreds of tables, adding these classes to every left, center and right cell can be extremely time-consuming, not to mention boring. Whenever you find yourself having to repeat something hundreds of times when doing web design or programming, it usually means there is a better way.

Nth-Child

We use the "nth-child" selector in CSS to apply a style using parent-child relationships. This enables us to address the issue of aligning the contents of a table without having to add classes all over the place. To make the contents of the first column of all the inner tables left-aligned, I can do as follows (line 26 below):

```
19 ▾ table table {
20       border: 0;
21       width:100%;
22   }
23 ▾ table table td {
24       border:1px dashed #000;
25   }
26 ▾ table table td:nth-child(1) {
27       text-align:left;
28   }
29
30   |
```

Succession of Crops.	Fallow, one-third Tares.		
	£.	s.	d.
Rent and tithes	1	0	0
Poor-rates	0	3	6
Income tax	0	1	3

The selector "table table td:nth-child(1)" means: "Apply the following style to every cell that is inside a table that is inside a table, provided that it is the first child of its parent". The "parent" in question is of course the inner rows. And the "first child" merely means the first cell of each inner table. What, therefore, this convoluted syntax means is "the first cell of each inner table", meaning the cells that contain the pound symbol and the numbers below it. Note that above, now, the pound symbol and the numbers below it are all left-aligned.

We can now do the same for the shillings (lines 29-31):

```
29 ▾  table table td:nth-child(2) {
30        text-align:center;
31    }
32
33    |
```

Succession of Crops.	Fallow, one-third Tares.		
	£.	s.	d.
Rent and tithes	1	0	0
Poor-rates	0	3	6
Income tax	0	1	3

Above, the selector on line 29 means "the second cell of every row of every inner table", which naturally applies to all the middle cells of all the inner tables, which means the shilling symbol and all the numbers below it.

If you are finding it difficult to understand these new "nth-child" selectors, there is no need to worry. Even a seasoned web designer will have to exert a lot of mental effort in order to "decode" the meaning of the selector. In practice, the decoding is done through trial and error, for example by quickly adding a border or red color and seeing what happens.

You can simply skim through this section and not worry if things seem to get too complicated. Only with much practice will these selectors become easy to understand. It is sufficient to know that such selectors exist, and if you have a need for them in the future or run into them, you can come back to this section to read up more on them.

Now, we will make the pennies right-aligned (lines 32-34):

```
32 ▾ table table td:nth-child(3) {
33        text-align:right;
34 }
35
36
```

Succession of Crops.	Fallow, one-third Tares.		
	£.	s.	d.
Rent and tithes	1	0	0
Poor-rates	0	3	6
Income tax	0	1	3

The new selector means "third child of every row of every inner table", which refers to the pennies.

Let's now hide the dashed border by setting it to zero in order to see what the table really looks like (line 23 below):

```
23 ▾ table table td {
24        border:0px dashed #000;
25 }
26 ▾ table table td:nth-child(1) {
27        text-align:left;
28 }
29 ▾ table table td:nth-child(2) {
30        text-align:center;
31 }
32 ▾ table table td:nth-child(3) {
33        text-align:right;
34 }
35
36
```

The result is as follows:

Succession of Crops.	Fallow, one-third	Tares.	
	£.	s.	d.
Rent and tithes	1	0	0
Poor-rates	0	3	6
Income tax	0	1	3

In the original table below, there is a black border between the symbols and numbers on the right and the text on the left:

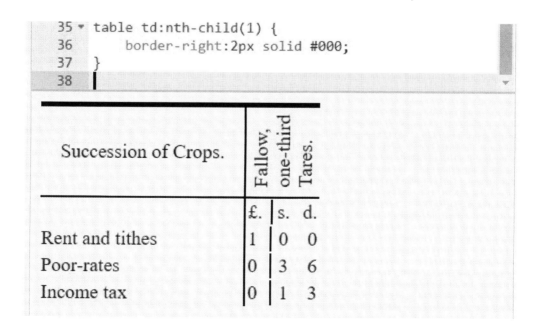

We can add the border using the "nth-child" selector we used earlier (lines 35-37 below):

```
35 ▾ table td:nth-child(1) {
36       border-right:2px solid #000;
37    }
38    |
```

Succession of Crops.	Fallow, one-third	Tares.	
	£.	s.	d.
Rent and tithes	1	0	0
Poor-rates	0	3	6
Income tax	0	1	3

The selector means "every first cell of every row of every table must have a right border of 2 pixels". We now have a right border that separates the text on the left ("Rent and tithes", etc.) from the symbols and numbers on the right.

Unfortunately, this definition also applies to the inner tables, making their first cells acquire unwanted right borders too (see the borders on the right of the pound symbol and the numbers below it). We hide these unwanted borders as follows (line 28 below):

```
26 ▼ table table td:nth-child(1) {
27        text-align:left;
28        border:0;
29   }
```

The result is as follows:

```
36 ▼ table td:nth-child(1) {
37        border-right:2px solid #000;
38   }
```

Succession of Crops.	Fallow, one-third Tares.		
	£.	s.	d.
Rent and tithes	1	0	0
Poor-rates	0	3	6
Income tax	0	1	3

On line 37, we declare that every first cell of every table should have a right border. But now, on line 28 we have declared that every first cell of every table *that is inside a table* should have no border. This new definition on line 28 is *more specific,* therefore it takes precedence and causes the unwanted borders to go away.

In the original, the pound, penny and shilling symbols have italic formatting. We achieve this as follows (lines 40-42):

```
40 ▾  table tr:nth-child(2) table {
41         font-style: italic;
42    }
43    |
```

Succession of Crops.	Fallow, one-third Tares.		
	£.	*s.*	*d.*
Rent and tithes	1	0	0
Poor-rates	0	3	6
Income tax	0	1	3

Above, our brand new selector means "a table that is inside the second row of a table". Which table satisfies this criterion? The table that contains the symbols, of course. Another way of reading the selector is: think of a table, think of the <tr> tags inside it, think of the second one, think of a table inside that. Reading it this way, you can easily pin down what is meant by the selector.

At this point we are nearly done recreating the table. We could do more work on it, but for simplicity's sake we will leave the table as it is.

First and Last Children

Instead of using nth-child(number), CSS also gives us the ":first-child" and ":last-child" pseudo-selectors, as follows.

Below, I have deleted the outer table from the code we used earlier and merged all the inner tables into a single table. I have also deleted most of the CSS:

```
 1▾ <table>
 2▾     <tr>
 3          <td>£.</td><td>s.</td><td>d.</td>
 4      </tr>
 5▾     <tr>
 6          <td>1</td><td>0</td><td>0</td>
 7      </tr>
 8▾     <tr>
 9          <td>0</td><td>3</td><td>6</td>
10      </tr>
11▾     <tr>
12          <td>0</td><td>1</td><td>3</td>
13      </tr>
14  </table>
15  |
```

```
 1▾ table {
 2      border-collapse:collapse;
 3      width:50%;
 4  }
 5▾ table tr {
 6      border-bottom:1px solid #000;
 7      text-align:center;
 8  }
 9  |
```

£.	s.	d.
1	0	0
0	3	6
0	1	3

Below, I have used the ":first-child" selector to give the first row of the table a black background and white text (lines 9-12):

```
 9▾ table tr:first-child {
10      background:#000;
11      color:#fff;
12  }
13  |
```

The selector on line 9 should be read as: think of a table, think of its tr tags, think of the one that is a first child. The result is as follows:

£.	s.	d.
1	0	0
0	3	6
0	1	3

Below, I have changed "first-child" to "last-child" on line 9, meaning that we are selecting, of all the rows of the table, the one that is a last child:

```
 9▾ table tr:last-child {
10      background:#000;
11      color:#fff;
12  }
13  |
```

Here is the result:

£.	s.	d.
1	0	0
0	3	6
0	**1**	**3**

Below, we use "table tr td:first-child" to select every first child of every row:

```
 9 ▾ table tr td:first-child {
10        background:#000;
11        color:#fff;
12    }
13
```

The selector should be read as: think of a table, think of its <tr> tags, think of the <td> tags inside them, think of the ones that are first children. This ends up applying to every first cell of every row. Here is the result:

£.	s.	d.
1	0	0
0	3	6
0	1	3

Changing "first-child" to "last-child", we end up selecting every final cell of every row:

```
 9 ▾ table tr td:last-child {
10        background:#000;
11        color:#fff;
12    }
13
```

Here is the result:

£.	s.	d.
1	0	**0**
0	3	**6**
0	1	**3**

There is no "middle-child" selector to help us select the middle cells. To style the middle column, we have to use the nth-child selector (line 9 below):

```
 9 ▾ table tr td:nth-child(2) {
10        background:#000;
11        color:#fff;
12   }
13   |
```

The result is as follows:

£.	s.	d.
1	0	0
0	3	6
0	1	3

Above, we use the selector on line 9 to select every second child of every row, which ends up selecting every middle cell.

Below, I have shortened the selector on line 9:

```
 9 ▾ table td:nth-child(2) {
10        background:#000;
11        color:#fff;
12   }
13   |
```

The result is as follows:

£.	s.	d.
1	0	0
0	3	6
0	1	3

Above, I have changed "table tr td:nth-child(2)" by removing the "tr". The result is the same as earlier, this does not change its meaning. One might have expected this shortened selector to select *the second cell of the table* rather than the second cell of every row of the table. The second cell of the table would have been the top middle cell, the one that contains "s.". But instead, CSS continues to select every second cell of *every row*. This is because CSS interprets the word "child" with respect to its immediate parent. We can even take away the word "table" from the selector and the result would still be the same (line 9 below):

```
 9 ▾ td:nth-child(2) {
10        background:#000;
11        color:#fff;
12 }
13
```

£.	s.	d.
1	0	0
0	3	6
0	1	3

Above, the selector on line 9 means "every cell that is a second child". Since each cell's parent is a row, "every cell that is a second child" means "every cell that is the second child of its row" (i.e. every <td> tag inside a <tr> tag).

Even and Odd Children

CSS offers us even and odd selectors that can come in very handy when trying to make a table look pretty, as follows (line 9 below):

```
 1 ▾ table {
 2        border-collapse:collapse;
 3        width:50%;
 4 }
 5 ▾ table tr {
 6        border-bottom:1px solid #000;
 7        text-align:center;
 8 }
 9 ▾ tr:nth-child(even) {
10        background:#000;
11        color:#fff;
12 }
13
```

£.	s.	d.
1	0	0
0	3	6
0	1	3

Above, on line 9, I have declared that every row that is even should have a black background with white text. This ends up making the second and fourth rows have this style, without affecting the rest. Below, I have changed the word "even" to "odd" (line 9):

```
 9 ▾ tr:nth-child(odd) {
10        background:#000;
11        color:#fff;
12   }
13   |
```

£.	s.	d.
1	0	0
0	3	6
0	1	3

Now, the first and third rows are affected. "tr:nth-child(odd)" should be read as: Every row that is an odd child of its parent. The table has four rows, we could select each row using tr:nth-child(1), tr:nth-child(2), tr:nth-child(3) and tr:nth-child(4). When we write tr:nth-child(odd), the browser looks at the children and selects nth-child(1) and nth-child(3) of the table, i.e. the ones that have an odd number.

Even and odd formatting is useful when trying to make a large table more readable, as follows:

```
 1 ▾ <table>
 2 ▾     <tr>
 3           <td>£.</td><td>s.</td><td>d.</td>
 4           <td>£.</td><td>s.</td><td>d.</td>
 5           <td>£.</td><td>s.</td><td>d.</td>
 6           <td>£.</td><td>s.</td><td>d.</td>
 7       </tr>
 8 ▾     <tr>
 9           <td>1</td><td>0</td><td>0</td>
10           <td>1</td><td>0</td><td>0</td>
11           <td>1</td><td>0</td><td>0</td>
12           <td>1</td><td>0</td><td>0</td>
13       </tr>
 1   |
```

```
 1 ▾ table {
 2        border-collapse:collapse;
 3        width:50%;
 4   }
 5 ▾ table tr {
 6        text-align:center;
 7   }
 8 ▾ tr:nth-child(even) {
 9        background:#ccc;
10   }
11   |
```

£.	s.	d.	£.	s.	d.	£.	s.	d.	£.	s.	d.
1	0	0	1	0	0	1	0	0	1	0	0
0	3	6	0	3	6	0	3	6	0	3	6
0	1	3	0	1	3	0	1	3	0	1	3
0	1	3	0	1	3	0	1	3	0	1	3
0	1	3	0	1	3	0	1	3	0	1	3

Having the even rows appear different from the odd ones helps the reader avoid losing their place when looking at the table or copying figures from it.

Table Headings

HTML offers us the <th> tag when working with tables. This tag is used to declare column and row headings, as follows (lines 3 and 4 of the HTML):

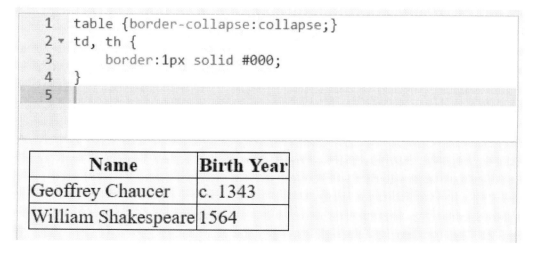

```
1   <table>
2       <tr>
3           <th>Name</th>
4           <th>Birth Year</th>
5       </tr>
6       <tr>
7           <td>Geoffrey Chaucer</td>
8           <td>c. 1343</td>
9       </tr>
10      <tr>
11          <td>William Shakespeare</td>
12          <td>1564</td>
13      </tr>
14  </table>
```

```
1   table {border-collapse:collapse;}
2   td {
3       border:1px solid #000;
4   }
5
```

Name	Birth Year
Geoffrey Chaucer	c. 1343
William Shakespeare	1564

Above, we have used <th> tags for the "Name" and "Birth Year" cells. This declares that these cells are column headings, meaning that they describe what comes underneath them.

By default, the <th> elements get bold formatting and centered text, to distinguish them from the rest of the cells. Above, we have given table cells a black border. But since the border is applied to the <td> tag (line 2 of the CSS), it does not apply to the <th> tags.

In order to put the <th> tags inside borders too, we add "th" to the selector on line 2:

```
1   table {border-collapse:collapse;}
2   td, th {
3       border:1px solid #000;
4   }
5
```

Name	Birth Year
Geoffrey Chaucer	c. 1343
William Shakespeare	1564

The <th> can also be used for row headings, not just column headings. Below, we have a simple multiplication table:

```
 i  1▾  <table>
    2▾      <tr>
    3              <th>X</th><th>1</th><th>2</th>
    4          </tr>
    5▾      <tr>
    6              <th>1</th><td>1</td><td>2</td>
    7          </tr>
    8▾      <tr>
    9              <th>2</th><td>2</td><td>4</td>
   10          </tr>
   11  </table>
    1  |
```

```
    1  table {border-collapse:collapse;}
    2▾ td, th {
    3      border:1px solid #000;
    4      padding:5px;
    5  }
    6▾ th {
    7      background:#999;
    8      color:#fff;
    9  }
   10  |
```

X	1	2
1	1	2
2	2	4

Above, we use <th> tags both for the first row *and* the first column. On line 3 of the HTML, we have only <th> tags. On the next row on line 6, we start out with a <th> tag, then use <td> for the rest of the cells. We repeat the same for line 9 of the HTML. In this way, we create a table that has headings both at the top and to the left. We can give these headings special formatting as we have done above, helping improve the table's appearance and hopefully making it more readable.

6.
The Links between Us

HTML stands for Hypertext Markup Language. Ted Nelson coined the term "hypertext" in 1963. In 1989, Tim Berners-Lee came up with a way of putting the idea of hypertext into practice, and from this the web was born. At its most basic level, hypertext refers to text that "links" to other text. Imagine you have a magical book that embodies the concept of hypertext. When reading the book's table of contents, if you were to press on any title, the book would immediately start flipping its pages until it gets to the title you pressed. And if you had a hypertext library, if a book referenced a certain page of another book, pressing that reference would immediately cause that other book to come flying through the air and open up at exactly that page.

Hypertext recreates that magical library on a computer. It allows us to have documents that "link to" other documents, and a simple click is sufficient to take us from one document to another document. In the real world, going from one document to another could mean going from one floor of a large library to another. Computers make things easy by instantly bringing up the document we want, except when we have a slow internet connection.

Below, we have folder inside of which there are two HTML documents:

Name	Date modified
document_1.html	2/9/2018 9:36 AM
document_2.html	2/9/2018 9:31 AM

Inside document1.html we have the following:

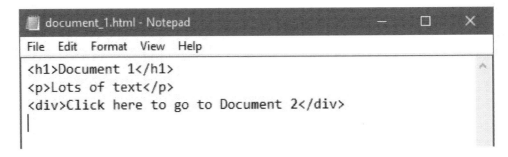

Opening document_1.html in a browser, we get the following:

At the moment, clicking on where it says "Click here" will not do anything, since we haven't created a link yet.

To create the link, we modify the document as follows:

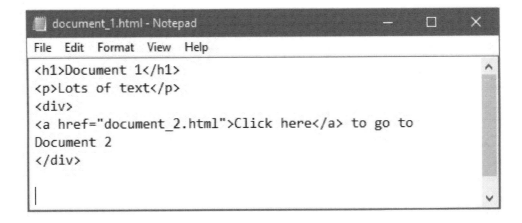

In HTML, we create links using the <a> tag, short for "anchor tag". The "href" attribute of the anchor tag determines what document the tag links to, and the text inside the anchor tag (between the <a> and </a>) determines what the "link text" is going to be.

If we now open the document again in a browser, this is what we see:

When we click on the underlined text that says "Click here", the browser opens up document_2.html:

We will now edit document_2.html in Notepad to turn the "Click here" into a link:

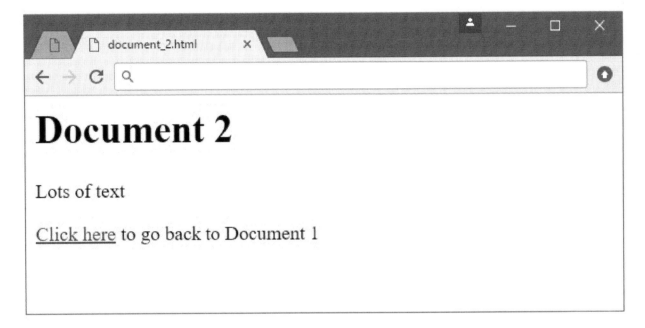

Opening document_2.html again in a browser, this is what we get:

Document 2

Lots of text

Click here to go back to Document 1

Now, if we click "Click here" above, it opens up Document 1. And inside Document 1, clicking "Click here" takes us again to Document 2. In this way, we have two documents that link to each other.

Let's now go to JSTinker to explore links further. Below, we have an anchor tag that links to Google.com:

```
1   <a href="http://www.google.com">
2       Go to Google</a>
```

Here is what it looks like:

Go to Google

Note the way we have written the URL of Google.com: http://www.google.com. The "http://" is necessary when linking to an "external" document, meaning to a document or web page that is not on your own website or server. Without the "http://" part, the browser will try to find a document on your computer or server that is named www.google.com.

The text that says "Go to Google" has no influence on what happens when a user clicks the link. For example, we can even lie as follows:

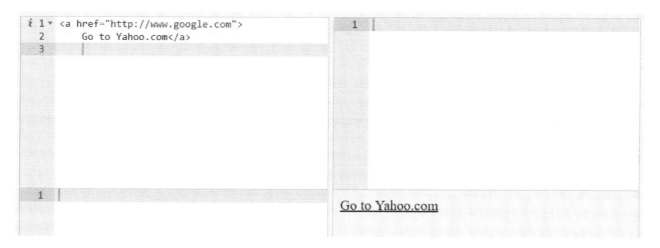

Above, the link text says "Go to Yahoo.com", but the "href" tag links to google.com. It is the "href" tag that matters when it comes to the link's behavior, meaning that if you click the link, you will actually go to Google, not Yahoo. This technicality is used by certain deceptive websites to make users think that the link is taking them somewhere where in reality it takes them somewhere completely different.

Links are necessary for "navigation", meaning for letting users go from somewhere in your website to somewhere else. Below, I created a rudimentary website that links to a few pages:

```
1  <h1>My Website</h1>
2  <a href="/home">Home</a>
3  <a href="/about">About Me</a>
4  <a href="/portfolio">Portfolio</a>
5  <a href="/contact">Contact Me</a>
6
```

My Website

Home About Me Portfolio Contact Me

The reason the links appear side-by-side is that <a> tags by default are *inline* elements. They do not take up a whole line.

Below, we have taken away the underline formatting of the links (line 2 of the CSS below):

```
1  a {
2      text-decoration:none;
3  }
4
```

My Website

Home About Me Portfolio Contact Me

Below, we add border and padding to the links (lines 3 and 4):

```
1  a {
2      text-decoration:none;
3      border:1px solid #000;
4      padding:5px;
5  }
6
```

My Website

Home | About Me | Portfolio | Contact Me

Below, we make the font size of the links smaller (line 5):

```
1 ▾ a {
2        text-decoration:none;
3        border:1px solid #000;
4        padding:5px;
5        font-size:12px;
6   }
```

My Website

Home | About Me | Portfolio | Contact Me

What if we wanted all the rectangles to have the same width? We cannot give the links a width because links are inline. Therefore first we must turn them into block or inline-block elements. Below, we turn them into inline-block (line 6):

```
1 ▾ a {
2        text-decoration:none;
3        border:1px solid #000;
4        padding:5px;
5        font-size:12px;
6        display:inline-block;
7   }
```

My Website

Home | About Me | Portfolio | Contact Me

Below, we give the links a width of 13%:

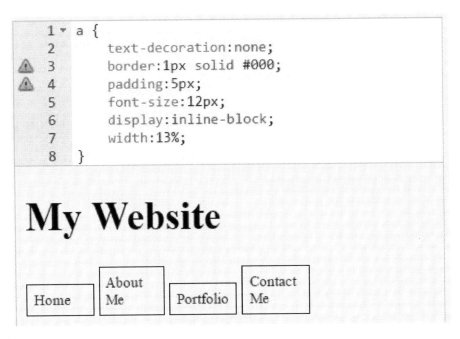

Above, since the width is too small to contain all of the text of each link, some of the links get broken up into two lines. To make the links look more uniform, we add a height (line 8):

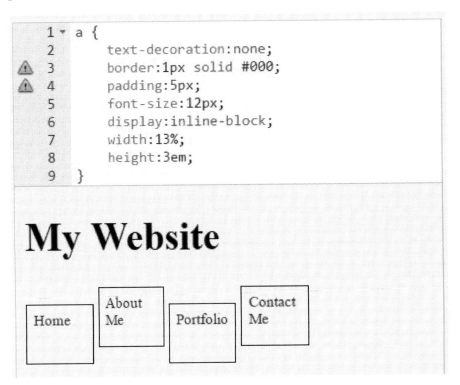

The result is strange because of the "inline-block" display property, which makes the browser make its own choices on how to display the links. In order to have better control over their appearance, we have to use "display:block" instead (line 6 below):

```
1 ▾ a {
2       text-decoration:none;
3       border:1px solid #000;
4       padding:5px;
5       font-size:12px;
6       display:block;
7       width:13%;
8       height:3em;
9 }
```

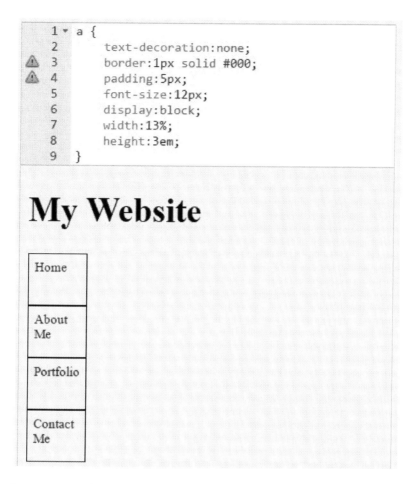

My Website

Home
About Me
Portfolio
Contact Me

Above, we run into a new issue. The "display:block" property makes each link take up a whole line. We therefore have to use floating to make them appear side-by-side (line 7 below):

```
1 ▾ a {
2       text-decoration:none;
3       border:1px solid #000;
4       padding:5px;
5       font-size:12px;
6       display:block;
7       float:left;
8       width:13%;
9       height:3em;
10 }
```

Here is the result:

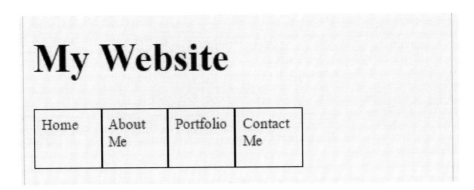

Above, our links are now side-by-side and have a uniform appearance. Below, we add a right margin (line 10) in order to make the links separate:

```
1   a {
2       text-decoration:none;
3       border:1px solid #000;
4       padding:5px;
5       font-size:12px;
6       display:block;
7       float:left;
8       width:13%;
9       height:3em;
10      margin-right:0.5em;
11  }
```

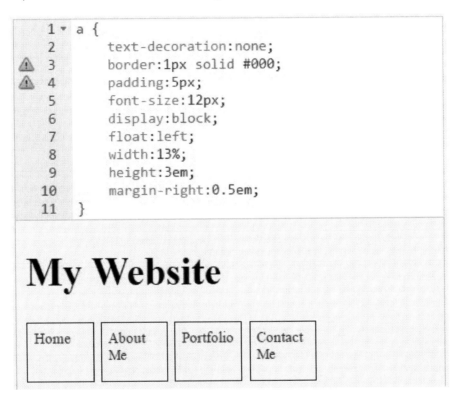

Using "border-radius" and "text-align", we add some extra styling (lines 11 and 12):

```
10      margin-right:0.5em;
11      text-align:center;
12      border-radius:25%;
13  }
```

Here is the result:

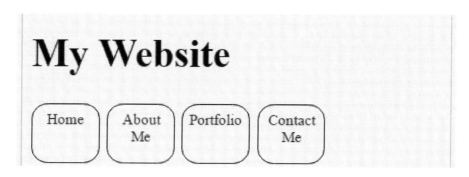

You may notice the way the texts are too close to the top borders (the word "Home" is much closer to the top border of its box than to its bottom border). We can fix this by adding extra top padding, as follows on line 5 below:

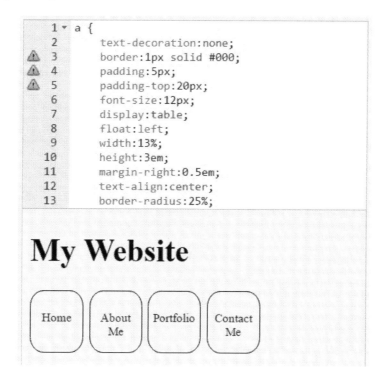

```
 1  a {
 2      text-decoration:none;
 3      border:1px solid #000;
 4      padding:5px;
 5      padding-top:20px;
 6      font-size:12px;
 7      display:table;
 8      float:left;
 9      width:13%;
10      height:3em;
11      margin-right:0.5em;
12      text-align:center;
13      border-radius:25%;
```

The links are now too tall, because the padding is added onto the existing height of 3 ems. Below I have reduced the height to 2 ems (line 10):

Now the texts are too close to the lower borders. By fiddling with the height and the top padding, we may eventually achieve a decent appearance. We could also simply increase the width of the buttons so that phrases like "About Me" appear on one line instead of two (line 8 below):

Above, I have increased the width while reducing the padding and removing the border radius.

You may have run into certain websites where if you hover the mouse over a link or button (buttons are often merely links with added styling), the button's shape changes. This is done using the CSS ":hover" pseudo-selector. Below, I have add hover styling on lines 12 to 15 so that if the user hovers their mouse pointer over one of the links, the link acquires a black background and white text:

Above, my mouse pointer is hovering over the "About Me" link to make its hover styling visible.

We also have access to the ":visited" pseudo-selector. This enables us to give a visited link a special styling. A visited link is a link that has already been viewed by the user. Below, I have declared that links already visited by the user should appear gray (lines 16-18), and as can be seen, the "About Me" link has become gray because the user has already visited it.

It is useful to give links visited formatting because it helps users know which links they have visited and which ones they have not. Below is a screenshot from the website opensourceshakespeare.org where Shakespeare's sonnets are listed:

Individual sonnets

1	21	41	61	81	101	121	141
2	22	42	62	82	102	122	142
3	23	43	63	83	103	123	143
4	24	44	64	84	104	124	144
5	25	45	65	85	105	125	145
6	26	46	66	86	106	126	146
7	27	47	67	87	107	127	147
8	28	48	68	88	108	128	148
9	29	49	69	89	109	129	149
10	30	50	70	90	110	130	150
11	31	51	71	91	111	131	151
12	32	52	72	92	112	132	152
13	33	53	73	93	113	133	153
14	34	54	74	94	114	134	154
15	35	55	75	95	115	135	
16	36	56	76	96	116	136	
17	37	57	77	97	117	137	
18	38	58	78	98	118	138	
19	39	59	79	99	119	139	
20	40	60	80	100	120	140	

Plays + Sonnets + Poems + Concordance + Character Search + Advanced Search + About OSS

Above, the sonnets I have already looked at (such as 1, 16, 30 and 31) have a red color (or gray, if you are viewing this in black and white), while the rest are black. This helps me keep track of the ones I have "visited" (i.e. viewed) and the ones I have not visited yet.

It is, however, unusual to have an item in the navigation menu change its appearance whether the user has visited them or not. We can force the links in our website to not change appearance even if they are visited by adding the ":visited" selector to the main select for the links (line 1 below):

```
 1 ▼  a, a:visited {
 2          text-decoration:none;
⚠ 3          border:1px solid #000;
 4          font-size:12px;
⚠ 5          padding:3px;
 6          display:table;
 7          float:left;
 8          width:18%;
 9          margin-right:0.5em;
10          text-align:center;
11      }
```

My Website

| Home | About Me | Portfolio | Contact Me |

Above, we have declared that links and visited links should both have the same exact styling.

We will now add a paragraph underneath the menu (lines 6-8 of the HTML):

```
 𝑖  1   <h1>My Website</h1>
    2   <a href="/home">Home</a>
    3   <a href="/about">About Me</a>
    4   <a href="/portfolio">Portfolio</a>
    5   <a href="/contact">Contact Me</a>
    6 ▼ <p>Welcome to my website. Visit
    7 ▼ <a href="http://example.com">my other
    8   website here</a>.</p>
    9   |
   10
```

Here is the result:

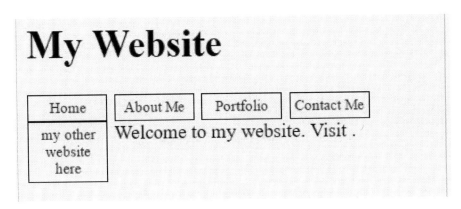

Above, notice the strange appearance of the new link. That is because on line 1 of the CSS, we have declared that *all* links should have such a style, which naturally affects this link too even though it is inside a paragraph. To avoid this issue, we will have to put our navigation links inside their own <div> (lines 2 and 7 below):

```
 1    <h1>My Website</h1>
 2    <div class="nav">
 3        <a href="/home">Home</a>
 4        <a href="/about">About Me</a>
 5        <a href="/portfolio">Portfolio</a>
 6        <a href="/contact">Contact Me</a>
 7    </div>
 8    <p>Welcome to my website. Visit
 9    <a href="http://example.com">my other
10    website here</a>.</p>
```

Above, the new <div> has a class of "nav". We can now use this class to restrict the CSS styling only to links inside this <div> (lines 1 and 12 below):

```
 1 ▾  .nav a, .nav a:visited {
 2         text-decoration:none;
 3         border:1px solid #000;
 4         font-size:12px;
 5         padding:3px;
 6         display:table;
 7         float:left;
 8         width:18%;
 9         margin-right:0.5em;
10         text-align:center;
11     }
12 ▾  .nav a:hover {
13         background:#000;
14         color:#fff;
15     }
```

My Website

| Home | About Me | Portfolio | Contact Me |

Welcome to my website. Visit <u>my other website here</u>.

Above, our styles now apply to the navigation items, but they leave the link inside the paragraph alone so that it continues to have its default appearance.

Opening Links in New Tabs

When browsing the web, clicking a link takes you to a new page on the same website, making you leave the old page you were looking at. For example, when looking at the Falcon Heavy article on Wikipedia, if I click the link to SpaceX, it will take me to the Wikipedia article about SpaceX. I could also open the link in a new tab by right-clicking on it and choosing "Open link in new tab", as shown below:

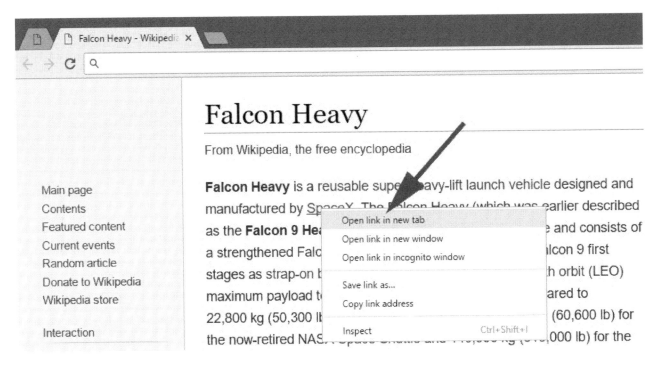

Now, the article about SpaceX opens up in a new tab, meaning the article about Falcon Heavy continues to remain open:

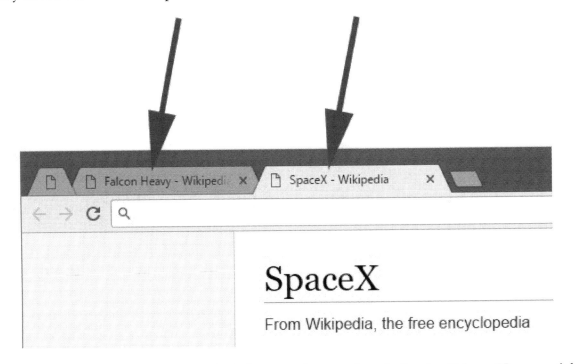

Above, I have placed two arrows. The left one points to the tab for the Falcon Heavy article, and the right arrow points to the newly opened SpaceX article's tab.

When you place a link on your website, by default the link will open in the same tab, rather than in a new tab. We can force a link to open in a new tab using the "target" attribute, as follows:

```
1   <h1>Ikram's Website</h1>
2   <p>
3       <a href="http://example.com"
4       target="_blank">Click here</a>
5       to visit some other website.
6   </p>
7
```

Here is what it looks like:

Ikram's Website

Click here to visit some other website.

Above, on line 3 of the HTML we have an <a> tag that links to example.com. I have broken up the tag into multiple lines for your viewing convenience. On line 4, we have a "target" attribute whose value is "_blank" (note the underscore). This tells the browser to open this link in a new tab. If a user clicks on it, a new tab will open, as if they had chosen "Open link in a new tab" by right-clicking on the link.

It is common practice to make internal links (links on your website that point to other pages on your website) open in the same tab (by not using a "target" attribute), and to make external links (links pointing to other websites) open in a new tab by using the "target" attribute with the "_blank" value.

This page intentionally left blank

7.
A New Look at HTML

So far, the HTML documents I have shown you how to create have not been proper HTML documents, even though they show up properly when opened up. In this chapter, I will introduce proper HTML while also introducing various other interesting concepts.

A proper HTML document starts with what is known as a document type declaration. This declaration tells the browser what language our document is written in, since besides HTML, we also have languages like SGML. We also have multiple flavors of HTML, such as XHTML. In this book, we are using the latest version of HTML, which is HTML5. To start an HTML5 document, we declare it as follows:

```
1    <!DOCTYPE HTML>
2
3
4
5
6
```

Above, note the way the tag starts with an exclamation mark. This is not an HTML tag, the HTML tags haven't started yet. Rather, it declares that everything below it is going to be HTML.

In the past, the DOCTYPE declaration was quite long, here is an example (the declaration takes up two lines):

```
1    <!DOCTYPE HTML PUBLIC "-//W3C//DTD HTML 4.01//EN"
2    "http://www.w3.org/TR/html4/strict.dtd">
3
```

With HTML5, it was simplified to merely <!DOCTYPE HTML>.

The next item on the list for creating proper HTML documents is <html> tag. This tag is going to contain everything else we create:

```
1   <!DOCTYPE HTML>
2 ▾ <html>
3
4   </html>
5
6
7
```

Next, we add a <head> and a <body> tag:

```
1   <!DOCTYPE HTML>
2 ▾ <html>
3 ▾     <head>
4
5       </head>
6
7 ▾     <body>
8
9       </body>
10  </html>
```

The <head> tag will contain information about the document, this can include CSS styles and JavaScript code. The <body> tag contains the actual contents of the document, meaning any headings, images, paragraphs, etc. that we have in our document.

The first thing to do in the <head> tag is to declare our "character set", as follows:

```
1   <!DOCTYPE HTML>
2 ▾ <html>
3 ▾     <head>
4           <meta charset="UTF-8">
5       </head>
6
7 ▾     <body>
8
9       </body>
10  </html>
```

You may remember the snowman we used in the chapter about lists. That snowman is "Unicode character" and can only properly show up if the document has a Unicode character set. Above, using the <meta> tag and its "charset" attribute, we declare that our document uses the UTF-8 character set, which is the character set most commonly used on the Internet. If instead of UTF-8 we write "ISO-8859-15" (a character set used for the Latin-derived alphabets), the snowman and other Unicode characters will show up as a jumbled mess of random characters.

There is no need to worry about character sets. It is sufficient to know the meta tag on line 4 in your HTML helps make the world a slightly better place.

The next thing we add is the <title> tag, as follows (line 5 below):

```
1    <!DOCTYPE HTML>
2 ▾  <html>
3 ▾      <head>
4            <meta charset="UTF-8">
5            <title>Welcome!</title>
6        </head>
7
8 ▾      <body>
9
10       </body>
11   </html>
12
13
```

The <title> tag determines the title of your document that is shown as the name of the browser tab where the document is shown, as follows:

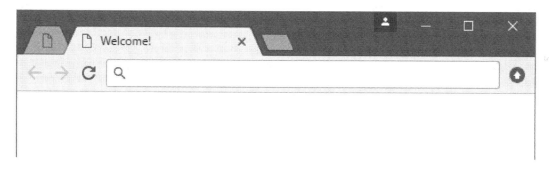

Above, the document is empty because we have not added anything to the <body> tag. But notice the "Welcome!" at the very top (above the magnifier icon). That is where the contents of our <title> tag are shown. When doing a web search (such as on Google), it is the contents of the <title> tag that are usually shown to users to tell them what the link contains. For example, below I have done a Google search for "wiki falcon heavy":

About 639,000 results (0.43 seconds)

Falcon Heavy - Wikipedia
https://en.wikipedia.org/wiki/Falcon_Heavy ▾
Falcon Heavy is a reusable super heavy-lift launch vehicle designed and manufactured by SpaceX. The
Falcon Heavy is a variant of the Falcon 9 vehicle and consists of a strengthened Falcon 9 rocket core
with two additional Falcon 9 first stages as strap-on boosters. This increases the low Earth orbit (LEO)
maximum ...
List of Falcon 9 and Falcon ... · Falcon 5 · Delta IV Heavy · Dragon 2

Falcon Heavy Demonstration Mission - Wikipedia
https://en.wikipedia.org/wiki/Falcon_Heavy_Demonstration_Mission ▾
The **Falcon Heavy** Demonstration Mission was the first attempt by SpaceX to launch a **Falcon Heavy**
rocket, on 6 February 2018 at 20:45 UTC. The launch introduced the **Falcon Heavy** as the most powerful
rocket currently in operation, producing five million pounds-force (22,000,000 N) of thrust and having
more than twice ...

The top search result says "Falcon Heavy - Wikipedia". Clicking on this link, we are taken to a Wikipedia article:

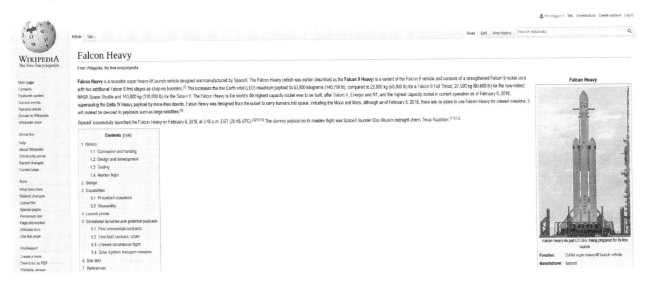

Notice that above, the document's visible title is "Falcon Heavy", it is not "Falcon Heavy - Wikipedia", yet Google shows us the title as "Falcon Heavy - Wikipedia". The reason is the Wikipedia page's <title> tag. If we right-click on an empty area of this article and click "View page source", we will be able to see the HTML for the article:[13]

---

[13] Depending on which browser you are using, the wording for "View page source" can change. The above screenshot is from the Chromium Web Browser.

SpaceX successfully launched the Falcon Heavy on February 6, 2018, at 3:45 p.m. EST (20:45 UTC).[3][9][10] The dummy payload on its maiden flight was SpaceX founder Elon Musk's midnight cherry Tesla Roadster.[11][12]

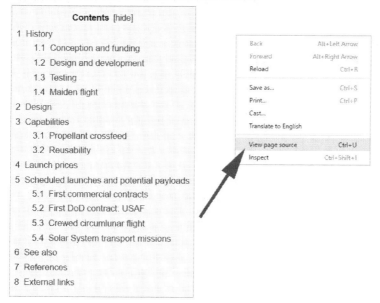

Below is a screenshot of the HTML:

```
1  <!DOCTYPE html>
2  <!-- saved from url=(0042)https://en.wikipedia.org/wiki/Falcon_Heavy -->
3  <html class="client-js ve-not-available" lang="en" dir="ltr"><head><meta
   http-equiv="Content-Type" content="text/html; charset=UTF-8">
4
5  <title>Falcon Heavy - Wikipedia</title>
6  <script>document.documentElement.className =
   document.documentElement.className.replace( /(^|\s)client-nojs(\s|$)/,
   "$1client-js$2" );</script>
7  <script>(window.RLQ=window.RLQ||[]).push(function()
```

Above, note the <title> tag on line 5, whose contents say "Falcon Heavy - Wikipedia". It is based on this <title> tag that in the Google results we saw the page's title as "Falcon Heavy - Wikipedia" rather than merely "Falcon Heavy".

Back to our document, we can now start adding actual content to our document, as follows (lines 9 and 10 of the HTML below):

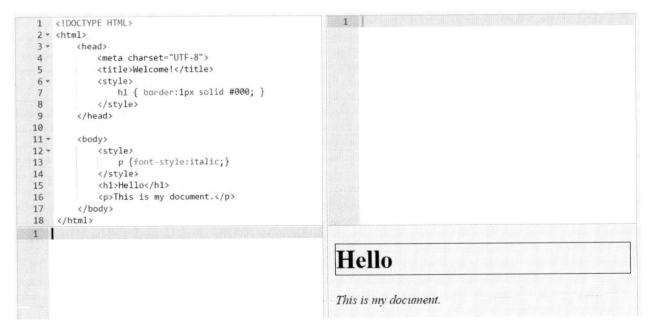

```
 1    <!DOCTYPE HTML>
 2 ▾  <html>
 3 ▾      <head>
 4              <meta charset="UTF-8">
 5              <title>Welcome!</title>
 6          </head>
 7
 8 ▾      <body>
 9              <h1>Hello</h1>
10              <p>This is my document.</p>
11          </body>
12      </html>
13
14
15
 1
```

Hello

This is my document.

All of our HTML document's contents should reside inside the <body> tag. This rule does not apply to CSS. We can add a <style> tag for CSS inside the <head> or the <body> tags, it doesn't matter (lines 7 and 13):

```
 1    <!DOCTYPE HTML>
 2 ▾  <html>
 3 ▾      <head>
 4              <meta charset="UTF-8">
 5              <title>Welcome!</title>
 6 ▾          <style>
 7                  h1 { border:1px solid #000; }
 8              </style>
 9          </head>
10
11 ▾      <body>
12 ▾          <style>
13                  p {font-style:italic;}
14              </style>
15              <h1>Hello</h1>
16              <p>This is my document.</p>
17          </body>
18      </html>
 1
```

Hello

This is my document.

Above, I have added a black border around the <h1> tag using the <style> tag on lines 6-8. This tag resides inside the <head> tag. Below that, I have given italic formatting to the <p> tag using the other <style> tag on lines 12-14. This tag resides inside the <body> tag.

We cannot place any contents outside the <head> and <body> tags. Anything you add must either be added to <head> or <body>. Stuff outside these tags is not proper HTML.

Page Backgrounds

The <body> tag gives us a way of applying styles to the whole document. Below, I have a folder with a picture in it called "doodles.png"[14]. I also have an HTML document called "test.html". This document contains the HTML from above.

Name	Date modified
doodles.png	8/9/2017 6:12 AM
test.html	2/10/2018 8:26 AM

Opening "test.html" in a browser, this is what we get:

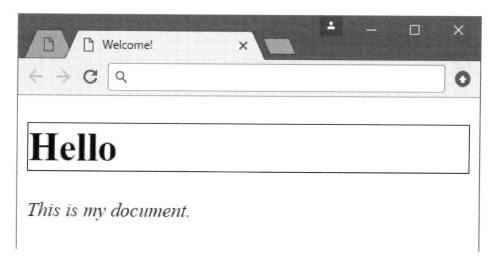

Below, we will add the "doodles.png" picture as a background for the <body> tag (line 8 below):

```
1   <!DOCTYPE HTML>
2   <html>
3       <head>
4           <meta charset="UTF-8">
5           <title>Welcome!</title>
6           <style>
7               h1 { border:1px solid #000; }
8               body {background:url(doodles.png)}
9           </style>
10      </head>
```

The result is that the background is now applied to the whole document:

---

[14] Taken from the free background patterns website subtlepatterns.com.

To work further with the background, I will now put the code inside JSTinker and move the style for the <body> tag into the CSS box:

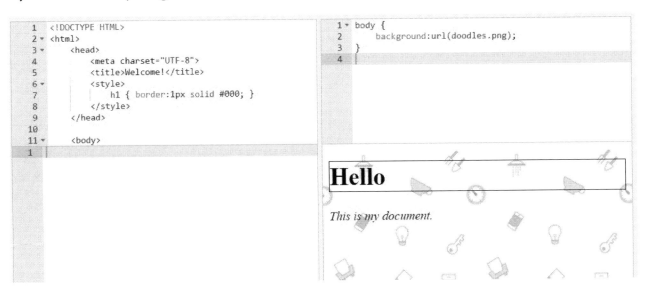

Above, since JSTinker is a playground for HTML and CSS, the background on the <body> only applies to the HTML preview on the bottom right, rather than to JSTinker itself.

Using the "background-size" property, we can make the background image smaller or larger (i.e. we can "scale" it), as follows (line 3):

```
1 ▾  body {
2        background:url(doodles.png);
3        background-size:100px;
4    }
5    |
```

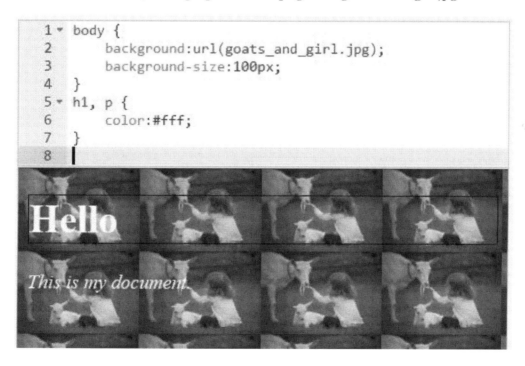

Above, the "100px" value we gave to the "background-size" property determines the width of the background image. The background's original size (i.e. the size of the image file doodles.png) is 400 pixels, so by declaring it here to be 100 pixels, we force it to become one fourth as large as before. The result is that the doodles are much smaller now.

By default, a background is repeated over and over again to make it fill up all the space it can. We can illustrate this by changing "doodles.png" to "goats_and_girl.jpg" from earlier:

```
1 ▾  body {
2        background:url(goats_and_girl.jpg);
3        background-size:100px;
4    }
5 ▾  h1, p {
6        color:#fff;
7    }
8    |
```

Above, I have also made the <h1> and <p> elements white to make them more visible. Notice the way the picture is repeated over and over again. Also notice the way the picture is smaller than we saw in the past, since the "background-size" property on line 3 is making it have a width of 100 pixels.

Using the "background-repeat" property, we can declare that the background should not be repeated (line 4 below):

```
1 ▾ body {
2       background:url(goats_and_girl.jpg);
3       background-size:100px;
4       background-repeat:no-repeat;
5   }
6 ▾ h1, p {
7       color:#fff;
8   }
```

We can also have the background repeat horizontally by using the "repeat-x" value for the "background-repeat" property (line 4 below):

```
1 ▾ body {
2       background:url(goats_and_girl.jpg);
3       background-size:100px;
4       background-repeat:repeat-x;
5   }
6 ▾ h1, p {
7       color:#fff;
8   }
```

Changing "repeat-x" to "repeat-y", the background is made to repeat vertically:

```
1 ▾ body {
2        background:url(goats_and_girl.jpg);
3        background-size:100px;
4        background-repeat:repeat-y;
5    }
6 ▾ h1, p {
7        color:#fff;
8    }
```

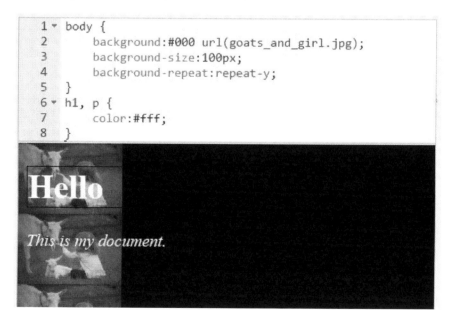

Besides giving the <body> tag an image background, we can also give it a color background while keeping the image, as follows (line 2 below):

```
1 ▾ body {
2        background:#000 url(goats_and_girl.jpg);
3        background-size:100px;
4        background-repeat:repeat-y;
5    }
6 ▾ h1, p {
7        color:#fff;
8    }
```

Above, we have declared that the background of the <body> should be black, we have also given it a URL for an image. This results in a black background except where the image is shown.

Below, I have given the doodles background to the <h1> tag and given the text a black color, while keeping everything else the same (lines 9-13):

```
 1 ▾ body {
 2        background:#000 url(goats_and_girl.jpg);
 3        background-size:100px;
 4        background-repeat:repeat-y;
 5    }
 6 ▾ h1, p {
 7        color:#fff;
 8    }
⚠ 9 ▾ h1 {
10        background:url(doodles.png);
11        color:#000;
12        background-size:200px;
13    }
```

Above, the background on the <h1> element extends beyond the text, since the background is applied to the <h1> element's box, similar to a border.

Block Quotes

The <blockquote> HTML tag is used to add quotation (i.e. indented paragraphs) to a document, as follows (lines 10-12 of the HTML):

```
 1    <!DOCTYPE HTML>
 2 ▾  <html>
 3 ▾      <head>
 4            <meta charset="UTF-8">
 5            <title>Welcome!</title>
 6        </head>
 7
 8 ▾      <body>
 9            <p>George Eliot said:</p>
10 ▾          <blockquote>Blessed is the man who, having
11            nothing to say, abstains from giving us wordy
12            evidence of the fact.</blockquote>
13        </body>
```

Here is the result:

> ## George Eliot said:
>
> > Blessed is the man who, having nothing to say, abstains from giving us wordy evidence of the fact.

By default, a <blockquote> element has extra margin on the right and left. We could achieve the same effect by giving a <p> tag extra margin. The benefit of a <blockquote> element is semantics. By using it, even a robot will be able to distinguish the fact that this is a quotation, whereas if we had use a <p> tag, the robot would see it as any other paragraph.

Many websites add special CSS to <blockquote> elements to make the quotations in an article prettier. Below, we have used the ":before" pseudo-selector to add a big curly quote to the beginning of the <blockquote> element:

```
1   blockquote:before {
2       content:"“";
3       font-size:250%;
4   }
5
```

> ## George Eliot said:
>
> > 66
> > Blessed is the man who, having nothing to say, abstains from giving us wordy evidence of the fact.

Above, we have put a curly left quote inside the "content" property and given it a font size of 250%. The result is that there is now a big curly quote at the beginning of the quotation. We can now add further CSS to make it look better:

```
1 ▾ blockquote:before {
2       content:"""";
3       font-size:350%;
4       color:#999;
5       position:relative;
6       top:20px;
7       left:-10px;
8 }
```

George Eliot said:

" " Blessed is the man who, having nothing to say, abstains from giving us wordy evidence of the fact.

Above, I have given the curly quote a gray color. I have also given it relative positioning and increased its distance from the top (forcing it downward) while giving it a negative left distance (forcing it to move leftward). I have also increased the font size to 350%.

The quotation now looks good, but there are some problems. There is now too much space between the quotation and the paragraph above it. This is caused by the very large font size of the quotation mark we added. There is also uneven line spacing inside the quotation. The space between lines one and two is much larger than the space between lines two and three. This, too, is caused by the overly large quotation mark.

We have multiple strategies for dealing with this problem. One way is to give the quotation mark a very small "line-height" property (line 8 below):

```
1 ▾ blockquote:before {
2        content:"“";
3        font-size:350%;
4        color:#999;
5        position:relative;
6        top:20px;
7        left:-10px;
8        line-height:0.1em;
9    }
```

George Eliot said:

     “ Blessed is the man who, having nothing to say, abstains from giving us wordy evidence of the fact.

Above, on line 8, we have given the quotation mark a "line-height" of 0.1 ems. This tells the CSS to pretend as if the quotation mark is only one tenth as high as it really is, causing its extreme height to be ignored.

Another strategy would be to give the quotation mark a "display:block' property and make it float:

```
 1 ▾ blockquote:before {
 2        content:"“";
 3        font-size:350%;
 4        color:#999;
 5        position:relative;
 6        top:20px;
 7        left:-10px;
 8        display:block;
 9        float:left;
10    }
```

George Eliot said:

     “ Blessed is the man who, having nothing to say, abstains from giving us wordy evidence of the fact.

By making the quotation mark float, it stops messing with the <blockquote> element's text. The floating has caused the quotation mark's position to be recalculated. Earlier, it was part of the <blockquote>'s text. It is now a block that is no longer part of the text. We can verify this by using a border. Below, I have given a border to the quotation mark while removing the "display:block" and "float:left" properties:

```
 1 ▼ blockquote:before {
 2       content:"""";
 3       font-size:350%;
 4       color:#999;
 5       position:relative;
 6       top:20px;
 7       left:-10px;
 8       line-height:0.1em;
 9       border:1px solid #000;
10   }
```

George Eliot said:

" Blessed is the man who, having nothing to say, abstains from giving us wordy evidence of the fact.

Below, I again change the quotation back to "display:block" and "float:left" (lines 8 and 9):

```
 1 ▼ blockquote:before {
 2       content:"""";
 3       font-size:350%;
 4       color:#999;
 5       position:relative;
 6       top:20px;
 7       left:-10px;
 8       display:block;
 9       float:left;
10       border:1px solid #000;
11   }
```

George Eliot said:

Blessed is the man who, having nothing to say, abstains from giving us wordy evidence of the fact.
"

Notice the way the quotation mark's triangle is on the left of the text, separate from it.

Below, I change the "top" and "left" properties in order to make the quotation mark appear at its proper place (lines 6 and 7):

```
1 ▾ blockquote:before {
2       content:"""";
3       font-size:350%;
4       color:#999;
5       position:relative;
6       top:-15px;
7       left:-10px;
8       display:block;
9       float:left;
10      border:1px solid #000;
```

The result is as follows:

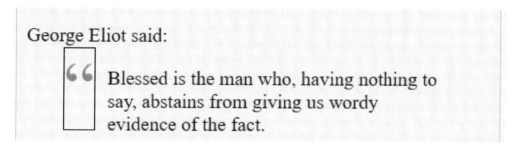

Now, setting the border to zero, this is the result we have achieved (line 10 below):

```
1 ▾ blockquote:before {
2       content:""";
3       font-size:350%;
4       color:#999;
5       position:relative;
6       top:-15px;
7       left:-10px;
8       display:block;
9       float:left;
10      border:0px solid #000;
11 }
```

George Eliot said:

❝ Blessed is the man who, having nothing to
    say, abstains from giving us wordy
    evidence of the fact.

This is different from the "line-height" fix we used earlier and looks less good. With the "line-height" fix, the quotation mark remained part of the text so that it nudged the word "Blessed" toward the right, giving it a nice stylistic appearance. But now that the quotation mark is a block element that floats, it no longer interacts with the text that way. Now, the word "Blessed" is directly above "say".

IDs

Throughout this book, I have used classes to identify particular elements and give them special styling, as follows:

```
1    <div class="animal dog">Rover</div>
2    <div class="animal dog">Gaspode</div>
3    <div class="animal dog">Sophie</div>
4    <div class="animal cat">Misty</div>
```

Here is the CSS and its result:

```
1 ▾  .dog:after {
2        content: "woof";
3        font-size:80%;
4        color:#999;
5        margin-left:10px;
6        font-style:italic;
7    }
8 ▾  .cat:after {
9        content:"mew";
10       font-size:80%;
11       color:#999;
12       font-style:italic;
13       margin-left:10px;
14   }
15   |
```

Rover *woof*
Gaspode *woof*
Sophie *woof*
Misty *mew*

Above, we have used the ":after" pseudo-selector to add the words "woof" to the end of the dog names and "mew" to the end of the cat name by making use of the "dog" and "cat" classes.

The special thing about classes is that they are *reusable*. You can add the "animal", "dog" or "cat" classes to any number of elements and have them all acquire the same formatting.

Instead of using classes, we can use IDs. For example, below I have given Gaspode the ID of "rons-pet" (line 2 of the HTML):

```
i 1    <div class="animal dog">Rover</div>
  2    <div class="animal dog" id="rons-pet">Gaspode</div>
  3    <div class="animal dog">Sophie</div>
  4    <div class="animal cat">Misty</div>
```

Below, I have used the ID of "rons-pet" to give this element special styling (lines 15-19 of the CSS):

```
15 ▾  #rons-pet {
16         font-size:120%;
17         letter-spacing:0.2em;
18         border:1px solid #000;
19     }
```

Rover *woof*

G a s p o d e *w o o f*

Sophie *woof*

Misty *mew*

On line 15, we have the selector "#rons-pet". We already know that we use a dot in front of a class name. In front of an ID, we use the hash character (#). On line 17, I use a new propety, "letter-spacing", which is used to increase or decrease the space between each letter of a word. Note how there is a lot of extra space between the letters of "Gaspode", as if it is written as "G a s p o d e". The same has happened to the "woof" for Gaspode.

It is bad practice to use IDs for styling, which is why I have not made use of them in this book.IDs have very high "specificity", leading to something called "specificity wars". I will not go into the details of this, it is sufficient to know that it is best to avoid IDs for styling.

IDs, however, are very useful for another purpose. They enable us to create "jump links" that enable a user to jump from one section of a document to another.

Below, we have two of Shakespeare's sonnets on the same HTML document:

```
 1   <!DOCTYPE HTML>
 2 ▾ <html>
 3 ▾     <head>
 4            <meta charset="UTF-8">
 5            <title>Shakespeare's Sonnets</title>
 6        </head>
 7
 8 ▾     <body>
 9            <h2 style='text-align: center'>SONNET I<br></h2>
10 ▾         <p>From fairest creatures we desire increase,<br>
11   That thereby beauty's rose might never die,<br>
12   But as the riper should by time decease,<br>
13   His tender heir might bear his memory:<br>
14   But thou, contracted to thine own bright eyes,<br>
```

Below, I have scrolled down on the HTML preview to show you the beginning of the second sonnet:

Within thine own bud buriest thy content
And, tender churl, makest waste in niggarding.
  Pity the world, or else this glutton be,
  To eat the world's due, by the grave and thee.

SONNET II

When forty winters shall beseige thy brow,
And dig deep trenches in thy beauty's field,
Thy youth's proud livery, so gazed on now,

Using IDs, we can create a table of contents at the top of the document to help users immediately jump to the sonnet they want. This is helpful for large documents and articles. The title "Sonnet I" is an <h2> tag (see line 9 above), we give it an ID of "sonnet-1" below (line 9 of the HTML):

```
 1   <!DOCTYPE HTML>
 2 ▾ <html>
 3 ▾     <head>
 4           <meta charset="UTF-8">
 5           <title>Shakespeare's Sonnets</title>
 6       </head>
 7
 8 ▾     <body>
 9 ▾         <h2 id="sonnet-1"
10           style='text-align: center'>SONNET I<br></h2>
11 ▾         <p>From fairest creatures we desire increase,<br>
12  That thereby beauty's rose might never die,<br>
13  But as the riper should by time decease,<br>
14  His tender heir might bear his memory:<br>
```

Below, we scroll down to line 29 of the HTML in order to give the title for the second sonnet an id of "sonnet-2":

```
20  And only herald to the gaudy spring, <br>
21  Within thine own bud buriest thy content<br>
22  And, tender churl, makest waste in niggarding.<br>
23      Pity the world, or else this
24  glutton be,<br>
25      To eat the world's due, by
26  the grave and thee.
27  </p>
28
29  <h2 id="sonnet-2" style='text-align: center'>SONNET II<br>
30 ▾         <p>When forty winters shall beseige thy brow,<br>
31  And dig deep trenches in thy beauty's field,<br>
32  Thy youth's proud livery, so gazed on now,<br>
33  Will be a tatter'd weed, of small worth held:<br>
```

Going back to the top of the document, I add two new <a> tags right after the <body> tag (lines 9 and 10):

```
 8 ▾     <body>
 9           <a href="#sonnet-1">Sonnet I</a>
10           <a href="#sonnet-2">Sonnet II</a>
11
12 ▾         <h2 id="sonnet-1"
```

Notice the special syntax we used for the "href" attribute of the <a> tags on lines 9 and 10. The hash character (#) tells the browser that this is a reference to an ID on the document. Here is what the links look like:

256

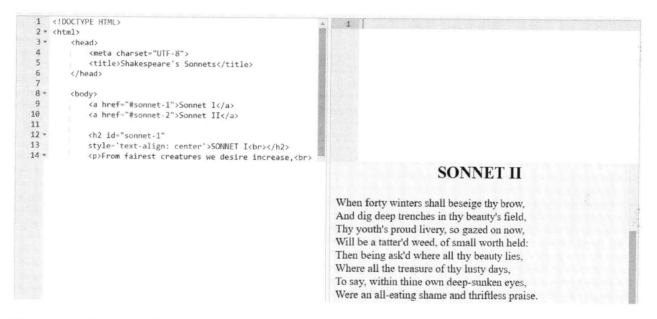

If a user clicks "Sonnet II", the browser will immediately jump to any element on the document that has an ID of "sonnet-2". Below, I have clicked on the Sonnet II link, which causes the browser to scroll down to Sonnet II:

```
1    <!DOCTYPE HTML>
2    <html>
3        <head>
4            <meta charset="UTF-8">
5            <title>Shakespeare's Sonnets</title>
6        </head>
7
8        <body>
9            <a href="#sonnet-1">Sonnet I</a>
10           <a href="#sonnet-2">Sonnet II</a>
11
12           <h2 id="sonnet-1"
13           style='text-align: center'>SONNET I<br></h2>
14           <p>From fairest creatures we desire increase,<br>
```

SONNET II

When forty winters shall beseige thy brow,
And dig deep trenches in thy beauty's field,
Thy youth's proud livery, so gazed on now,
Will be a tatter'd weed, of small worth held:
Then being ask'd where all thy beauty lies,
Where all the treasure of thy lusty days,
To say, within thine own deep-sunken eyes,
Were an all-eating shame and thriftless praise.

We can make use of IDs to send users to a specific section of a document that happens to be on another website. Below, I have created a link that takes users to the "Capabilities" section of the Falcon Heavy article on Wikipedia:

```
1    <a
2    href="https://en.wikipedia.org/wiki/Falcon_Heavy#Capabilities">
3    Click here</a> to view the "Capabilities" section
4    of the Falcon Heavy article on Wikipedia.
5
```

Here is what the link looks like:

Click here to view the "Capabilities" section of the Falcon Heavy article on Wikipedia.

If a user clicks that link, the following will open up in their browser:

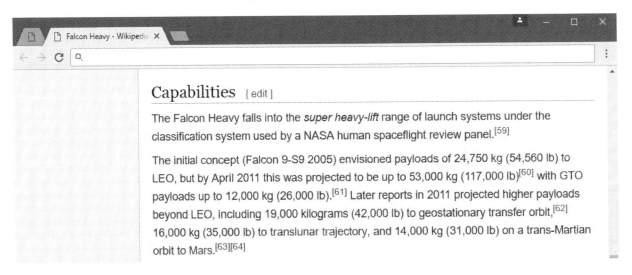

The "href" attribute of the <a> tag is made up of the link to the Wikipedia article:

https://en.wikipedia.org/wiki/Falcon_Heavy

This is followed by the ID of the element that we want to take users to:

#Capabilities

This only works because Wikipedia helpfully adds IDs to its headings. If we look at the HTML for the Wikipedia article, we will see that the id "Capabilities" is defined on a <span> tag inside the <h2> tag for the Capabilities heading (line 383 below):

```
383  <h2><span class="mw-headline" id="Capabilities">Capabilities</span><span class="mw-editsection">
     <span class="mw-editsection-bracket">[</span><a href="https://en.wikipedia.org/w/index.php?
     title=Falcon_Heavy&amp;action=edit&amp;section=7" title="Edit section: Capabilities">edit</a><span
     class="mw-editsection-bracket">]</span></span></h2>
384  <p>The Falcon Heavy falls into the <i>super heavy-lift</i> range of launch systems under the
     classification system used by a NASA human spaceflight review panel.<sup id="cite_ref-hsf200910_59-
     0" class="reference"><a href="https://en.wikipedia.org/wiki/Falcon_Heavy#cite_note-hsf200910-59">
     [59]</a></sup></p>
```

Subscripts and Superscripts

Below, we have an exerpt from the article on water in *The Standard Electrical Dictionary* by T. O'Conor Sloane (1892):

```
1   <p>A compound whose molecule consists of two atoms of
2   hydrogen and one atom of oxygen; formula, H2O. Its specific
3   gravity is 1, it being the base of
4   the system of specific gravities of solids and liquids. If
5   pure, it is almost a non-conductor of
6   electricity.</p>
```

Using the <sub> tag (which stands for "subscript"),we can give the H_2O formula its proper appearance and semantics (line 2 below):

```
1   <p>A compound whose molecule consists of two atoms of
2   hydrogen and one atom of oxygen; formula, H<sub>2</sub>O.
3   Its specific gravity is 1, it being the base of
4   the system of specific gravities of solids and liquids. If
5   pure, it is almost a non-conductor of
6   electricity.</p>
7   |
8
```

The paragraph now looks thus:

A compound whose molecule consists of two atoms of hydrogen and one atom of oxygen; formula, H_2O. Its specific gravity is 1, it being the base of the system of specific gravities of solids and liquids. If pure, it is almost a non-conductor of electricity.

There is, however, an issue. The <sub> tag forces its line to expand downwards, causing its line to have more space below it than the rest of the lines, leading to an uneven appearance. We can fix this by giving <sub> elements a very small "line-height" property (line 5 below):

```
1 ▾ p {
2       font-size:20px;
3 }
4 ▾ sub {
5       line-height:0.1em;
6 }
7 |
```

A compound whose molecule consists of two atoms of hydrogen and one atom of oxygen; formula, H_2O. Its specific gravity is 1, it being the base of the system of specific gravities of solids and liquids. If pure, it is

Above, the <sub> tag stops exerting influence on the height of its line, making it fit in properly with the rest of the text.

We also have the <sup> tag for creating superscripts, as follows:

```
1  ax<sup>2</sup> + bx + c = 0
```

```
1
```

```
1 ▾ p {
2       font-size:20px;
3 }
4 ▾ sup {
5       line-height:0.1em;
6 }
7 |
```

$ax^2 + bx + c = 0$

The <sup> tag, similar to the <sub> tag, messes with the line height of its own line, therefore giving it a small "line-height" property (line 5 above) helps prevent it from messing up the appearance of its paragraph.

Images

Below, we have the picture of a giant rubber duck floating on a river in Hong Kong:

The rubber duck's picture is too large, therefore in the CSS I have given it a width of 400 pixels (line 2 of the CSS above) to make it appear smaller. By default, images have automatic height; reducing the width will cause the browser to also reduce the height, in this way keeping the image's "aspect ratio" intact.

Below, I have given the image a height besides its width (line 3 below):

Above, note the way the image is squished. By giving the image both a width and a height, we are twisting it in order to make it fit this exact width and height. To prevent squishing, we must always either keep the width undefined, or the height undefined, so that the browser may have the freedom to automatically adjust them. Below, I have kept the height of 100 pixels while removing the width defintion:

```
1 ▾ img {
2       height:100px;
3 }
4 |
```

Above, now that the width definition is gone, the browser adjusts the width of the image to make it smaller *in proportion* to its height, so that the image does not get skewed.

Images take a "height" and "width" attribute that we can use to give them the size we want, as follows:

```
1   <img height="100" src="rubber_duck.jpg" />
2 |
```

Above, the height attribute of 100 that I added is *not* CSS. It is HTML. Note the way there are no units after the 100, the browser automatically assumes pixels. The result is exactly the same as giving the image a CSS height of 100 pixels. If we define both the width and height, we again run the risk of twisting the image:

The height and width attributes can be useful in cases where you want to quickly determine the width or height of an image without having to bother writing CSS (some systems do not even let you write CSS, limiting you to the use of the width and height attributes). If we had dozens of images and we wanted each one to have a specific width or height, it would be quicker to use the width and height attributes rather than having to add a unique class to each image then write a CSS definition for it.

Alternate Texts

Image tags take an "alt" attribute that we can use to tell search engines and blind people what the image portrays. On line 2 of the HTML below, I have added an "alt" attribute that gives a brief description of the image:

```
1  <img width="300"
2  alt="Giant rubber duck floating on river in Hong Kong"
3  src="rubber_duck.jpg" />
4
```

A blind person who is using a screen reader (a program that reads out the contents of web page to them) will now hear this description read out to them, helping them know what the image is even though they cannot see it.

Another benefit is that "alt" attributes help search engines understand the contents of images. If you have web page for a museum that shows dozens of items, if an image has an alt attribute of "Medieval crossbow from Spain", when a user searches on Google for "medieval crossbow from Spain", Google will show them that image from the museum's website (among others). Without the "alt" tag, Google may have no idea what the image portrays, so that the image will not come up in web searches.

Another benefit of an alt attribute is that if for some reason the image fails to load, the user will still see the alt text, helping them know what the image is without seeing it:

Giant rubber duck floating on river in
Hong Kong

8.
Beautifying Text

In Latin alphabets, we have two types of fonts; serif fonts and sans-serif fonts:

The letter "A" on the left has serifs, while the letter "A" on the right lacks them. The serifs are the stuff at the bottom of the "A" on the left that make it look like it is wearing slippers. Below, we have a serif "H" on the left and a sans-serif "H" on the right:

Above, the serif "H" on the left has the serifs both at the top and the bottom:

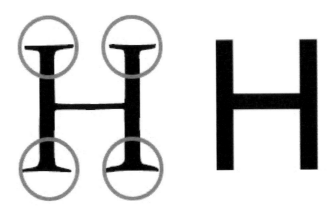

Serif fonts in general have a more classical appearance, while sans-serif fonts ("sans" is French for "lacking", "without") have a more modern appearance. In CSS, we can declare that a certain text should be either serif or sans-serif without specifying the font (line 2 below):

```
i 1    <p>This is some text</p>
  2 |
```

```
1▾ p {
2      font-family:sans-serif;
3      font-size:30px;
4  }
5  |
```

```
1 |
```

This is some text

Above, on line 2 of the CSS, I have declared that the <p> element should have a sans-serif font. In general, this declaration is used after specifying a font, as follows:

```
1▾ p {
2      font-family:'Roboto Condensed', sans-serif;
3      font-size:30px;
4  }
```

Here is the result:

This is some text

Above, on line 2, I have declared that the <p> element should use the 'Roboto Condensed' font, after which I have written 'sans-serif'. This tells the browser to use the Roboto Condensed font *if the user has this font*, and if they don't have it, it tells the browser to use the default sans-serif font of the user's system.

You can declare as many fonts as you like (separated by commas). The browser will try to use the first one if the user has it. If they don't, the browser will fall back on the second font specified, and if they don't, it will fall back on 'sans-serif'.

Below, on line 2, we have an example of three font declarations, ending with 'serif':

```
1 ▼  p {
2        font-family: 'Goudy Old Style', Centaur, serif;
3        font-size:30px;
4    }
5    |
```

This is some text

Text Shadows

Text "text-shadow" property is used to add a shadow to a text. Below, we have a quotation from Shakespeare:

By the pricking of my thumbs,
Something wicked this way comes.

On line 4 below, I define a text shadow:

```
1 ▼  p {
2        font-family: Centaur, serif;
3        font-size:30px;
4        text-shadow:2px 2px 2px #ccc;
5    }
```

Here is the result:

By the pricking of my thumbs,
Something wicked this way comes.

The "text-shadow" property's value is defined similarly to the "box-shadow" property. We define a top distance, a left distance and a size, followed by a color. Using the interplay between the text color and the shadow, we can create interesting effects, as follows (lines 4 and 5):

```
1   p {
2       font-family: Centaur, serif;
3       font-size:30px;
4       text-shadow:1px 1px 5px #ccc;
5       color:#ccc;
6   }
```

Here is the result:

By the pricking of my thumbs,
Something wicked this way comes.

Some websites use a very subtle shadow to make their text have a nice-looking sheen, as follows:

```
1 ▾ p {
2       font-family: Centaur, serif;
3       font-size:20px;
4       text-shadow:1px 1px 1px #fff;
5       color:#000;
6 }
7
8 |
```

By the pricking of my thumbs,
Something wicked this way comes.

Above, the HTML preview has a gray background. I have given the text a white "shadow", which creates a very subtle effect where the edges of the black text are brighter than the gray background.

Drop Caps

A drop cap is a large letter that is used at the beginning of a passage. Below is an example of a drop cap from *Stories from Lands of Sunshine* by Eleanor Riggs (1904). The drop cap is the large "J" that takes up multiple lines:

THE MAGNOLIA

JUST beyond New Orleans is a beautiful swamp of tall cypress trees and low palmettoes. It has dark little bayous with strange Indian names, and is the home of hundreds of birds. It is a narrow swamp, and winds like a tattered gray scarf about the shoulders of the old gray lake called Pont'chartrain. In recent years neat cottages have been built

We will now try to recreate something like the above. Below, I have typed some of the paragraph from above:

```
1  <p>Just beyond New Orleans is a beautiful swamp of
2  tall cypress trees and low palmettoes. It has
3  dark little bayous with strange Indian names,
4  and is the home of hundreds of birds. It is a narrow
5  swamp, and winds like a tattered gray scarf about...</p>
6
7
```

```
1  p {
2      font-family: 'Goudy Old Style', serif;
3      font-size:20px;
4  }
5
6
```

Just beyond New Orleans is a beautiful swamp of tall cypress trees and low palmettoes. It has dark little bayous with strange Indian names, and is the home of hundreds of birds. It is a narrow swamp, and winds like a tattered gray scarf about...

In order to add special styling to the letter "J", we put it in a <span> tag and give it a class of its own:

```
1  <p><span class="drop-cap">J</span>ust beyond New Orleans
2  is a beautiful swamp of tall cypress trees and low
```

It may seem strange to put a single letter of a word in a tag of its own, but this is commonly done for styling purposes. It doesn't actually affect the appearance of the text until we add CSS for it:

Just beyond New Orleans is a beautiful swamp of tall cypress trees and low palmettoes. It has dark little bayous with strange Indian names, and is the home of hundreds of birds. It is a narrow swamp, and winds like a tattered gray scarf about...

Let's now give the "drop-cap" class a large font size:

```
6  .drop-cap {
7      font-size:300%;
8  }
```

Here is the result:

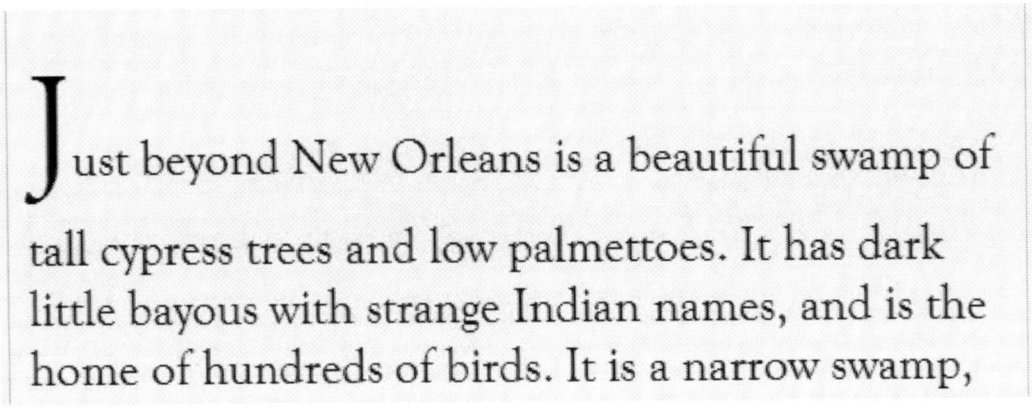

Just beyond New Orleans is a beautiful swamp of tall cypress trees and low palmettoes. It has dark little bayous with strange Indian names, and is the home of hundreds of birds. It is a narrow swamp,

Above, the "J" is now much larger. But it causes certain issues for us. It pushes the line right below it down, causing uneven line spacing. We can fix this by giving it a small line height (line 8 below):

```
6   .drop-cap {
7       font-size:300%;
8       line-height:0.1em;
9   }
```

Here is the result:

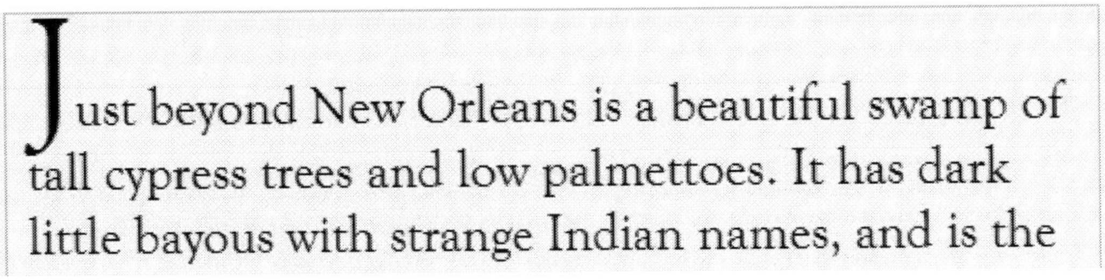

Just beyond New Orleans is a beautiful swamp of tall cypress trees and low palmettoes. It has dark little bayous with strange Indian names, and is the

Above, the lines are now evenly spaced.

The next thing to do is to push the "J" downwards. One might think of giving it an inline-block display property and a top margin (lines 9 and 10), as follows, but it doesn't work:

```
 6 ▾  .drop-cap {
 7        font-size:300%;
 8        line-height:0.1em;
 9        display:inline-block;
10        margin-top:20px;
```

J ust beyond New Orleans is a beautiful swamp of
tall cypress trees and low palmettoes. It has dark
little bayous with strange Indian names, and is the

The top margin on line 10 pushes the whole line down, not just the "J".

We can use relative positioning to push it down, as follows (lines 10 and 11):

```
 6 ▾  .drop-cap {
 7        font-size:300%;
 8        line-height:0.1em;
 9        display:inline-block;
10        position:relative;
11        top:20px;
12    }
```

J ust beyond New Orleans is a beautiful swamp of
tall cypress trees and low palmettoes. It has dark
little bayous with strange Indian names, and is the

The trouble is that the "J" gets overlaid onto the line below. If we were to use bottom padding to push the next line down (line 12 below), this would happen:

```
 6 ▾  .drop-cap {
 7        font-size:300%;
 8        line-height:0.1em;
 9        display:inline-block;
10        position:relative;
11        top:20px;
12        padding-bottom:40px;
13     }
```

J ust beyond New Orleans is a beautiful swamp of
tall cypress trees and low palmettoes. It has dark
little bayous with strange Indian names, and is the
home of hundreds of birds. It is a narrow swamp,

Above, all of the second line ends up going down, which is not what we want.

The proper solution is to use "display:block" and a left float:

```
 6 ▾  .drop-cap {
 7        font-size:300%;
 8        line-height:0.1em;
 9        display:block;
10        float:left;
11     }
```

J ust beyond New Orleans is a beautiful swamp of
tall cypress trees and low palmettoes. It has dark
little bayous with strange Indian names, and is the

Now, if were to give the drop cap a top margin (line 11 below), things will act a little more reasonably:

```
 6 ▾  .drop-cap {
 7        font-size:300%;
 8        line-height:0.1em;
 9        display:block;
10        float:left;
11        margin-top:0.45em;
12    }
```

J ust beyond New Orleans is a beautiful swamp of
tall cypress trees and low palmettoes. It has dark
little bayous with strange Indian names, and is the

Above, the "J" ends up being pushed down, and the line below it makes room for it by moving the word "tall" toward the right. You may notice that the "J" is now running into the word "little" below it. We can fix this by giving the drop cap a bottom margin (line 12 below):

```
 6 ▾  .drop-cap {
 7        font-size:300%;
 8        line-height:0.1em;
 9        display:block;
10        float:left;
11        margin-top:0.45em;
12        margin-bottom:0.5em;
```

J ust beyond New Orleans is a beautiful swamp of
tall cypress trees and low palmettoes. It has dark
little bayous with strange Indian names, and is
the home of hundreds of birds. It is a narrow

The bottom margin enlarges the footprint of the drop cap. It tells the browser to reserve this much empty space underneath the drop cap, which forces the text to move away from it.

Below, I have changed the font family of the text to the font known as Georgia (line 2 below):

```
 1 ▾  p {
 2        font-family: Georgia, serif;
 3        font-size:20px;
 4    }
```

Here is the result on our text:

Just beyond New Orleans is a beautiful swamp of tall cypress trees and low palmettoes. It has dark little bayous with strange Indian names, and is the home of hundreds of birds. It is a narrow swamp, and

Above, notice how there is now a little too much space underneath the drop cap. This is because what looks good in one font does not necessarily work for another font. When changing fonts, we sometimes have to readjust the CSS styling in order to make it look decent again. Below, I reduce the bottom margin (line 12), which reduces the amount of space reserved underneath the drop cap:

```
 6 ▾  .drop-cap {
 7        font-size:350%;
 8        line-height:0.1em;
 9        display:block;
10        float:left;
11        margin-top:0.45em;
12        margin-bottom:0.3em;
```

Just beyond New Orleans is a beautiful swamp of tall cypress trees and low palmettoes. It has dark little bayous with strange Indian names, and is the home of hundreds of birds. It is a narrow swamp, and

9.
Meeting the Inspector

Learning "inspection" is a crucial skill for any learner of HTML and CSS. Web browsers like Chromium, Chrome and Firefox come with an "inspector" that helps you peek into the code of the HTML document you are looking at. Below, inside the Chromium web browser, I have right-clicked on an empty area on the Falcon Heavy article on Wikipedia and chosen to click "Inspect":

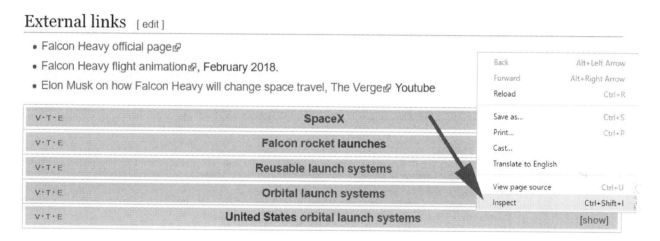

This causes the Chromium Inspector to appear, as follows:

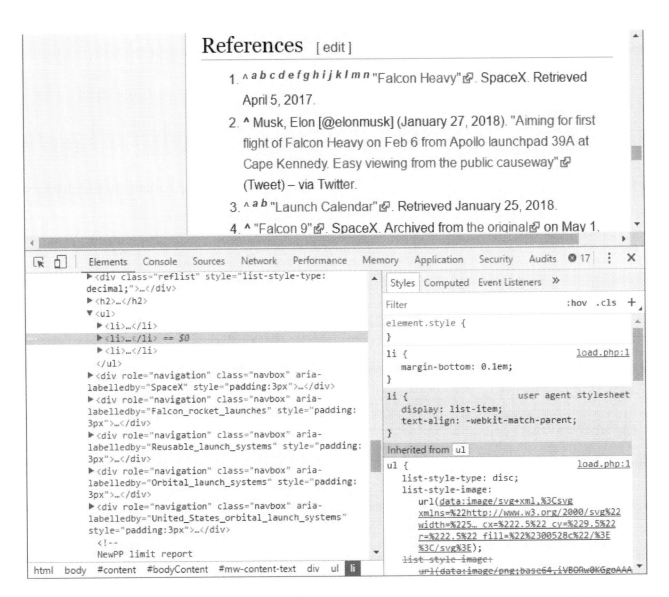

The above can be quite overwhelming for a beginner, but it is quite easy to work with it once you get used to it. On the left, we have direct access to the HTML of the document. On the right, we have access to the document's CSS.

Below, by scrolling up, I have found the HTML for the <h1> tag of the article (which says "Falcon Heavy"):

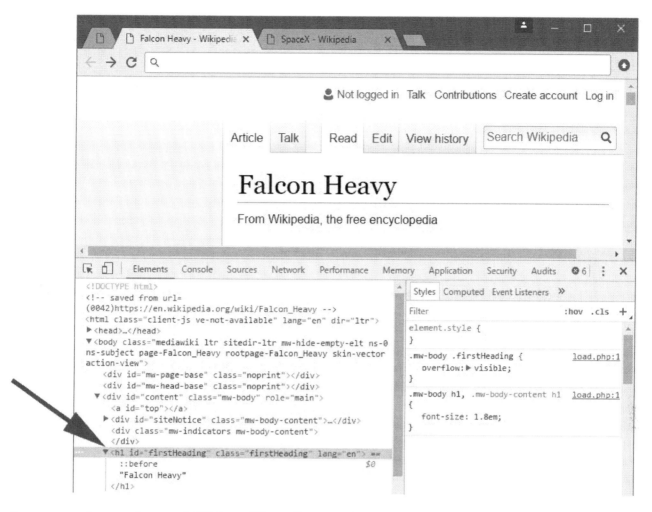

I can now change the word "Falcon Heavy" to anything I want by double-clicking the word "Falcon Heavy" in the inspector:

Pressing "Enter" ("return" on a Mac) makes my changes show on document:

Article Talk   Read   Edit   View history   Search Wikipedia   Q

Falcon Not So Heavy

From Wikipedia, the free encyclopedia

Do not worry; I am not actually vandalizing Wikipedia. By making changes in the inspector, I only change my own local "copy" of the article. This has no effect on the web page that others see.

Using the inspector, you can now impress your friends by telling them you can make changes to this or that website.

The inspector is also useful for testing our styles on a document in real-time. Below, I have a document open with Shakespeare's first sonnet on it:

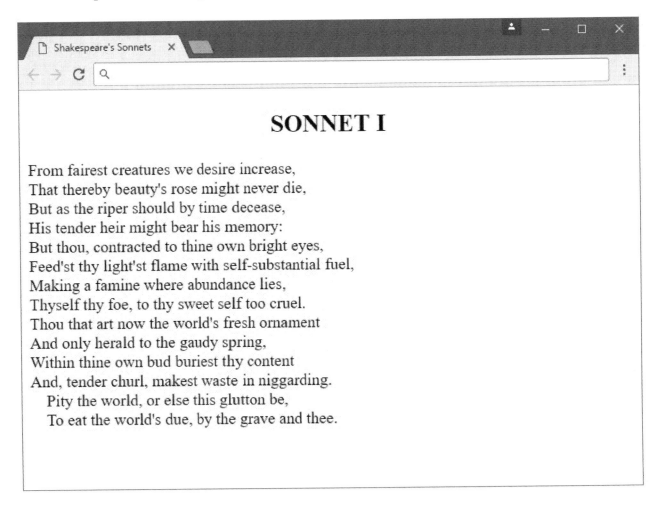

Below, I have opened the inspector:

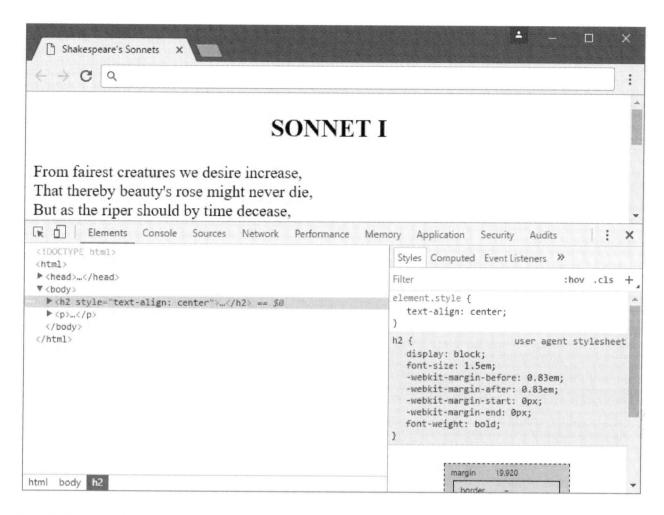

By clicking the little triangles on the left of the elements, I can expand them to make their contents visible. Below, I have clicked the triangle to the left of the <p> tag:

```
<!DOCTYPE html>
<html>
▶ <head>…</head>
▼ <body>
    ▶ <h2 style="text-align: center">…</h2> == $0
      ▼ <p>
          "From fairest creatures we desire increase,"
          <br>
          "
          That thereby beauty's rose might never die,"
          <br>
          "
          But as the riper should by time decease,"
          <br>
          "
          His tender heir might bear his memory:"
```

Let's say we want to test out some styles on the <p> tag. We first have to select it by clicking on it in the inspector:

281

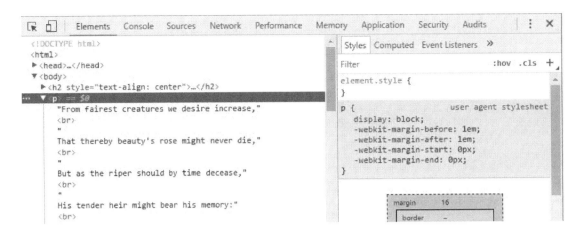

Now, on the right side I can add styles to the <p> tag by clicking the "element.style" box on the right. I start typing "font" and the inspector offers me various CSS properties starting with the word "font":

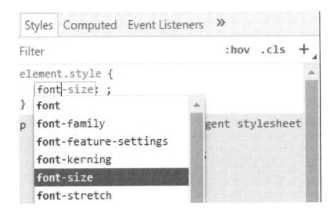

I click on "font-size":

Now, I will press the "tab" button on my keyboard (you can also press Enter/return) and typing "150%" as the new value of the "font-size" property:

Above, notice the way that the text of the sonnet is now larger. Also notice that in the HTML preview on the left of the inspector, the new style we added is added as a new "style" attribute on the <p> tag. Anything we add in the "element.style" area is added to the element as a style attribute.

Below, I have selected the <h2> tag on the left of the inspector and added a number of CSS properties on the right, changing the appearance of the word "Sonnet I":

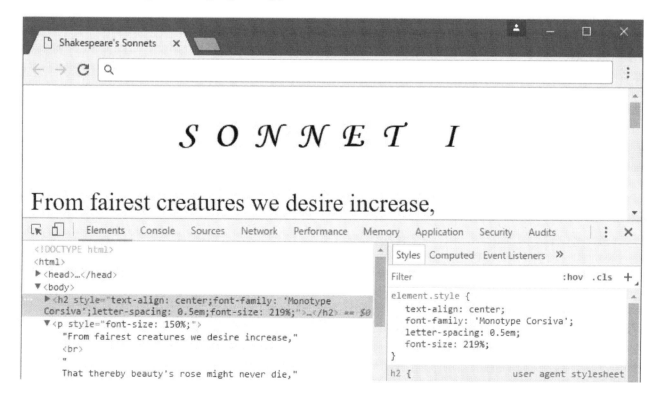

Any changes you make to the document will be lost when you close the tab. There is no way to save the changes you make. Using the inspector is entirely for "inspecting" a document's HTML and CSS to find out more about it.

Below, we have a very simple HTML document with two names on it:

By opening the inspector, I can check what is causing the word "Gaspode" to appear so large:

Above, on the left I have clicked on the <div> tag that contains the word "Gaspode". On the right, I can see the styles that apply to it. The inspector is telling me that there is an italic formatting on the "animal" class, and a 150% font-size on the "dog" class.

We can also make changes to the styles that are on a class. Below, on the right, I have added a 1px border on the "animal" class. The result is that both animal names get a border:

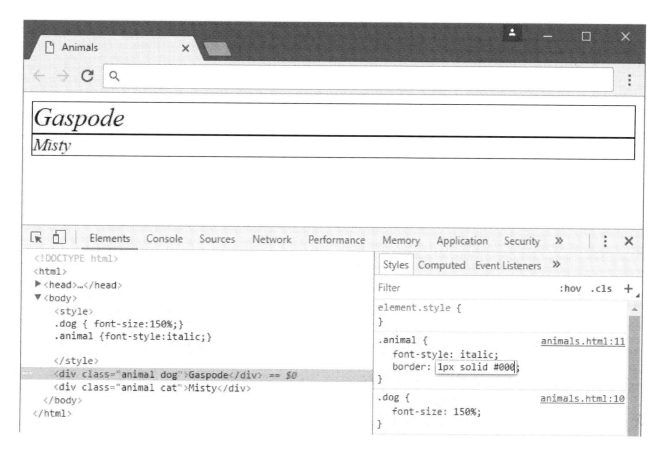

I can even add a brand new class to an element and style that class. On the left side of the inspector, by double-clicking on the class names of an element we can add new classes to it or remove classes. Below, I have added the class "terrier" to the <div> for Gaspode:

```
        </style>
        <div class="animal dog terrier">Gaspode</div> == $0
        <div class="animal cat">Misty</div>
      </body>
    </html>
```

Now I can create a new CSS rule for the "terrier" class by lcicking on the plus icon on the top right of the CSS part of the inspector:

Once I click the plus icon, the inspector creates a new CSS section for me and suggests a selector:

I refuse the suggestion and instead type ".terrier" only:

I now add some styles to the "terrier" class. I give it a "font-family" property of "Roboto Condensed' (this is the name of a font) and a padding of 10 pixels. The result can be seen above the inspector.

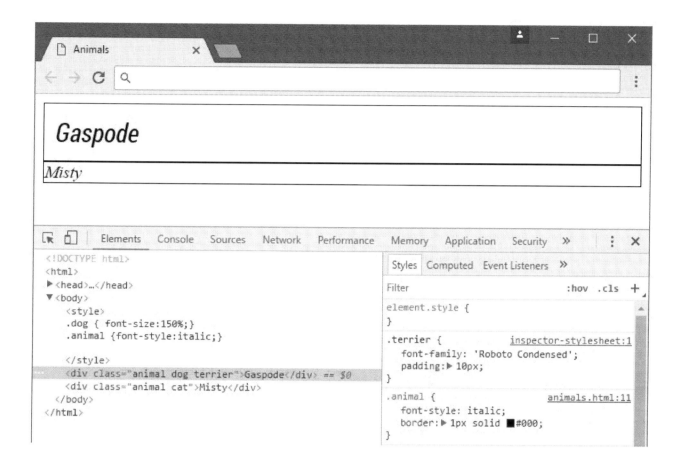

This page intentionally left blank

10.
Creating Your First Layout

In this chapter, we will bring together what we have learned so far in order to make a "real" web page. We will study the scenario of turning a non-web design into a web design, which is how professional web designers often do their work. The designs are created on paper or inside a program like Vizio or Photoshop. The design is then given to a web designer who writes the HTML and CSS necessary to recreate the design on the web.

Above, we have a page from a magazine that we will turn into a web page. The page is from a 1836 edition of a London ladies' magazine known as *The Court Magazine*.

Below is a screenshot of the folder in which I will be putting my files:

At the moment, the folder only contains one file. The file is the decorative picture from the magazine page. Below, I have opened the image in Microsoft Paint in order to show you what it looks like:

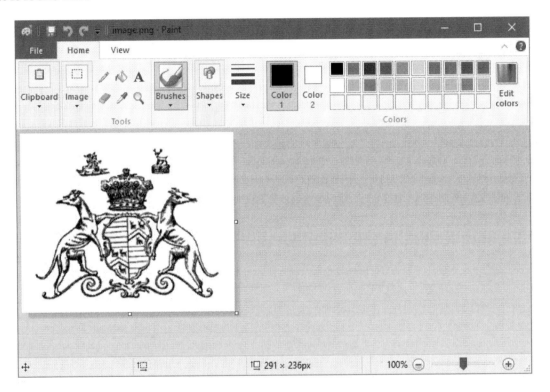

Below, I have created a new file called magazine.html (using the method of clicking an empty area, choosing New -> New Text Document and renaming the Next Text Document.txt to magazine.html):

Below, I open magazine.html in Notepad++[15], which is a highly useful (and free!) code editing program:

---

[15] You can download it at notepad-plus-plus.org. If you are using a Mac, you can get a free code editor at brackets.io.

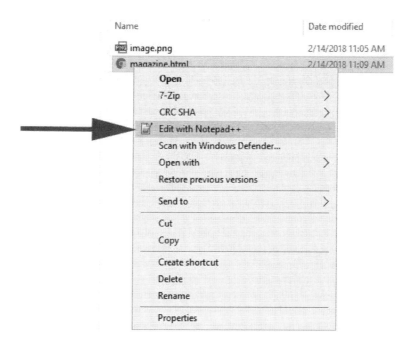

Note: You will not see the option "Edit with Notepad++" until you have downloaded and installed the Notepad++ program.[16]

Below is a picture of the magazine.html file opened in Notepad++:

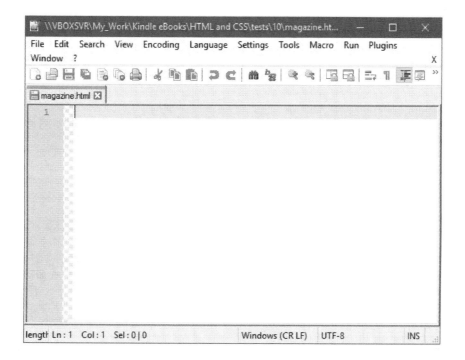

---

[16] You can Google "How to install notepad++" to find videos and tutorials on installing this program on your computer.

Below, I have entered the code for a barebones HTML document:

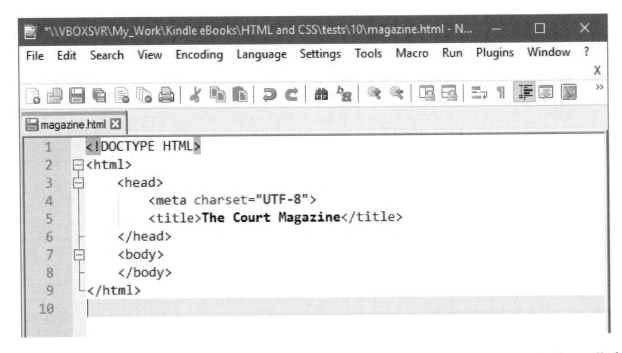

It is common to put images in their own folder, there I will create a new folder called "images" and move the image file into it:

It is also common to put CSS in a separate file in its own folder. For this reason, we will create a new folder:

Inside the "css" folder we will create a new file called "styles.css":

Below, I have also opened the "styles.css" file in Notepad++, so that I can have easy access to it:

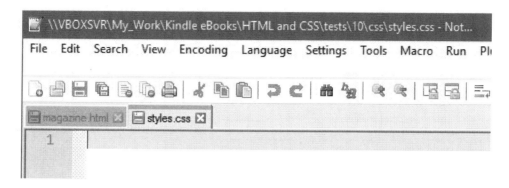

We will now tell our html document to get its CSS from this new file, as follows (line 6 below):

```
 1   <!DOCTYPE HTML>
 2   <html>
 3       <head>
 4           <meta charset="UTF-8">
 5           <title>The Court Magazine</title>
 6           <link rel="stylesheet" type="text/css" href="css/styles.css"/>
 7       </head>
 8       <body>
 9       </body>
10   </html>
11
```

Above, we use the <link> tag that we have not used before. This tag, similar to the <meta> tag, does not have a closing tag. Using the "rel" attribute, we declare that this is a stylesheet. In the "type" attribute, we write "text/css". Using the "href" attribute, we declare where the file is located. The path we declare is "css/styles.css", which tells the browser to look in a folder called "css" and to find a file inside that folder named "styles.css".

We will now test to see if everything is working properly by adding a test <h1> tag on line 9:

```
 8       <body>
 9           <h1>TEST</h1>
10       </body>
```

In "styles.css", we will give the <h1> a special formatting, such as a border:

I will now open "magazine.html" in a browser:

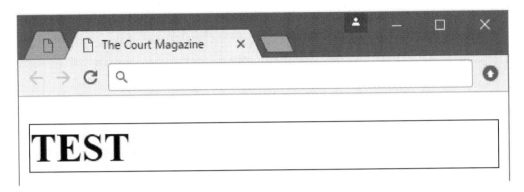

Above, we can see that everything is working properly. The title tag "The Court Magazine" can be seen at the top (above the magnifier icon), and the <h1> element now has the black border which we declared inside the "styles.css" file.

We will now work on creating a masthead for our magazine website. A masthead is the top part of a website where the site's logo is shown along with other things. Below is a picture of the website for Britain's Royal Society. The masthead is the top part where you see the word "The Royal Society" on the left and a magnifier and stacked rectangles icon on the right:

The masthead is shown on most pages of a website, depending on the design choices of the creators. Below, I have navigated to the "Grants" page of the Royal Society's website. Notice that the masthead remains the same:

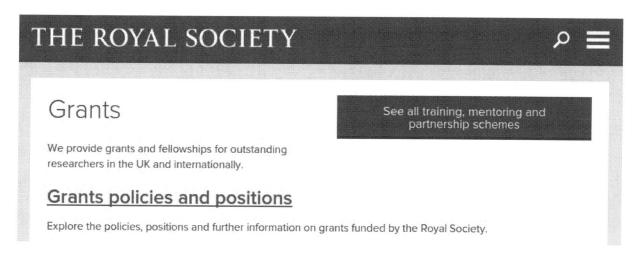

For our website, we will have to take our inspiration from the picture of the magazine page that we saw earlier:

It is complicated to generate curved text in HTML/CSS, therefore for the purposes of this book we will reuse the above title from the picture of the magazine page. Below, I put the above image inside the images folder:[17]

Name		Date modified
image.png		2/14/2018 11:05 AM
magazine_title.png		2/15/2018 10:58 AM

We now use a new tag to create the masthead for our website. This tag is the <header> tag (not to be confused with the <head> tag):

---

[17] Those wishing to follow along can download the image files (and the rest of the files used throughout this chapter) at the author's website here: http://hawramani.com/the-court-magazine

```
8    ⊟        <body>
9    ⊟            <header>
10   ⊟                <div class="logo">
11                       <img src="images/magazine_title.png" />
12                   </div>
13               </header>
```

The <header> tag does not accomplish anything special when it comes to styling. Instead of <header>, one can merely use a <div>. It is better to use the <header> tag, however, because this is semantically more appropriate. It allows robots (such as search engines) to know this is the masthead of the website, helping them avoid the mistake of thinking the masthead is the actual content of the site.

Inside the <header> tag, I have placed a <div> with a class of "logo", and inside that div, I have placed the <img> tag for the magazine title.

This is what our document looks like now in a browser:

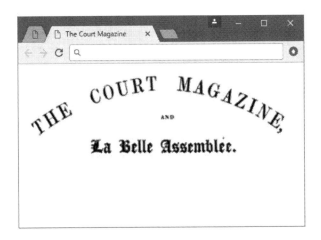

Next, we will define the navigation section of the website:

```
8    ⊟        <body>
9    ⊟            <header>
10   ⊟                <div class="logo">
11                       <img src="images/magazine_title.png" />
12                   </div>
13   ⊟                <nav>
14                       <a href="">Home</a>
15                       <a href="">About</a>
16                       <a href="">Contact</a>
17                   </nav>
18               </header>
19           </body>
```

Above, I have created a new tag for the navigation. This is the <nav> tag. Similar to the <header> tag, the <nav> is like a <div> and does not come with any special formatting. Inside it I have created a few links. The links at the moment have empty "href" attributes, since we do not yet know where the links should go.

Next will create the contents of the article:

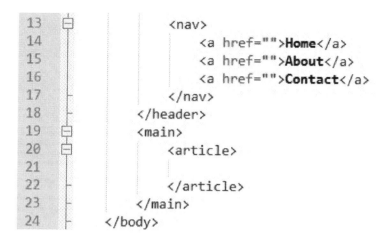

To define the main content area of a website, we use the <main> tag. Inside it, we use an <article> tag to define the article area. The <main> tag may also contain ads, videos and other elements not having to do with the article.

Remember that we had an image at the top of the article, below we add that and below it we add the title of the article:

```
20    <article>
21        <img src="images/image.png" />
22        <h1>Genealogical Memoir of Lady Mary Vyner</h1>
23    </article>
```

Here is what our document looks like in the browser:

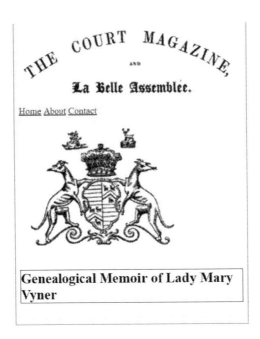

It does not look very pretty, but we will leave the styling for a little later. It is now time to add the contents of the article. Instead of typing up the contents, I will use some "filler" text. This is used by web designers to test out their designs without having to write out long paragraphs. The most commonly used filler text is "lorem ipsum", which is made up of Latin words. Below is a picture of a number of <p> tags I have added below the <h1> tag filled with the "lorem ipsum" text:

```
20   <article>
21       <img src="images/image.png" />
22       <h1>Genealogical Memoir of Lady Mary Vyner</h1>
23       <p>Lorem ipsum dolor sit amet, id sed doctus dissentias, putant perpetua consequat cu has.
24       Ut everti denique mediocrem pri, te tation ridens moderatius vel. Cu vim inani oporteat.
25       Ne natum intellegam pri, diam equidem ornatus in vis.</p>
26       <p>Eam ad epicurei prodesset expetendis, id alii nibh posidonium vix, vim in feugiat
27       vivendum mnesarchum. Id mel dicat graeco semper, nostrud scriptorem no vim.
28       Maiorum nostrum patrioque id vis, laudem scripta mei te. Te vis dolores explicari.</p>
29       <p>Ei nec homero propriae. Corpora platonem iracundia vel at. Movet probatus sed ad.
30       Cu vim solum voluptaria dissentias, postea epicurei cu usu. Solet
31       periculis has te, laoreet signiferumque pri id, per molestiae eloquentiam eu.</p>
32       <p>Mel id aliquip definiebas philosophia, et illud utamur usu. Eam ignota invidunt in.
33       Menandri invenire euripidis eu pro, mel mutat solet eu. Ex timeam nominati constituto mei.</p>
34       <p>Euripidis voluptatibus te vis, duo dicat propriae omittantur an. Usu ad nostrud offendit,
35       no quem nostro legimus duo. Quo ad debet dolore offendit, eu suas labores sensibus sit.
36       Sed blandit philosophia ut.</p>
37   </article>
```

Adding Styles

It is now time to style our creation. The first thing to do is to make the logo smaller, as follows:

Above, I have removed the border styling I had added earlier to the <h1>tag. The selector ".logo img" means "an image located inside an element that has the class of 'logo'". The result is as follows:

Home About Contact

Genealogical Memoir of Lady Mary Vyner

Lorem ipsum dolor sit amet, id sed doctus dissentias, putant perpetua consequat cu has. Ut everti denique mediocrem pri, te tation ridens moderatius vel. Cu vim inani oporteat. Ne natum intellegam pri, diam equidem ornatus in vis.

Below, I center-align the logo image by giving the "logo" class a "text-align" property of "center" (line 2 below). The "text-align" property applies to all inline elements inside an element, and since the "img" tag inside the "logo" class is inline, it ends up being center-aligned.

```
1  .logo {
2        text-align:center;
3  }
4  .logo img {
5        width:230px;
6  }
7
```

Here is the result:

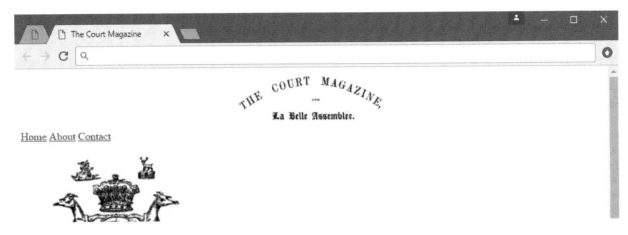

If we had placed the "text-align: center" property inside the ".logo img" selector (as follows on line 6), nothing would have happened:

```
1  .logo {
2
3  }
4  .logo img {
5        width:230px;
6        text-align:center;
7  }
8
```

The reason is that the "text-align" property applies to the *contents* of an element. If we want the image to be center-aligned inside the "logo" div (as we do), we have to declare the "text-align" property on the "logo" <div> on line 2. Declaring "text-align" on line 6 above means "center the image's contents inside the <img> tag", which means nothing when it comes to the image's position inside its container <div>. It's like saying "Hang this painting centered inside its own frame on the wall." This tells you nothing about where it should go on the wall. If you are a little confused, there is no need to worry. I have seen seasoned web designers put "text-align" on inline elements then wonder why nothing happens.

We will now add a subtle border underneath the logo <div> (line 3 below):

```
1   .logo {
2       text-align:center;
3       border-bottom:1px solid #ccc;
4   }
5   .logo img {
6       width:230px;
7   }
8
```

Here is the result:

THE COURT MAGAZINE
AND
La Belle Assemblee.

Home About Contact

Below, I center-align the navigation links:

```
9    nav {
10       text-align:center;
11   }
```

Note that I did not write ".nav" but merely "nav" as the selector. This is because in our HTML we are using a <nav> tag, the word "nav" here is a tag name rather than a class name. To refresh your memory, here is what we have in the HTML:

```
<header>
    <div class="logo">
        <img src="images/magazine_title.png" />
    </div>
    <nav>
        <a href="">Home</a>
        <a href="">About</a>
        <a href="">Contact</a>
    </nav>
</header>
```

Here is the result of the center-align we declared above:

The center-aligning works because the <a> tags are inline elements. If we turn them to block elements and make them float as follows, the center-aligning will stop working:

```
 9   ⊟nav {
10        text-align:center;
11   └}
12
13   ⊟nav a {
14        display:block;
15        float:left;
16   └}
```

Here is the result:

If we take away the "float:left" on line 15 but keep "display:block", this takes place:

Above, each <a> tag takes up a full line due to the "display:block". But they *inherit* the "text-align:center" property from the container, so that they end up being centered inside their own boxes. *They are not centered inside the <nav> tag.* We can verify this by adding a border to the <a> tags (line 15 below):

```
13   ⊟nav a {
14        display:block;
15        border:1px solid #000;
16   └}
```

Here is the result:

Above, each <a> tag takes up a whole line and is not centered inside <nav>. But the text of the <a> tags themselves are centered within their own boxes due to inheritance.

Centering things inside things leads to much confusion among web designers due to interplay between block elements, inline elements and inheritance. It takes months of experience to get a "feel" for how these things work together. I am afraid that for now, you are doomed to hundreds of hours of trial and error before things start to make intuitive sense. When confused, it is almost always useful to put a border on the elements you are working with (as I did on line 15 above). This helps you know where the elements begin and end and can help you visualize the problem.

Back to our regular programming, below I have removed the "display:block" property and the border and given a top margin to the <a> tags (line 14):

```
 9   nav {
10       text-align:center;
11   }
12
13   nav a {
14       margin-top:5px;
15   }
```

Here is the result:

Nothing happened because the <a> tags are inline elements. Inline elements do not take margins. What we can do instead is give a top margin to the <nav> tag (line 11 below), which is a block tag and can take a margin:

```
 9    ┌nav {
10    │      text-align:center;
11    │      margin-top:5px;
12    └}
13
14    ┌nav a {
15    │
16    └}
```

Here is the result:

Notice how there is some space above the navigation links now, separating them from the border above them.

Below, I have added a large number of CSS properties to the navigation links:

```
14    ┌nav a {
15    │      text-decoration:none;
16    │      text-transform:uppercase;
17    │      letter-spacing:2px;
18    │      color:#999;
19    │      text-shadow:1px 1px 1px #ccc;
20    │      padding-left:0.6em;
21    │      padding-right:0.6em;
22    └}
```

Here is the result:

Below, I use the ":hover" pseudo-selector to give the links a special appearance when a user hovers their mouse pointer over them:

```
24    ⊟nav a:hover {
25          text-shadow:3px 3px 3px #ccc;
26    └}
```

Below is a picture of what the "ABOUT" link looks like with a mouse hovering over it:

The CSS I added on line 25 above causes the shadow of the text to become wider and longer, making the links have a dynamic appearance when a user hovers their mouse pointer over them.

I will now add a border underneath the navigation as follows (line 12 below):

```
9     ⊟nav {
10          text-align:center;
11          margin-top:5px;
12          border-bottom:1px solid #ccc;
13    └}
```

Here is the result:

The bottom border we added is too close to the links. There are various ways of fixing this. Below I add bottom padding to the <nav> element (line 13 below):

```
9     ⊟nav {
10          text-align:center;
11          margin-top:5px;
12          border-bottom:1px solid #ccc;
13          padding-bottom:5px;
14    └}
```

Here is the result:

The bottom padding I added means there should be a space of 5 pixels on the bottom of the <nav> element between this element and its contents. This ends up creating a 5 pixel space between the navigation links and their container (the <nav> element).

Next we turn our attention to the article. Currently, this is what it looks like:

Genealogical Memoir of Lady Mary Vyner

Lorem ipsum dolor sit amet, id sed doctus dissentias, putant perpetua consequat cu has. Ut everti denique mediocrem pri, te tation ridens moderatius vel. Cu vim inani oporteat. Ne natum intellegam pri, diam equidem ornatus in vis.

We have to center the image inside the article. Here is what the HTML looks like:

```
<main>
    <article>
        <img src="images/image.png" />
        <h1>Genealogical Memoir of Lady Mary Vyner</h1>
```

Unfortunately, we cannot center-align the image at the moment because, as already mentioned, putting "text-align:center" on an <img> tag does nothing. And if we were to put "text-align:center" on the <article> tag, this will work, except that it will make everything else inside it center-aligned also, which is not something we necessarily want. In order to get around this issue, we put the <img> tag inside a container (lines 21-23 below):

```
19   <main>
20       <article>
21           <div class="image-contaier">
22               <img src="images/image.png" />
23           </div>
24           <h1>Genealogical Memoir of Lady Mary Vyner</h1>
```

Now, we can declare the contents of the "image-container" <div> to be center-aligned, which will center-align the image:

```
30   .image-container {
31       text-align:center;
32   }
```

Here is the result:

The image is a bit too big, so we will change its size using the "width" HTML attribute (rather than CSS) (line 22 below):

```
20   <article>
21       <div class="image-container">
22           <img src="images/image.png" width="200" />
23       </div>
24       <h1>Genealogical Memoir of Lady Mary Vyner</h1>
```

The benefit of doing things this way is that, as has already been mentioned, it helps us quickly set the size of an image inside an article without having to write CSS, and sometimes editing CSS can require a lot of extra work, for example if you are using a content management system like WordPress or Drupal.

Here is the result:

HOME   ABOUT   CONTACT

Genealogical Memoir of Lady Mary Vyner

Next we move on to the title of the article. Below I have added some CSS to styles.css using the selector "article h1", meaning "<h1> tags that happen to be inside <article> tags".

```
34   article h1 {
35        text-align:center;
36        text-transform:uppercase;
37        font-size:15px;
38        letter-spacing:3px;
39   }
```

Here is the result:

GENEALOGICAL MEMOIR OF LADY MARY VYNER

Lorem ipsum dolor sit amet, id sed doctus dissentias, putant perpetua consequat cu has. Ut everti denique mediocrem pri, te tation ridens moderatius vel. Cu vim inani oporteat. Ne natum intellegam pri, diam equidem ornatus in vis.

Let's now take a look at the original article and see what is left to be done:

We are actually done. The article's text is in two columns, but we do not recreate this because columns are not suited to the web and introduce various styling and readability issues.

Adding a Wrapper

Below, I have placed all of the contents of the <body> inside a div with the class of "outer-wrapper" (lines 9 and 42 below):

```
8    <body>
9        <div class="outer-wrapper">
10           <header>
11               <div class="logo">
12                   <img src="images/magazine_title.png" />
13               </div>
14               <nav>
15                   <a href="">Home</a>
16                   <a href="">About</a>
17                   <a href="">Contact</a>
18               </nav>
19           </header>
20           <main>
21               <article>
22                   <div class="image-container">
23                       <img src="images/image.png" width="200" />
24                   </div>
25                   <h1>Genealogical Memoir of Lady Mary Vyner</h1>
26                   <p>Lorem ipsum dolor sit amet, id sed doctus dissentias, putant perpetua consequat cu has.
27                   Ut everti denique mediocrem pri, te tation ridens moderatius vel. Cu vim inani oporteat.
28                   Ne natum intellegam pri, diam equidem ornatus in vis.</p>
29                   <p>Eam ad epicurei prodesset expetendis, id alii nibh posidonium vix, vim in feugiat
30                   vivendum mnesarchum. Id mel dicat graeco semper, nostrud scriptorem no vim.
31                   Maiorum nostrum patrioque id vis, laudem scripta mei te. Te vis dolores explicari.</p>
32                   <p>Ei nec homero propriae. Corpora platonem iracundia vel at. Movet probatus sed ad.
33                   Cu vim solum voluptaria dissentias, postea epicurei cu usu. Solet
34                   periculis has te, laoreet signiferumque pri id, per molestiae eloquentiam eu.</p>
35                   <p>Mel id aliquip definiebas philosophia, et illud utamur usu. Eam ignota invidunt in.
36                   Menandri invenire euripidis eu pro, mel mutat solet eu. Ex timeam nominati constituto mei.</p>
37                   <p>Euripidis voluptatibus te vis, duo dicat propriae omittantur an. Usu ad nostrud offendit,
38                   no quem nostro legimus duo. Quo ad debet dolore offendit, eu suas labores sensibus sit.
39                   Sed blandit philosophia ut.</p>
40               </article>
41           </main>
42       </div>
43   </body>
```

Wrappers are commonly used in order to give websites a more defined appearance. Below I add a border on the "outer-wrapper" div inside styles.css:

Now, the whole web page is enclosed in a border:

Below, I add a margin to the "outer-wrapper" <div>, which increases the space between it and the browser window:

```
1  .outer-wrapper {
2      border:1px solid #ccc;
3      margin:25px;
4  }
```

Here is the result:

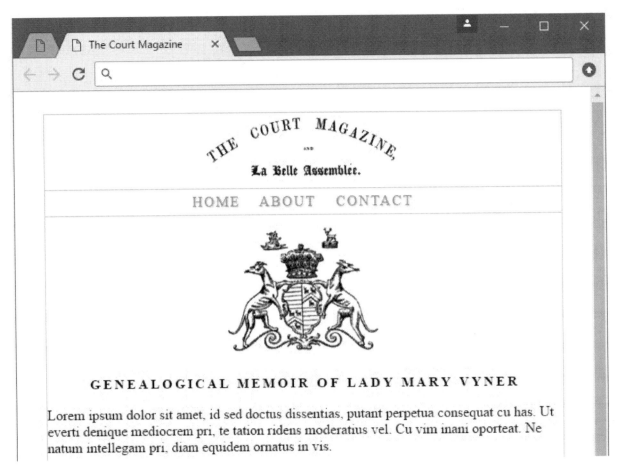

Below, I give the wrapper some more styling:

```
1  .outer-wrapper {
2      border:1px solid #ccc;
3      margin:25px;
4      border-radius:15px;
5      box-shadow:5px 5px 15px #000;
6  }
```

Here is what the design looks like now:

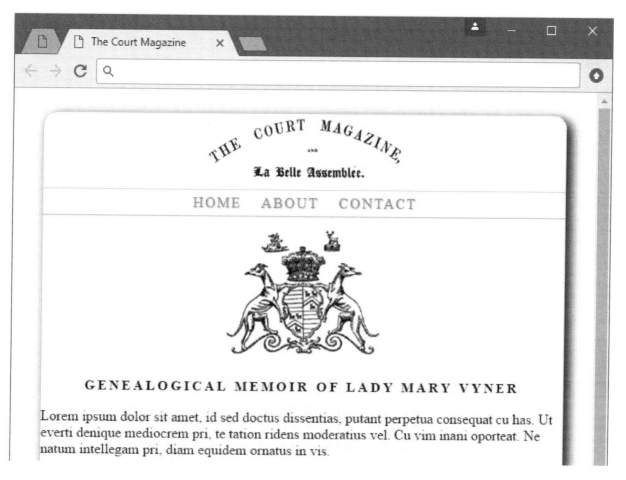

In order to give the website a more professional appearance, below I add a background pattern (taken from subtlepatterns.com) to the <body> tag (lines 1-3 below):

```css
1  body {
2      background:url("../images/symphony.png");
3  }
4
5  .outer-wrapper {
6      border:1px solid #ccc;
7      margin:25px;
8      border-radius:15px;
9      box-shadow:5px 5px 15px #000;
10 }
```

Here is what the design looks like now:

GENEALOGICAL MEMOIR OF LADY MARY VYNER

Lorem ipsum dolor sit amet, id sed doctus dissentias, putant perpetua consequat cu has. Ut everti denique mediocrem pri, te tation ridens moderatius vel. Cu vim inani oporteat. Ne natum intellegam pri, diam equidem ornatus in vis.

It doesn't look good because the "outer-wrapper" <div> is transparent, so that the background on the <body> tag shows through it. We remedy the situation by adding a white background to the "outer-wrapper" (line 10 below):

```
1  body {
2      background:url("../images/symphony.png");
3  }
4
5  .outer-wrapper {
6      border:1px solid #ccc;
7      margin:25px;
8      border-radius:15px;
9      box-shadow:5px 5px 15px #000;
10     background:white;
11 }
```

Here is the result:

Now, there is a patterned background *outside* the website's contents. The background is applied to the <body> tag, but since the "outer-wrapper" div has a white background, the patterned background does not show through it, it ends up only showing up on the outer edge of the website.

On line 2 of the CSS above, you may have noticed the strange URL we used ("../images/symphony.png"). This is known as a relative path. The two dots tell the browser to go to the parent folder, look for a folder named "images", then look for a file named "symphony.png". It is necessary to do this because we have written this CSS inside the file "styles.css". If you remember, this file is inside its own folder:

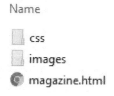

If we had not written the two dots, the browser would have tried to find the "images" folder inside the "css" folder, which is wrong. The two dots inside "style.css" tell the browser "don't look inside the folder where I am located, but go outside me and look down from there". The browser goes outside the folder for "styles.css", ending up looking at the folder that contains "magazine.html" and the two folders "css" and "images". It then starts looking from there for a folder named "images" and inside that for a file named "symphony.png". This is like telling someone who is looking for something to go look in another room.

In the screenshot of the design shown earlier, notice the way the magazine logo is too close to the top edge. We fix this by giving the "logo" div some top padding (line 17 below):

```
13    .logo {
14        text-align:center;
15        border-bottom:1px solid #ccc;
16        padding-top:20px;
17    }
```

Here is the result:

The same issue exists in the article:

GENEALOGICAL MEMOIR OF LADY MARY VYNER

Lorem ipsum dolor sit amet, id sed doctus dissentias, putant perpetua consequat cu has. Ut everti denique mediocrem pri, te tation ridens moderatius vel. Cu vim inani oporteat. Ne natum intellegam pri, diam equidem ornatus in vis.

Notice the way the "Loerm ipsum" is too close to the left edge. We fix this by giving the <article> tag some padding:

```
48    article {
49        padding:0 10px;
50    }
```

Here is the result:

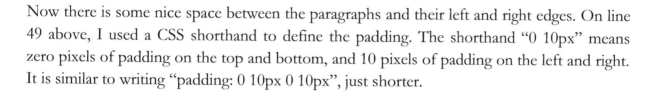

Now there is some nice space between the paragraphs and their left and right edges. On line 49 above, I used a CSS shorthand to define the padding. The shorthand "0 10px" means zero pixels of padding on the top and bottom, and 10 pixels of padding on the left and right. It is similar to writing "padding: 0 10px 0 10px", just shorter.

Adding a Sidebar

Most websites have a sidebar which provides extra links and information. Below is a picture of the Royal Society's website. The page being displayed is the "Mission and priorities" page. The main content of the page is on the left, while there is a picture and download links on the right. This right section is the sidebar:

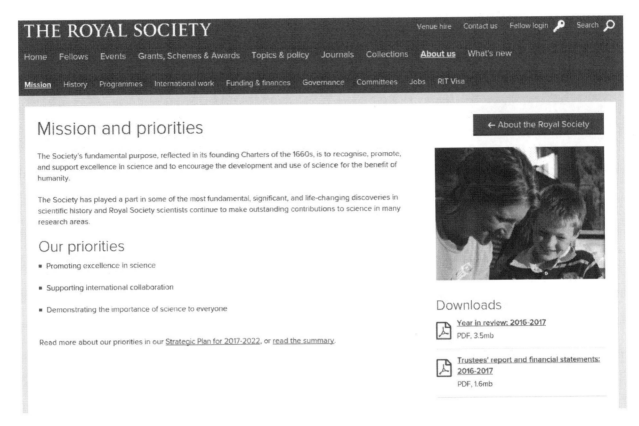

Below, we add a new <div> with a class of "sidebar" to our HTML document (see the bottom):

```
<main>
    <article>
        <div class="image-container">
            <img src="images/image.png" width="200" />
        </div>
        <h1>Genealogical Memoir of Lady Mary Vyner</h1>
        <p>Lorem ipsum dolor sit amet, id sed doctus dissentias, putant perpetua consequat cu has.
        Ut everti denique mediocrem pri, te tation ridens moderatius vel. Cu vim inani oporteat.
        Ne natum intellegam pri, diam equidem ornatus in vis.</p>
        <p>Eam ad epicurei prodesset expetendis, id alii nibh posidonium vix, vim in feugiat
        vivendum mnesarchum. Id mel dicat graeco semper, nostrud scriptorem no vim.
        Maiorum nostrum patrioque id vis, laudem scripta mei te. Te vis dolores explicari.</p>
        <p>Ei nec homero propriae. Corpora platonem iracundia vel at. Movet probatus sed ad.
        Cu vim solum voluptaria dissentias, postea epicurei cu usu. Solet
        periculis has te, laoreet signiferumque pri id, per molestiae eloquentiam eu.</p>
        <p>Mel id aliquip definiebas philosophia, et illud utamur usu. Eam ignota invidunt in.
        Menandri invenire euripidis eu pro, mel mutat solet eu. Ex timeam nominati constituto mei.</p>
        <p>Euripidis voluptatibus te vis, duo dicat propriae omittantur an. Usu ad nostrud offendit,
        no quem nostro legimus duo. Quo ad debet dolore offendit, eu suas labores sensibus sit.
        Sed blandit philosophia ut.</p>
    </article>
</main>
<div class="sidebar">

</div>
```

Below, I add a test <h2> tag to the sidebar <div> (line 43 below):

```
42    ┌      <div class="sidebar">
43    ┤          <h2>Test</h2>
44    └      </div>
```

Below is the result. The sidebar <div> shows up at the bottom the page, as follows:

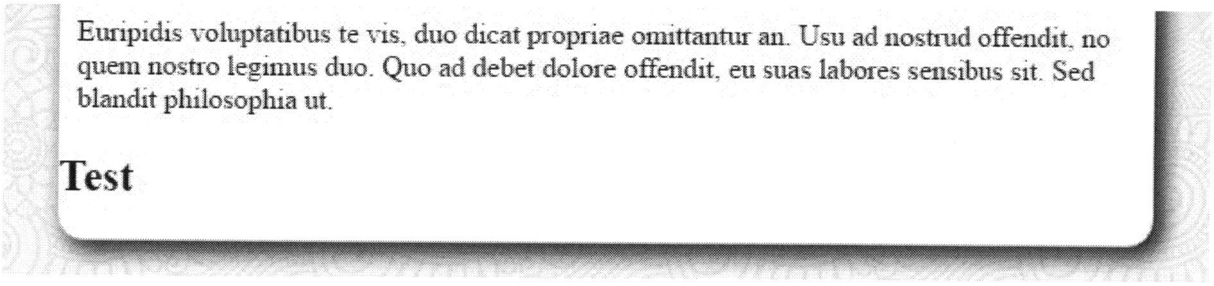

Euripidis voluptatibus te vis, duo dicat propriae omittantur an. Usu ad nostrud offendit, no quem nostro legimus duo. Quo ad debet dolore offendit, eu suas labores sensibus sit. Sed blandit philosophia ut.

Test

In order to make the sidebar show up on the right side of the page, we need to use floating.

```
59    main {
60        float:left;
61        width:65%;
62    }
63    .sidebar {
64        float:right;
65        width:30%;
66    }
```

Here is the result:

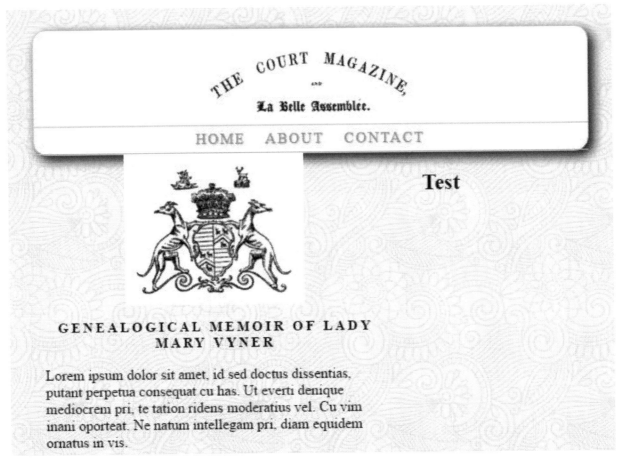

Above, the sidebar is now showing up properly on the right. Except that now the wrapper <div> has collapsed, causing the patterned background of the <body> tag to show through.

The solution to this is to use what is known as a "clear fix". The clear fix solves a problem inherent to floating, the problem of the container collapsing. We need to something to force the container not to collapse, but to stretch it so that it can encapsulate the whole design as it is supposed to. In order to create this fix, we need to add a new <div> outside our floating elements (i.e. outside the <main> tag and the sidebar <div>). The new <div> has to be outside these and after them (lines 45-47 below):

```
41      </main>
42      <div class="sidebar">
43          <h2>Test</h2>
44      </div>
45      <div class="clearfix">
46
47      </div>
```

In the CSS, we give the clearfix <div> a "clear:both" property:

```
67    .clearfix {
68        clear:both;
69    }
```

Here is the result:

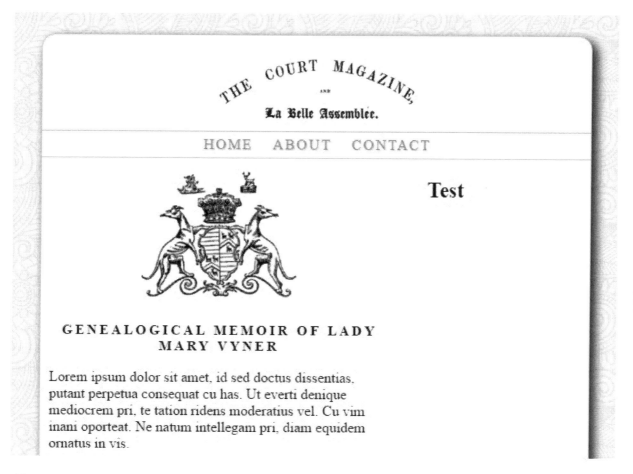

Above, now everything shows up perfectly. If you are a bit unclear on why the clear fix is needed, do not worry, it takes a lot of practice before these things start to make intuitive sense.[18]

Above, notice the way the image above the article's title is now not in the center of the whole page. The reason is that we shrunk the <main> tag's contents to 65%, so the image is now centered within the context of this shrunken <main> tag. The same applies to the <h1> tag inside the <article> tag. It too is centered with respect to the <main> tag. This is a good thing since we do not want the contents of the <main> tag to spill over onto the sidebar.

---

[18] The clear fix I used above is good enough for most cases, but there are far more complicated solutions that are sometimes needed. You can do a web search for "clear fix" to read more on them.

We will now add some real content to the sidebar <div>. I have removed the test <h2> tag and added a "Popular Right Now" section which links to various popular articles on the magazine to encourage readers read them. I use an unordered list for the links:

```
42    <div class="sidebar">
43        <h2>Popular Right Now</h2>
44        <ul>
45            <li><a href="">The Christmas Cattle Show for 1835</a></li>
46            <li><a href="">A Day in the Val D'Aosta</a></li>
47            <li><a href="">Proverbs Out of Use</a></li>
48            <li><a href="">Literature of the Month</a></li>
49        </ul>
50    </div>
```

Here is the result:

Below I add some styling to the <h2> tag inside the sidebar:

```
71    .sidebar h2 {
72         font-size:16px;
73         font-weight:bold;
74         font-style:italic;
75         letter-spacing:2px;
76         color:#666;
77    }
```

Here is the result:

To make the list prettier, I remove the default bullet points (line 80 below) and add my own custom Unicode bullet using the ":before" pseudo-selector:

```
79    .sidebar ul {
80         list-style:none;
81    }
82    .sidebar li:before {
83         content:"❀"
84    }
```

This is what the links look like now:

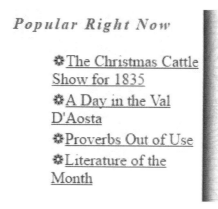

Above, there is a lot of space between the links and the left side. This is caused by the default padding that the browsers adds on the <ul> tag. In order to cancel it out, we do as follows:

```
79   .sidebar ul {
80       list-style:none;
81       padding:0;
82   }
```

Here is our sidebar now:

Popular Right Now

❀ The Christmas Cattle Show
for 1835
❀ A Day in the Val D'Aosta
❀ Proverbs Out of Use
❀ Literature of the Month

Below, we use padding to increase the space between the bullet points and the text:

```
83   .sidebar li:before {
84       content:"❀";
85       padding:5px;
86   }
```

Here is the result:

Popular Right Now

❀ The Christmas Cattle
Show for 1835
❀ A Day in the Val D'Aosta
❀ Proverbs Out of Use
❀ Literature of the Month

Below, I add some styling to the sidebar links:

```
88  .sidebar li a {
89      font-family: Centaur, serif;
90      color:#000;
91      font-size:1.3em;
92      text-decoration:none;
93  }
```

Here is the result:

Popular Right Now

❁ The Christmas Cattle
Show for 1835
❁ A Day in the Val
D'Aosta
❁ Proverbs Out of Use
❁ Literature of the
Month

To increase the spacing between each link and the next, I add a bottom margin to the <li>
tags:

```
83  .sidebar li {
84      margin-bottom:10px;
85  }
```

Here is the result:

Popular Right Now

❁ The Christmas Cattle
Show for 1835

❁ A Day in the Val
D'Aosta

❁ Proverbs Out of Use

❁ Literature of the
Month

Now, we add a new section to the sidebar called "Drawing of the Month", as follows (lines 51 and 52 below):

```
42    <div class="sidebar">
43        <h2>Popular Right Now</h2>
44        <ul>
45            <li><a href="">The Christmas Cattle Show for 1835</a></li>
46            <li><a href="">A Day in the Val D'Aosta</a></li>
47            <li><a href="">Proverbs Out of Use</a></li>
48            <li><a href="">Literature of the Month</a></li>
49        </ul>
50
51        <h2>Drawing of the Month</h2>
52        <img class="drawing-of-the-month" src="images/drawing_of_the_month.png" />
53    </div>
```

Here is what it looks like:

Above, the drawing is too big and spills out of the sidebar. We fix this with a bit of CSS:

```
97    .sidebar img.drawing-of-the-month {
98        width:200px;
99    }
```

Above, we have declared that an <img> tag inside the sidebar <div> that has the class name of "drawing of the month" should have a width of 200 pixels. The selector "img.drawing-of-

326

the-month" (note the lack of a space between "img" and ".drawing-of-the-month") means an <img> tag having a class of "drawing-of-the-month". If there was a space between "img" and ".drawing-of-the-month", that would have meant "an element with a class of drawing-of-the-month". But without the space, the meaning is that the class name should be on the <img> tag itself.

Here is the result:

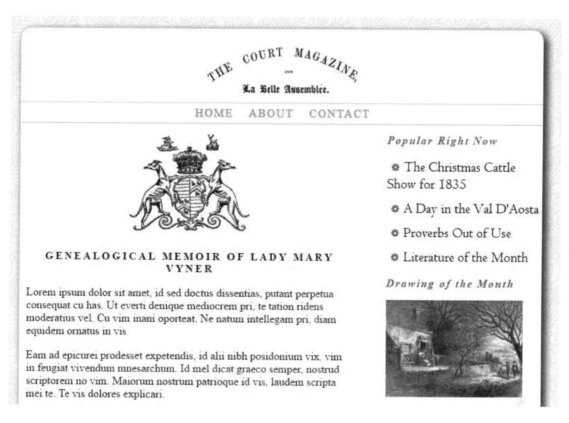

We could help users see a bigger version of the drawing by clicking on it if we put the <img> tag inside an <a> tag that links to the image itself, as follows (lines 52 and 54 below):

```
51    <h2>Drawing of the Month</h2>
52    <a href="images/drawing_of_the_month.png">
53        <img class="drawing-of-the-month" src="images/drawing_of_the_month.png" />
54    </a>
```

Above, we have an <a> tag that links to the image file. If a user clicks on it, they will see the full image in their browser window, as follows:

The appearance of the sidebar does not change in any way when we put the image inside an <a> tag:

The only thing that changes is that when a user clicks on the image, they will be taken to the full image.[19]

---

[19] Note that in a professional design people usually do not link to image files. They would instead link to a new page on their website that has the image on it shown in a larger size. In this way users will continue to see the website's logo and the rest of its design while viewing the picture.

Let's now add a border to the left of the sidebar to separate it from the main content (line 66 below):

```
63    .sidebar {
64        float:right;
65        width:30%;
66        border-left:1px solid #ccc;
67    }
```

Here is the result:

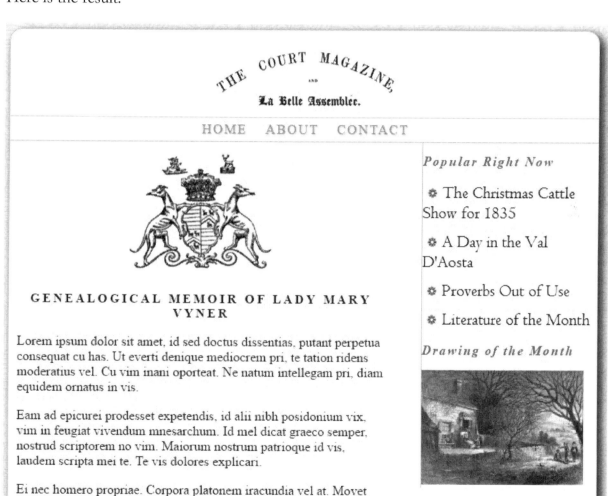

Above, the sidebar's border is too close to the sidebar's contents. We fix this by giving the sidebar a left padding (line 67 below):

```
63  .sidebar {
64      float:right;
65      width:30%;
66      border-left:1px solid #ccc;
67      padding-left:10px;
68  }
```

Here is the result:

HOME   ABOUT   CONTACT

GENEALOGICAL MEMOIR OF LADY MARY VYNER

Popular Right Now

❀ The Christmas Cattle Show for 1835

❀ A Day in the Val D'Aosta

❀ Proverbs Out of Use

❀ Literature of the Month

There is, however, an issue. If we look lower down on the page, we see that the sidebar's border does not extend fully to the bottom as we would expect:

Lorem ipsum dolor sit amet, id sed doctus dissentias, putant perpetua consequat cu has. Ut everti denique mediocrem pri, te tation ridens moderatius vel. Cu vim inani oporteat. Ne natum intellegam pri, diam equidem ornatus in vis.

Eam ad epicurei prodesset expetendis, id alii nibh posidonium vix, vim in feugiat vivendum mnesarchum. Id mel dicat graeco semper, nostrud scriptorem no vim. Maiorum nostrum patrioque id vis, laudem scripta mei te. Te vis dolores explicari.

Ei nec homero propriae. Corpora platonem iracundia vel at. Movet probatus sed ad. Cu vim solum voluptaria dissentias, postea epicurei cu usu. Solet periculis has te, laoreet signiferumque pri id, per molestiae eloquentiam eu.

Mel id aliquip definiebas philosophia, et illud utamur usu. Eam ignota invidunt in. Menandri invenire euripidis eu pro, mel mutat solet eu. Ex timeam nominati constituto mei.

Euripidis voluptatibus te vis, duo dicat propriae omittantur an. Usu ad nostrud offendit, no quem nostro legimus duo. Quo ad debet dolore offendit, eu suas labores sensibus sit. Sed blandit philosophia ut.

Drawing of the Month

Above, the sidebar's border ends a little after the Drawing of the Month image. This is because the sidebar <div> ends there, since it only gets as long as its contents require. There is no simple CSS fix for this to make the sidebar the same height as the article. One thing we could do is give the sidebar a bottom border (line 67 below):

```
63   .sidebar {
64       float:right;
65       width:30%;
66       border-left:1px solid #ccc;
67       border-bottom:1px solid #ccc;
68       padding-left:10px;
69   }
```

Here is the result:

Lorem ipsum dolor sit amet, id sed doctus dissentias, putant perpetua consequat cu has. Ut everti denique mediocrem pri, te tation ridens moderatius vel. Cu vim inani oporteat. Ne natum intellegam pri, diam equidem ornatus in vis.

Eam ad epicurei prodesset expetendis, id alii nibh posidonium vix, vim in feugiat vivendum mnesarchum. Id mel dicat graeco semper, nostrud scriptorem no vim. Maiorum nostrum patrioque id vis, laudem scripta mei te. Te vis dolores explicari.

Ei nec homero propriae. Corpora platonem iracundia vel at. Movet probatus sed ad. Cu vim solum voluptaria dissentias, postea epicurei cu usu. Solet periculis has te, laoreet signiferumque pri id, per molestiae eloquentiam eu.

Drawing of the Month

The bottom border gives the sidebar a completed appearance and does not look too bad (we can add some bottom padding to increase the distance between the drawing and the border.

Another solution is to give the sidebar a minimum height, as follows (line 67 below):

```
63   .sidebar {
64       float:right;
65       width:30%;
66       border-left:1px solid #ccc;
67       min-height:800px;
68       padding-left:10px;
69   }
```

The "min-height" property means the element should never get smaller in height than this. A minimum height of 800 pixels means the sidebar should never be smaller than 800 pixels in height. This is different from giving it a "height" of 800 pixels, because if we give it a "height" of 800 pixels and later on we add extra stuff to the sidebar so that its height increases beyond 800 pixels, the content will spill out of the sidebar since the 800 pixel height does not allow it to grow. But with "min-height", we ensure that it has a minimum height while allowing for future growth.

Here is the result:

Lorem ipsum dolor sit amet, id sed doctus dissentias, putant perpetua consequat cu has. Ut everti denique mediocrem pri, te tation ridens moderatius vel. Cu vim inani oporteat. Ne natum intellegam pri, diam equidem ornatus in vis.

Eam ad epicurei prodesset expetendis, id alii nibh posidonium vix, vim in feugiat vivendum mnesarchum. Id mel dicat graeco semper, nostrud scriptorem no vim. Maiorum nostrum patrioque id vis, laudem scripta mei te. Te vis dolores explicari.

Ei nec homero propriae. Corpora platonem iracundia vel at. Movet probatus sed ad. Cu vim solum voluptaria dissentias, postea epicurei cu usu. Solet periculis has te, laoreet signiferumque pri id, per molestiae eloquentiam eu.

Mel id aliquip definiebas philosophia, et illud utamur usu. Eam ignota invidunt in. Menandri invenire euripidis eu pro, mel mutat solet eu. Ex timeam nominati constituto mei.

Euripidis voluptatibus te vis, duo dicat propriae omittantur an. Usu ad nostrud offendit, no quem nostro legimus duo. Quo ad debet dolore offendit, eu suas labores sensibus sit. Sed blandit philosophia ut.

Drawing of the Month

Above, note the way the sidebar's border extends right to the bottom of the page. Not only that, but the sidebar now pushes the outer wrapper downward, so that there is now space underneath the article too.

Adding a Footer

A footer is the bottom part of a website where the copyright notice and some other items are placed. Below is a picture of the Royal Society's website's footer (the large gray area):

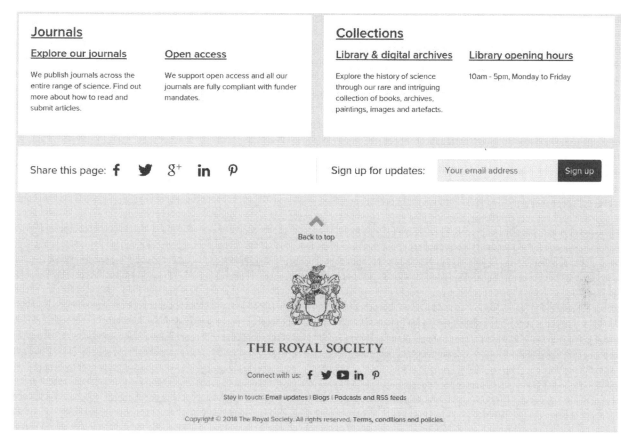

Above, the footer contains a "back to top" link, a logo, links to social media, a copy right notice, and links to the website's terms and conditions.

In HTML, we create footers using the <footer> tag, which is a semantic tag similar to <main> and <header>. Below, I have added a <footer> tag after the clear fix <div>, inside the outer wrapper <div> (lines 60-62):

```
51          <h2>Drawing of the Month</h2>
52          <a href="images/drawing_of_the_month.png">
53              <img class="drawing-of-the-month" src="images/drawing_of_the_month.png" />
54          </a>
55      </div>
56      <div class="clearfix">
57
58      </div>
59
60      <footer>
61      Copyright &copy; 2018. All Rights Reserved.
62      </footer>
63      </div>
64  </body>
```

Here is the result:

Copyright © 2018. All Rights Reserved.

In the <footer> tag, I used the © HTML entity which stands for the copyright symbol. We will now add some CSS in order to improve the appearance of the footer:

```
104  footer {
105      border-top:1px solid #ccc;
106      text-align:center;
107      font-size:80%;
108  }
```

Here is the result:

Copyright © 2018. All Rights Reserved.

Let's add some padding to give the footer some breathing space (line 108 below):

```
104  footer {
105      border-top:1px solid #ccc;
106      text-align:center;
107      font-size:80%;
108      padding:10px 0;
109  }
```

334

The property "padding:10px 0" is shorthand for creating 10 pixels of padding at the top and bottom and zero pixels on the left and right. Here is the result:

We could also copy the Royal Society's website's design by putting the footer outside the main website's design. We accomplish that by moving the <footer> tag outside the outer wrapper <div>:

```
60          </div>
61          <footer>
62              Copyright &copy; 2018. All Rights Reserved.
63          </footer>
64      </body>
```

Above, the <footer> tag is now right before the <body> tag's closing tag. Here is the result:

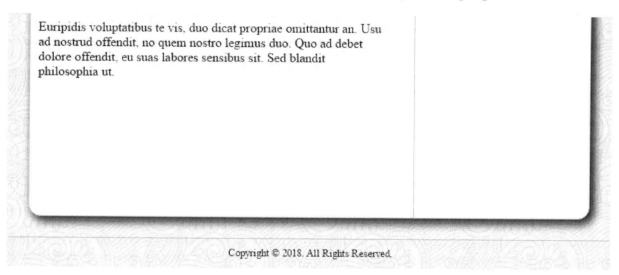

Euripidis voluptatibus te vis, duo dicat propriae omittantur an. Usu ad nostrud offendit, no quem nostro legimus duo. Quo ad debet dolore offendit, eu suas labores sensibus sit. Sed blandit philosophia ut.

We no longer have a need for the top border on the <footer> tag. Below I have removed it:

Thanks to using centering and percentages, our site expands and collapses based on the width of the user's browser window. Below is what the site looks like if a user views it on a large screen:

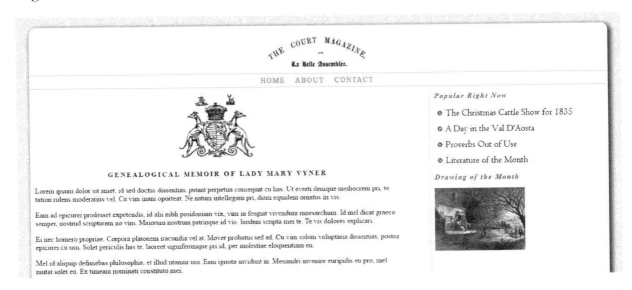

Above, note the way the site's logo and the article's picture continue to be properly centered within the design. And notice how the article's area and the sidebar have both grown in width.

Below is what the site looks like on a small screen:

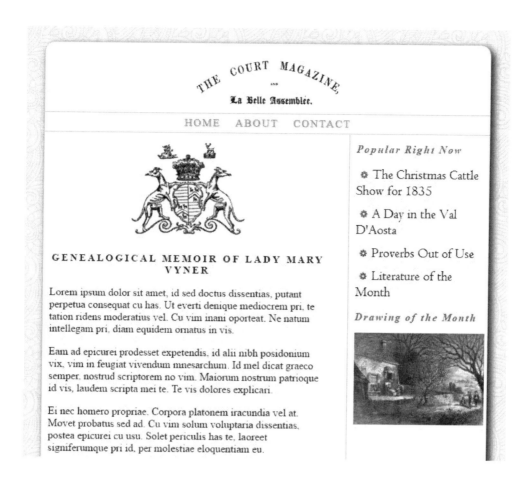

Fixed Width Sites

It is sometimes desirable for a website to have the same width regardless of the size of the screen. We can achieve this by giving the outer wrapper <div> a width (line 11 below):

```
5   .outer-wrapper {
6       border:1px solid #ccc;
7       margin:25px;
8       border-radius:15px;
9       box-shadow:5px 5px 15px #000;
10      background:white;
11      width:700px;
12   }
```

Here is the result:

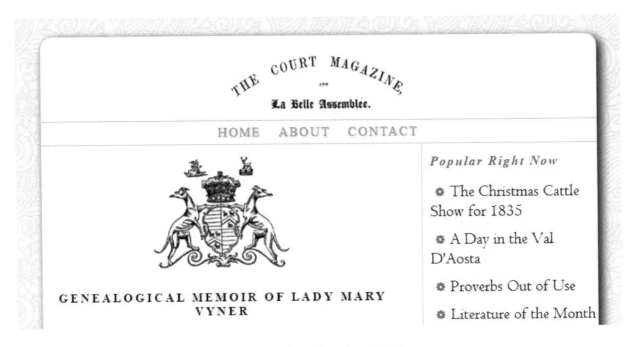

Now, if I view the site on a larger screen, here is what I will see:

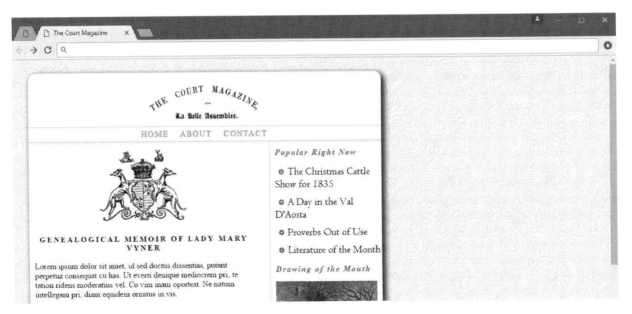

Above, the browser window has expanded, but the contents of the site remain the same width. Generally when doing this, we want the site to be centered rather than being stuck to one side of the screen. This is called "centering a layout" and there are various ways of going about it.

In the present layout, we will accomplish centering using an automatic margin. Currently, the outer wrapper has the following CSS:

```
 5  .outer-wrapper {
 6      border:1px solid #ccc;
 7      margin:25px;
 8      border-radius:15px;
 9      box-shadow:5px 5px 15px #000;
10      background:white;
11      width:700px;
12  }
```

We change line 7 above as follows:

```
 5  .outer-wrapper {
 6      border:1px solid #ccc;
 7      margin:25px auto;
 8      border-radius:15px;
 9      box-shadow:5px 5px 15px #000;
10      background:white;
11      width:700px;
12  }
```

Above, we added the word "auto" to the end of the margin property. This shorthand means that we want 25 pixels of margin at the top and bottom, and *automatic* margins on the left and right. Automatic margins are calculated by the browser in a way that centers the element. Here is the result:

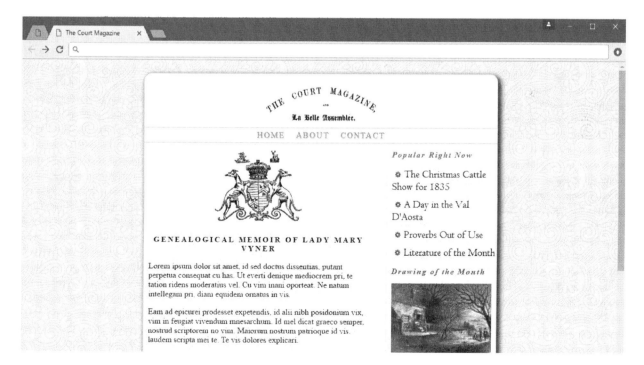

Above, the website is now properly centered within the browser window.

Centering a layout in CSS is notoriously confusing due to the interactions between one <div> and another and their various properties (floats, positioning).

Another form of centering uses positioning as follows (lines 13-15):

```
6   .outer-wrapper {
7       border:1px solid #ccc;
8       margin:25px auto;
9       border-radius:15px;
10      box-shadow:5px 5px 15px #000;
11      background:white;
12      width:700px;
13      position:absolute;
14      left:50%;
15      margin-left:-350px;
16  }
```

Above, we use a special trick. We cause the outer wrapper to be 50% distant from the left edge. This by itself is not enough, because this 50% distance pushes the outer wrapper and its contents too far to the left, as follows:

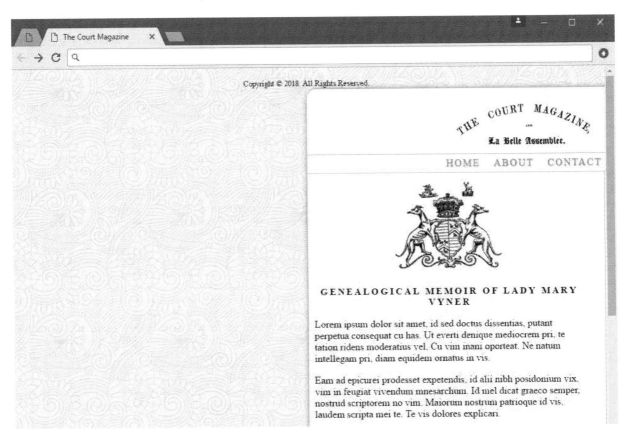

Above, the design is pushes so far to the left that we cannot even see the sidebar. The "margin-left:-350px" fixes this by moving the outer wrapper leftwards by 350 pixels. Here is the result:

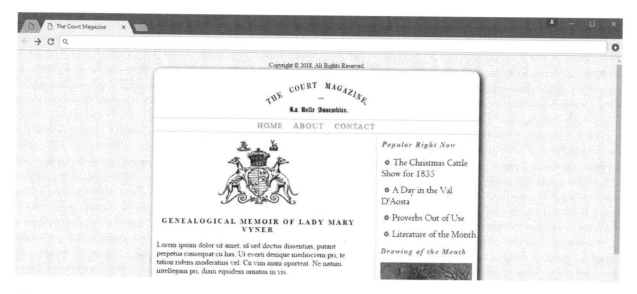

Above, now the website is properly centered. The 350 figure is the width of the outer wrapper div (700 pixels) divided by two. If you are confused about why this works, there is no need to worry. It is sufficient to know that this is a trick that works. You give something a 50% left distance, then give it a negative margin that is half the size of the element. This trick only works if you are dealing with an element that has a specific width defined for it.

Above, you may have noticed that the copyright notice is now at the top. This is because by making the outer wrapper absolutely positioned, it ends up hovering over the document and other elements will entirely ignore its presence. As far as the <footer> tag is concerned, there is nothing above it, so it shows up at the very top of the document.

In order to fix that, we have to put the absolute positioning on another <div> that contains both the outer wrapper and the <footer>. Below, I have created a new <div> with the class of "outer-outer-wrapper". The name is a bit silly, in a professional design you would name it "outer-wrapper" and the old outer wrapper would be renamed "inner-wrapper". But to avoid confusion, I will keep the new <div>'s class name as "outer-outer-wrapper":

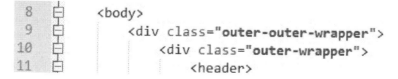

```
 8      <body>
 9          <div class="outer-outer-wrapper">
10              <div class="outer-wrapper">
11                  <header>
```

This new <div> contains everything, including the outer wrapper and the footer. Below is the new CSS we add to styles.css for the new outer outer wrapper (lines 5-10 below):

```
 5   .outer-outer-wrapper {
 6       width:700px;
 7       position:absolute;
 8       left:50%;
 9       margin-left:-350px;
10   }
11   .outer-wrapper {
12       border:1px solid #ccc;
13       margin:25px auto;
14       border-radius:15px;
15       box-shadow:5px 5px 15px #000;
16       background:white;
17       width:700px;
18   }
```

Above, the old outer wrapper no longer has absolute positioning. I have moved the absolute positioning definition to the new outer outer wrapper. This new <div> must have a width similar to the outer wrapper in order for the centering calculation to work.

Here is the result:

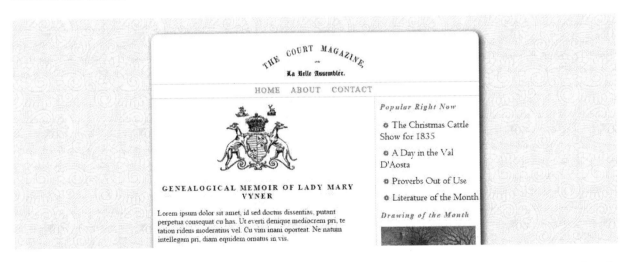

Above, everything is now working perfectly. We have a secret "outer outer" wrapper that is not showing up, but that is causing the whole design to be centered.

Creating a Contact Page

In this section, we will create a new page for the magazine where users can contact the magazine's owners. Here is what our site's folder looks like at the moment:

Below, I create a new empty HTML document named "contact.html":

Below, I have opened "contact.html" inside Notepad++:

Now, I will copy and paste all of the contents of "magazine.html" inside "contact.html", as follows:

```
1    <!DOCTYPE HTML>
2    <html>
3        <head>
4            <meta charset="UTF-8">
5            <title>The Court Magazine</title>
6            <link rel="stylesheet" type="text/css" href="css/styles.css"/>
7        </head>
8        <body>
9            <div class="outer-outer-wrapper">
10               <div class="outer-wrapper">
11                   <header>
12                       <div class="logo">
13                           <img src="images/magazine_title.png" />
14                       </div>
15                       <nav>
16                           <a href="">Home</a>
17                           <a href="">About</a>
18                           <a href="">Contact</a>
19                       </nav>
20                   </header>
21                   <main>
22                       <article>
23                           <div class="image-container">
24                               <img src="images/image.png" width="200" />
25                           </div>
26                           <h1>Genealogical Memoir of Lady Mary Vyner</h1>
27                           <p>Lorem ipsum dolor sit amet, id sed doctus dissentias, putant perpetua consequat cu has.
28                           Ut everti denique mediocrem pri, te tation ridens moderatius vel. Cu vim inani oporteat.
29                           Ne natum intellegam pri, diam equidem ornatus in vis.</p>
```

Copying and pasting saves a lot of work, since we want the contact page to look similar to the rest of the site. Instead of building the page from scratch, we use the HTML for "magazine.html" as a template. Below, I change the title of the new page to "Contact Us – The Court Magazine" (line 5):

```
3        <head>
4            <meta charset="UTF-8">
5            <title>Contact Us - The Court Magazine</title>
6            <link rel="stylesheet" type="text/css" href="css/styles.css"/>
7        </head>
8        <body>
```

Above, notice that on line 6 we refer to the "styles.css" file, which "magazine.html" also refers to. We can have as many HTML documents as we want with all of them using the same CSS file for styling.

Below, I have deleted the contents of the <article> tag, but I have kept everything else, such as the sidebar (and the footer):

```
21       <main>
22           <article>
23
24           </article>
25       </main>
26       <div class="sidebar">
27           <h2>Popular Right Now</h2>
```

344

Here is what the page looks like when opened in a browser:

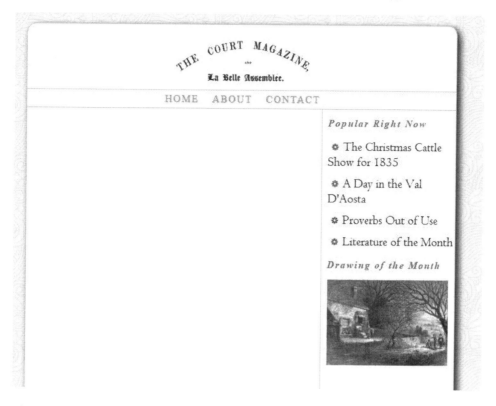

Above, we have the site's design showing up properly, with a blank space where the contact page's contents should go.

Below, we add the contact page's title:

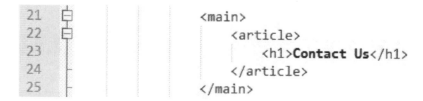

```
<main>
    <article>
        <h1>Contact Us</h1>
    </article>
</main>
```

Here is the result:

Next we will add an explanatory paragraph:

```
21      <main>
22          <article>
23              <h1>Contact Us</h1>
24              <p>Please use the form below to send us a message. You may also contact us
25              by emailing us at contact@example.com.</p>
26          </article>
27      </main>
```

Here is the result:

CONTACT US

Please use the form below to send us a message. You may also contact us by emailing us at contact@example.com.

Popular Right Now

❋ The Christmas Cattle Show for 1835

We can turn "contact@example.com" into an email link, which is a type of link that when clicked, opens up the user's email client (such as Outlook).

```
22      <article>
23          <h1>Contact Us</h1>
24          <p>Please use the form below to send us a message. You may also contact us
25          by emailing us at <a href="mailto:contact@example.com">contact@example.com</a>.</p>
26      </article>
```

Above, notice the special "mailto:" keyword used inside the "href" attribute (line 25). This tells the browser this is an email link. Here is what the page looks like now:

CONTACT US

Please use the form below to send us a message. You may also contact us by emailing us at contact@example.com.

Next, we start creating the contact form using the HTML <form> tag:

```
27  ⊟                        <form>
28
29  ⊢                        </form>
```

Next, I add a text input box to the form:

```
27  ⊟                <form>
28                       <label for="full-name">Full Name</label>
29                       <input type="text" id="full-name" name="full-name" /><br/>
30  ⊢                </form>
```

Here is what it looks like:

CONTACT US

Please use the form below to send us a message. You may also
contact us by emailing us at contact@example.com.

Full Name [   ]

The <label> tag on line 28 creates the "label" for the input. The "for" attribute on line 28 determines which input box the label is for, the input box is "full-name", meaning this label is related to an input box that has an ID of "full-name".

The "name" attribute on the <input> tag is used by the server and does not concern us here, it is sufficient to know that on a real website, this attribute matters to the programmers who work on the website's "back-end" (database, etc.).

Without a label, users will only an empty box, as follows:

CONTACT US

Please use the form below to send us a message. You may also
contact us by emailing us at contact@example.com.

[   ]

Instead of using a <label> tag, you could use a <div> or <p> tag to contain the word "Full Name", as follows:

```
27  ⊟                <form>
28                       <p>Full Name</p>
29                       <input type="text" id="full-name" name="full-name" /><br/>
30  ⊢                </form>
```

Here is what it looks like:

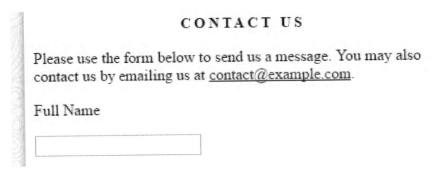

The above will work. The <label> tag, however, has benefits. The first is that blind users will be told by their screen reading program that the input box has a label of "Full Name" associated with it. Another benefit is that if a user clicks on the word "Full Name", the input box will immediately get a typing cursor in it, as follows:

Full Name

Next, we add a <textarea> tag where users can write down the message they want to send to the magazine:

```
27  <form>
28      <label for="full-name">Full Name</label>
29      <input type="text" id="full-name" name="full-name" /><br/>
30
31      <label for="message">Message</label>
32      <textarea id="message" name="message"></textarea>
33  </form>
```

Here is what it looks like:

The <textarea> tag allows users to type out a longer message than the <input> tag does, and it allows the use of the Enter/return key so that users can write multiple paragraphs if they want. Note that while the <input> tag is self-closing, the <textarea> tag requires a closing </textarea> tag.

Above, the form doesn't look too pretty, but we will leave styling for later.

Next, we add a submit button as follows (line 34):

```
 7     <form>
28         <label for="full-name">Full Name</label>
29         <input type="text" id="full-name" name="full-name" /><br/>
30
31         <label for="message">Message</label>
32         <textarea id="message" name="message"></textarea><br />
33
34         <input type="submit" value="Send Message!" />
35     </form>
```

Here is the result:

On line 34 above, the "type" attribute has a value of "submit", which tells the browser this is a submit button. The "value" attribute is "Send Message!", this determines the text that is shown to users inside the submit button.

We can now turn our attention to styling the form. In order to give our form a uniform appearance, we style the <label> tag as follows:

```
117    label {
118        display:block;
119        width:100px;
120        float:left;
121        text-align:right;
122    }
```

Here is the result:

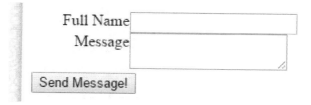

The equal width of the two labels causes the input and the text area to be aligned exactly above each other. We have to give the labels a "display:block" property since we they are inline elements by default and cannot take a width. We cause them to float left otherwis they would take up a whole line. We use "text-align:right" to align the label texts on the right, this helps them stay visually close to the input boxes they describe.

Below, we add a right padding to the <label> tag to create some space between the labels and the input boxes (line 122 below):

```
117    label {
118        display:block;
119        width:100px;
120        float:left;
121        text-align:right;
122        padding-right:10px;
123    }
```

Here is the result:

Next, we add some bottom margin to the input box:

```
125    input[type=text] {
126        margin-bottom:10px;
127    }
```

Above, we use a special CSS construct we have not met before. Remember that both the input box and the submit button are created using <input> tags, the only thing that distinguishes them is their "type" attribute in the HTML. In the CSS above, we are declaring that an input that has a "type" attribute of "text" should get a bottom margin of 10 pixels. This means that the CSS will only apply to the input box and not to the submit button.

Here is the result:

Full Name [   ]

Message [   ]

[Send Message!]

nstead of using "input[type=text]", we could have added a bottom margin to the ID of the input (#full-name), or we could have given the input a class name and put the CSS on that class. In CSS, there are usually multiple ways of achieving the same thing. The benefit of using "input[type=text]" is that if we add any new input boxes, the style will automatically apply to them too.

Next, we give the input and the textarea boxes the same width, as follows:

```
129    input[type=text], textarea {
130          width:60%;
131    }
```

Here is the result:

If you look carefully, you will notice that the input and the textarea are not actually the exact same width, despite giving them both a 200 pixel width. This is caused by a technical issue related to the way the browser calculates the width of an input versus the width of a textarea. The solution is to use the "box-sizing" CSS property, as follows (line 131 below):

```
129    input[type=text], textarea {
130          width:60%;
131          box-sizing:border-box;
132    }
```

The CSS property "box-sizing:border-box" property tells the browser to calculate the width of the input and the textarea with respect to their borders rather than their inner contents. The result is that they get the same apparent width:

Full Name

Message

Send Message!

Notice that the textarea is somewhat small. Below I have written a three-line message, when I go to line 3, line 1 stops showing due to scrolling out of view:

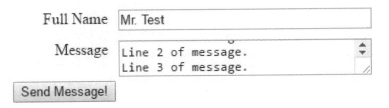

We can provide a better user experience by making the message writing area higher. To do this, we can either define a height in CSS, or use the "rows" attribute as follows:

```
<label for="message">Message</label>
<textarea rows="8" id="message" name="message"></textarea><br />
```

Above, I have created a "rows" attribute with a value of "8". This tells the browser that this textarea should be high enough to show eight lines of text at the same time. Here is what it looks like:

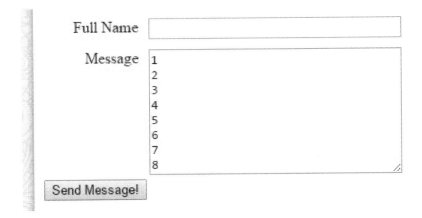

Above, I written down 8 lines, each line with a number on it.

Next, we style the submit button. We give it a left margin of 110 pixels to make it appear underneath the input boxes as follows:

```
134  input[type=submit] {
135      margin-left:110px;
136  }
```

Above, on line 134, I have used the "input[type=submit]" selector, meaning the style will only apply to inputs whose "type" attribute is "submit". Here is the result:

We can add all kinds of styling to a submit button, as follows:

```
134  ⊟input[type=submit] {
135         margin-left:110px;
136         border:1px solid #000;
137         color:#fff;
138         background:#666;
139         padding:5px;
140         text-shadow:1px 1px 0px #000;
141         font-size:120%;
142         font-family:Centaur, serif;
143         letter-spacing:2px;
144  └}
```

Here is the result:

By now, you may be wondering what happens if you type some stuff in the boxes and press the submit button. Where does the data go? On a real website, when you press the submit button, the data ends up being sent to the server where the website is located. The server has a program that accepts the data and saves it in a database, and perhaps sends an email to the website's owner with the contents of the message in it.

It is outside the scope of this book to teach how form submission works, since that is part of web development rather than HTML and CSS.

Where to go next...

At this point, you have acquired a basic training in HTML and CSS and you are ready to create your own website. A website must be "hosted" on a "server" for people to be able to see it on the internet. In my book *Cloud Computing for Complete Beginners* I teach how to create a website on a server that you yourself own and control. If your goal is to acquire the skills needed for a career in web design and development, then that book teaches the professional way for doing things.

And if you merely wish to have your own personal website and do not expect a huge amount of traffic, then you can do a web search for "how to host my own website" and you will find various tutorials for signing up for a "web host" and transferring your HTML, CSS and image files to the server via something called FTP.

Many web hosting services provide you with a "WordPress plan". This allows you to quickly get a beautiful and easy-to-manage website going while also giving you a lot of control over the HTML and CSS.

Made in the USA
Middletown, DE
03 September 2019